Trinidad Yoruba

Caribbean Archaeology and Ethnohistory

L. Antonio Curet, Series Editor

Trinidad Yoruba

From Mother Tongue to Memory

Maureen Warner-Lewis

The University of Alabama Press
Tuscaloosa

∞
The paper on which this book is printed meets the minimum requirements of American National Standard for Information Sciences–Permanence of Paper for Printed Library Materials, ANSI Z39.48-1984.

Cataloging-in-Publication Data available from the Library of Congress

ISBN-10: 0-8173-5582-0 (pbk. : alk. paper)
ISBN-13: 978-0-8173-5582-1 (pbk. : alk. paper)
ISBN 978-0-8173-8318-3 (electronic)

C

Contents

A

Acknowledgments

This book comes into print at a time when the Afrocentric and multicultural perspectives are increasingly gaining ground in the academy. This work, while not a product of the present phase, is however the outcome of revisionist approaches by indigenes to their sociohistorical realities. As part of the decolonization process, the Caribbean academy is redirecting its attention from European topics and, as a concomitant, has had to reevaluate inherited assumptions and methodologies. The ex-colonial scholar has therefore found himself or herself not solely with the task of "naming our landscape," as the poets Derek Walcott and Edward Kamau Brathwaite would say, but of analyzing and interpreting our own behaviors, our own societies, our own epistemologies.

This work is also Afrocentric in that it addresses the experience of Africans in one locale of the diaspora and examines the nature of their social and linguistic heritage as it was simultaneously retained, modified and discarded in a European-dominated island community. The profile of the Yoruba language is traced through its speakers' experience of slavery, postslavery indenture, and today's multiethnic and politically independent state.

Trinidad Yoruba: From Mother Tongue to Memory is a revision of my doctoral dissertation presented to the University of the West Indies in 1982 and entitled "The Yoruba Language in Trinidad." The topic had its genesis in 1965 with the suggestion of David Ọkẹ, a postgraduate colleague at the University of York in England, that given the retention of *shango* or *orisha* religion in Trinidad, a wider nexus of Yoruba cultural survivals was indicated. Once such queries were posed when fieldwork began in my homeland of Trinidad in 1966, it became evident that African linguistic and cultural retentions and memories were extensive. Where in the historiography there had largely been silence and ignorance regarding nineteenth-century Africa-born residents in the Caribbean (at most statistics of apparently little import), there was now recall of flesh-and-blood individuals and communities; there was even reproduction of their language by way of words, sentences, and songs in abundance! Cultural, historical, and linguistic gaps were being filled and continue to be fed by the ongoing mining of field data. For me this has meant that the Caribbean past and its present could no longer be perceived from a one-dimensional (i.e., European) point of view. The African dimension was persistent and alive in the social and psychological fabric, even though it was a factor that had been neglected and undervalued in all that was official, scholarly, and appropriate.

The memories and language skills of my informants must therefore be given the primary credit for enabling this book, for they have brought into visibility the lives, knowledge and worldview of themselves and their ancestors!

After a period of self-financing, this research received tangible support in 1971–1972 from the Senate Subcommittee for Linguistics and from the Research and Publications Committee at the University of the West Indies, Jamaica. In 1974–1975, Prof. David Ọkẹ together with Prof. Ade Oluwasanmi, Vice-Chancellor of the then University of Ifẹ (now the Ọbafẹmi Awolọwọ University), arranged a one-year lectureship for me with that university's Department of English. This visit enabled translation of field texts by Tẹlẹ Nadi and Tokunbọ (Shyllon) Adetunji, and afforded me the valuable scholarly assistance of Yoruba cultural specialists like Wande Abimbọla, Ọlasope Oyelaran, Akinwumi Iṣọla, George Ọlọmọla, and Bade Ajuwọn.

The guidance of Pauline Christie, John Rickford, Ann Jeffries, and Hubert Devonish in things linguistic has been of incalculable help to one whose primary discipline is literature; their generous gift of time and their nagging but insightful queries have pushed me to wrestle with issues and concepts beyond what I believed to be within my capacity. Mervyn Alleyne has always been generous with extended book loans. Monica Schuler alerted my attention to the relevance of post-Emancipation African immigration to the historical context of my field data, an issue that helped fine-tune my interview probings, and I was pleased to find that Keith Laurence had pioneered documentation in this field.

Other communities of help have been similarly institutional and personal. Within the institutional framework, the governments of Jamaica and Cuba sponsored my research visit to the José Martí National Library in Havana in1977; a British Council grant in 1980 enabled access to the library at the School of Oriental and African

Studies in London; a Fulbright Fellowship in 1989–1990 allowed use of the University of Florida Library in Gainesville and a visiting attachment with that university's Department of African and Oriental Languages and Literatures. The facilities and assistance of librarians at other centers have also been instrumental in providing secondary material: the University of the West Indies Library at Mona (Jamaica) and St. Augustine (Trinidad); the Parliamentary Library, Port of Spain; the University of Ifẹ; and Northwestern University, Evanston, Illinois. And from the inception of my university teaching career in 1970, the university administration, my departmental colleagues, and successive heads of the Department of English at the University of the West Indies, Mona, have cooperated by making possible study leaves and other facilities.

In the personal sphere, I wish to acknowledge publicly the physical hospitality, as well as moral and verbal encouragement of the late Edwina Oluwasanmi, Doris Brathwaite, and Roberta Gaskin, in addition to Arthur Drayton, Ebenezer and Doreen Ojurongbe, Cynthia Falode, Edward Kamau Brathwaite, Bob Gaskin, Alma Jordan, Gordon Rohlehr, Carol (Carrington) Cumberbatch, my deceased father, Carlton Warner, my mother, Eleene Warner, and my sister, Carol Warner. I also thank Windell Daley, whose competence and thoughtfulness minimized my involvement in housekeeping during the early 1980s. My husband, Rupert Lewis, and our two children have, through repeated sacrifices of absence and extended work hours, supported me morally, emotionally, and intellectually.

N

A Note on Ethnonyms

There is as yet no satisfactory term by which to refer to all persons of African descent. *Negro* is negatively value loaded. The issue becomes more problematic because this book treats of both continental Africans and their diasporan descendants of varying generations. I therefore distinguish by terminology between *Africans* (persons born in Africa), *African Creoles* (the designation coined by Africans to distinguish between themselves and their diasporan-born progeny), and *Blacks* (an unsatisfactory generic term to refer to both groups). In parallel fashion, the term *Whites* is used synonymously with *Europeans*. Where the two color references are used adjectively, they are lowercased, *black* and *white*.

Yoruba refers generically to speakers of the eponymic language and their descendants, whether on the African continent or in the Americas. *Trinidad Yoruba* restricts reference to the particular culture group and language formed on the island of Trinidad. Trinidad Yoruba is therefore a subgroup of the umbrella Yoruba ethnic community.

In keeping with recent revisioning, the historical terms *Indian* and *Amerindian* have been replaced by *native American*. This designation varies with *aboriginal*. *Indian* is reserved for persons born in India and their diasporan descendants. *Creole* is a complex term applied to a range of referents in Caribbean historical experience and culture. From the Caribbean perspective, *creole* means 'forged in the Americas, native to the Americas though genetically from elsewhere'. The issue of admixture is ancillary. The term as applied to persons is capitalized as an ethnic designation, but applied to culture, including language, it is lowercased. When, however, a particular creole language is cited, the term is uppercased; thus *French Creole*.

Uppercased *Maroon* refers to a runaway slave who establishes residence anywhere away from the plantation, whether individually or collectively. The concept of existence separate from the supervisory control of the Other is expressed by the adjective *maroon* and the abstract category *maroonage* /marunaž/.

O

Orthographic Guide

In setting out both Yoruba and Trinidad Yoruba, present Yoruba orthographic conventions have been largely followed. However, the ṣ of Yoruba orthography is retained in Yoruba language contexts, but is converted to *sh* in passages of continuous English text. Furthermore, with regard to Trinidad Yoruba I have used both *kp* and *p* to indicate variant phonetic realizations of the Trinidad Yoruba phoneme /p/, whereas standard Yoruba practice, as an economy measure, employs *p* to signal [kp], there being no contrasting [p] in the Yoruba phoneme inventory.

Similarly, where Yoruba orthography uses *y* before vowel + *n* to suggest [ny] followed by a nasalized vowel, I have regularized both Yoruba and Trinidad representations of the alveo-palatal nasal glide as *ny,* since Trinidad Yoruba more often than not utilizes only the palatal glide /y/ in this position. Trinidad Yoruba variant realizations of the Yoruba phoneme are thus indicated by *y* and *ny.* However, to avoid too radical a departure from Yoruba orthographic convention, nasality in the preceding vowel is conveyed by a syllable-final nasal consonant. Thus [ã] is spelled *an.*

Where, however, the nasal vowel is followed by a bilabial nasal in Trinidad Yoruba pronunciation, this fact is conveyed by a postvocalic *m,* its superscript vs. on-line position suggesting the relative weakness or strength respectively of its articulation. Postvocalic *nn* as in *Sa Liɔnn* suggests the articulation of the nasal consonant in contrast to the single *n* which is an index of nasality in the vowel.

With Fon words, on the other hand, nasalized vowels carry the nasal superscript ~ but no succeeding consonant; thus *vodũ.* In addition, [ɛ] and [ɔ] are indicated by these phonetic symbols in the spelling. Yoruba orthography, however, represents these sounds by ẹ and ọ respectively. These phones are represented in French and French Creole words by *è* and *ò* respectively.

There is variant treatment of tones throughout the book. Tone marks, now considered obligatory in Yoruba orthography, have been retained in the representation of Yoruba as opposed to Trinidad Yoruba words and texts; Trinidad Yoruba tones, being erratic, are not represented in Trinidad Yoruba texts, except where tone in Trinidad Yoruba is being discussed. On the other hand, in extended English language context, Yoruba names are written without tone indicators. By the reverse ṭoken, all Yoruba words, including names, carry tone values in the chapter most intimately concerned with phonology, chapter 5.

P

Phonological Symbols

Vowels

	Back	*High*	*Low*	*Rounded*	*Tense*
i	–	+	–	–	+
ɪ	–	+	–	–	–
e	–	–	–	–	+
ɛ	–	–	–	–	–
ə	+	–	–	–	–
a	+	–	+	–	+
ɑ	+	–	+	+	–
ɒ	+	–	+	+	–
ɔ	+	–	+	+	–
o	+	–	–	+	+
ʊ	+	+	–	–	–
u	+	+	–	+	+

Consonants

	Obstruent	*Continuant*	*Voiced*	*Anterior*	*Coronal*	*Back*	*High*
p	+	–	–	+	–	–	–
kp	+	–	–	+	–	+	+
ɓ	+	–	+	+	–	–	–
b	+	–	+	+	–	–	–
gb	+	–	+	+	–	+	+
t	+	–	–	+	+	–	–
d	+	–	+	+	+	–	–
k	+	–	–	–	–	+	+
g	+	–	+	–	–	+	+
f	+	+	–	+	–	–	–
v	+	+	+	+	–	–	–
s	+	+	–	+	+	–	–
z	+	+	+	+	+	–	–

	Obstruent	*Continuant*	*Voiced*	*Anterior*	*Coronal*	*Back*	*High*
š	+	+	−	−	+	−	+
ž	+	+	+	−	+	−	+
c	+	−	−	−	+	−	+
j	+	−	+	−	+	−	+
w	−	+	+	−	−	+	+
y	−	+	+	−	−	−	+
h	−	+	−	−	−	−	−
l	−	+	+	+	+	−	−
r	−	+	+	+	+	−	−
ɾ	−	+	+	+	+	−	−
m	−	−	+	+	−	−	−
n	−	−	+	+	+	−	−
ɲ	−	−	+	−	+	−	+
ŋ	−	−	+	−	−	+	+

=	syllable juncture
+	intersentential pause
#	sentence juncture

A

Abbreviations

adj	adjective
adv	adverb
ant	anterior
assoc	associative
c	consonant
C.O.	Colonial Office, London
compl	complement, complementizer
cond	condition
cont	continuous aspect
def	definer
DJE	*Dictionary of Jamaican English*
E	English
Eg	Ẹgba
Ek	Ekiti
Eng. Cr.	English Creole
emph	emphatic
equ	equative verb
EY	Eastern Yoruba
f	female
foc	focusing verb
Fr	French
Fr. Cr.	French Creole
fut	future
hab	habitual aspect
hyp	hypothetical
id	identity
Ij	Ijẹsha
Ijb	Ijẹbu
imp	imperative
intens	intensifier
interr	interrogative
L_2	second language
loc	locative
m	male
N	noun

neg	negator
NP	noun phrase
num	numeral
Ø	zero occurrence
obj	object
ord	ordinal
pl	plural
Port	Portuguese
Pr	personal pronoun
P.R.O.	Public Record Office
prog	progressive aspect
rel	relative
S	sentence
sg	singular
Span	Spanish
subj	subject
SVO	Subject + Verb + Object sequence
SY	Standard Yoruba
TE	Trinidad English
TY	Trinidad Yoruba
v	vowel
V	verb
vol	volitive
VP	verb phrase
Y	Yoruba

Trinidad Yoruba

I

Introduction

Study of African Languages in the Caribbean

In the anglophone Caribbean, historiography has moved to embrace documentation and analysis of the lives and social conditions of the poor and underprivileged only within the last two decades. Before then, history concerned itself largely with official policies and therefore continued to promulgate the ideologies of the ruling classes. Among these ideologies are racist attitudes toward African peoples and their cultural forms. And since, within these conceptual parameters, Africans had no culture and no history, the issue of their contribution to Caribbean society could not arise. Similarly, it was inconceivable that African languages could exist here since Africans did not speak languages: they spoke mumbo-jumbo. Enlightened opinion in recent years credits them with speaking "dialects." In popular parlance, this means "corrupt speech forms."

On the other hand, by an inconsistency of logic, the official historical record has asserted that slaves sharing the same language (their capacity for speech communication now admitted) were systematically distributed to different plantations. This statement must have some basis of truth relative to official *intention,* but it has been repeated ad nauseam with little questioning of its unrealizeability in *fact.* The preponderance of certain ethnic groups on any one cargo, the irregularity of slave-ship arrivals in the face of pressing labor needs, planters' preferences for certain ethnic types, the social intercourse between slaves of neighboring plantations, the employment of slaves on public projects related to construction, maintenance, and commerce, particularly in urban centers—all these real-life factors militated against the isolation of African slaves on the basis of their linguistic affiliation.

Another misconception successfully implanted is that slavery was a monolithic system initiated some four centuries ago. This concept has, on the one hand, distorted the contradictory and fluctuating nature of laws and social relationships in slave societies, and on the other, has distanced slavery in time. That institution, however, ended only a century and a half ago in the British and French West Indies, while it was abolished barely a century ago in Cuba and Brazil. That being the case, it is entirely conceivable that strong evidences of African cultural institutions should still linger in this geographical area.

In general, modern linguists have been slow to recognize the existence in this region of fragmentary as well as continuous African language discourse. Little specific attention has been focused in this direction. It is quite possible that more African language discourse remains concealed in ethnographic and musicological recordings than has been consciously sought in linguistic fieldwork.[1] Indeed, from the beginning, description of African linguistic behavior has been made in the context of investigation into African Caribbean religion and anthropology.

It would appear that very few missionaries took an interest in the cultural and linguistic practices of the slaves, considering that Africans were to be led away from all things heathenish and inducted into European systems of thought and action. However, among the exceptions was Rev. Georg Oldendorp, Moravian missionary-historian to the Danish West Indies. In the late eighteenth century he detailed the ethnic affiliations and customs of slaves, along with African words in frequent use, a limited number of vocabulary items in various languages and translations into several African languages of the sentence "Christ has washed me with his blood" (Oldendorp 1987: 201–2).

In the second decade of this century, J. Graham Cruickshank, who took a keen interest in the social manners and speech culture of the folk in British Guiana, penned two seminal articles on the African settlers in that territory (Cruickshank 1916, 1917). Cruickshank was stimulated in this direction at the same time that Fernando Ortiz was becoming seduced into sympathetic consideration of African Cuban history, philosophy and customs. Don Fernando's massive output on these subjects between 1906 and 1969 was to begin a virtual school of research dedicated to documentation of African retentions and African cultural influence in Cuba.

The lexicographic orientation was the first linguistic line of approach in the documentation of specific African speech communities in Cuba: thus Diaz Fabelo (1956, 1958), Cabrera (1970),

Deschamps Chappeaux (1967), González Huguet and Baudry (1967). Such lexical inventories and texts represent not only linguistic distillations from religious and anthropological field research but also incorporate data from explanatory *libretas* or notebooks which are kept, in idiosyncratic hispanicized orthography, by African religious practictioners in Cuba.[2] Apart from lexical, phraseological, and proverbial entries, *libretas* contain mystical and folkloric data. Other lexica based on usage in African-Caribbean religious communities are Comhaire-Sylvain (1955), Quesada (1973), and Elder (1988).

Lexica accompanied by etymological and morphophonological analyses include Dalby (1971), García González (1973), Valdés Acosta (1974), Bilby (1983), Bilby and Bunseki (1983), Carter (1986a and b), and Adetugbọ (1991). Semantics is the main thrust of Valdés Acosta (1986), and phonology the emphasis in Olmsted (1953) and Carter (1993).

Sociolinguistic studies include Warner (1970, 1971a), Hall-Alleyne (1984, 1990), and Adetugbọ (1991); while syntax has been treated in Warner (1971b). The present work is a revision of Warner-Lewis (1982), which subjected Trinidad Yoruba to multiple levels of linguistic analysis and noted features indicative of residual language function. The latter topic in relation to Jamaican Maroon Twi has been treated in Alleyne and Hall-Alleyne (1982).

Impact of African Languages on Caribbean Speech

The rarity in this century of African speech communities in the region coupled with the scarcity there of African linguists has meant that interest in African languages in the Caribbean has largely centered on the identification of Africanisms in Caribbean speech. Lexical Africanisms were in part the subject of Ortiz (1921) and became the sole focus of Ortiz (1922). For Jamaica, Cassidy and Le Page (1967) revealed a wealth of African loan words and calques, while Hall (1976) and Bilby (1985) have continued identification in specific domains. Other areal studies of African lexical retention are Daeleman (1972), Price (1975), McAndrew (1978), and Huttar (1985). Allsopp (1977), Holm (1993) and Baker (1993) cover the Caribbean generally.

Following close on the realization of a fair representation of African lexical items in Caribbean languages, linguistic attention turned to areas of grammatical and phonological influence. Analyses on the impact of tone-based African languages on tonal and intonation contours in Creoles have been offered by Lawton (1963), D'Costa and Berry (1971), Carter (1979), and Devonish (1989). Syntactic parallels have been pointed out by Relouzat (1971), Huttar (1971), Cassidy (1972), Lewis (1978), Dalphinis (1985), Smith, Robertson, and Williamson (1987), and Robertson (1993), among others. Alleyne (1980, 1988) has approached the issue across linguistic levels.

Discourse analogies are treated in Rickford and Rickford (1976), Warner-Lewis (1979), Edwards (1978), and Dalphinis (1985: 165–85).

In fact, the implications of morphosyntactic, phonological, and lexical components in the African-Caribbean connection has spawned a mass of linguistic analyses devoted to what has become a controversial issue: the redefinition—or is it the precise definition?—of the genetic relationship between Creoles and the African and European languages that have parented them.

The Research Project

This study offers a description of an African language—Yoruba—as used on the island of Trinidad in the southern Caribbean. The exercise is a pioneering one, in that it examines the historical and sociolinguistic context of Yoruba culture and language in Trinidad, in addition to setting out some of the most salient aspects of its phonology, syntax, and lexicon.

It is a study of largely mnemonic language competence based on a corpus generated by formerly active Yoruba language users. This linguistic situation is therefore qualitatively different from that described in Dorian (1981) in that Trinidad Yoruba (TY), unlike East Sutherland Gaelic, is already obsolescent, its residual active vehicle being largely that of song, and its residual domain being confined to religious ritual. Its main ritual setting is that of *orisha* ceremonial but may also extend to pre- and post-burial wakes for individuals previously connected with Yoruba culture, whether by ethnicity or through *orisha* devotion. At the same time, this research uncovered in Trinidad a competence in Yoruba discourse (i) which was inert and (ii) which extended beyond sacred topics and functions. No previous account or description of Yoruba language use on the island had been registered, and apart from passing remarks on the possible Yoruba origin of *orisha* chants by a few scholars, among them George Simpson in *The Shango Cult in Trinidad* (1965), no attention had been focused on Yoruba language retention.

In this context of mainly latent language competence, then, a distinction needs to be drawn between *major* or *primary* as against *secondary* informants/speakers. Of the seventy-odd informants interviewed over the research period, only eight qualify as primary speakers, three of whom were second-generation Yoruba descendants. The others were third-generation. The historical and linguistic data proferred by primary speakers were quantitatively greater and/or qualitatively better than those provided by secondary informants. The latter supplied lexical items only or produced texts displaying a higher degree of phonological deviance from the same texts presented by primary speakers. Both categories, however, provided sociolinguistic and anthropological information. *Tertiary* informants supplied little or no Yoruba text, but advanced sociolinguistic supporting data.

The lingustic analysis of Trinidad Yoruba is based on the output of the eight major speakers. Compared with Dorian's categories, however, the eight primary informants would most nearly qualify for semi-speaker status. But this would be a misleading term to apply in the context of inactive or noninteractive Yoruba language capacity, the brevity of connected discourse, and levels of xenoglossia or noncomprehension with respect to recollected texts. In addition, given their articulatory facility yet limited comprehension skills, they do not qualify as "passive bilinguals."

Nor do they fit easily into the categories hypothesized by Campbell and Muntzel (1989). Whether or not one excludes TY's ritual functionality for at least five of the informants, TY speakers may all be considered rememberers since both the ritual and nonritual uses of language were nonreciprocal. Of the two categories of rememberers analyzed in Campbell and Muntzel (1989), the competence of TY primary speakers most closely resembles that of the "surviving once-fully-competent" Salvadoran Lenca speaker. However, one needs to question the criteria or conditions for judging levels of competence prior to the period when researchers were investigating the subject. In addition, in the Trinidad scenario, it is improbable that the TY speakers under consideration were ever "fully competent" in the sense of commanding the stylistic range and syntactic versatility of mainstream Yoruba speakers, among whom mature first generation TY speakers would number. All the same, the competency levels of TY speakers and the linguistic features of TY bear comparison with those associated with the Lenca speaker: "The phonology is intact . . . but much of the lexicon is forgotten. . . . The grammar, as well, may be largely the same as the native model in its fully viable state, although actual production is characterized by fairly simple constructions and phrases, with reduced access to stylistic or pragmatic variants and complex sentences; such speakers are unable (at least initially) to produce a normal discourse" (Campbell and Muntzel 1989: 183–84).

However, the classification of this level of language use as typical of "radical language death" is at odds with the survival of TY in the context of "gradual death," that is, "the loss of a language due to gradual shift to the dominant language in language-contact situations" (1989: 185) albeit that such asymmetrical power relations between languages in contact were exacerbated by conditions of physical exile. Indeed, *one is prompted to question the very notion of language "death," at least in situations of language shift.* Perhaps the applicability of the notion should be limited to situations where speakers of a language suddenly become extinct. Perhaps, further, it may apply to language systems that have disappeared from active or passive use in situations of language contact, as, for instance, many African languages whose speakers came to Trinidad and other Caribbean islands. But such a judgement is only conditional, since assumption of extinction really resides in our inability to recognize residual elements of those language systems.

On the other hand, the Trinidad experience, being one of gradual language shift, supports the greater accuracy in these contexts of the term "obsolescence," since it suggests a low level of language functionality over an extended period of time, while avoiding pronouncement on the termination of either active or passive performative abilities in a language. It is noteworthy, for instance, that all languages known to have been used substantially in Trinidad over the last five hundred years still linger in use, qua identifiable language systems, whether revived for occasional use, spoken daily by older members of ethnic communities, or used for place and personal names by the total population.[3] Furthermore, by giving consideration—as will be done in Chapter 9—to the transfer of phonological, idiomatic, and syntactic elements from obsolescent to interactive languages, the notion of language "death" is modified, for what is at work by way of the survival of earlier elements in later languages is the *retention of essential features through transmutation of outer form.*

Let us return, however, to the specific issues raised by the categories of language death situations set out by Campbell and

Muntzel. One notes that they are not clearly differentiated, partly because they are event-specific, and partly because the causes of language "death" and levels of language competency in residual language situations are treated conjointly. Yet despite problems posed by the infancy of language obsolescence research and theory, the checkered language competence combinations in such situations have led to the recognition of a proficiency continuum, well attested in the case of TY.

At one end of the spectrum was third- and fourth-generation T, who never had productive competence in TY, whose passive comprehension skills were minimal, but who had copied down phrases and a lexicon from first- and second-generation speakers, in addition to which she had rehearsed sacred formulae in chant and speech, learned from a first-generation source. She equates with Campbell and Muntzel's Cacopera rememberer. In keeping with the phonological dominance of primary language in such a speaker's reproduction of ancestral language, stress replaced tone, and the phonetic sequences alien to English—[gb] and [kp]—were reinterpreted, though not in total conformity with English phonology, perhaps because some of the substitute consonant clusters like [bw] and [pw] exist in French Creole, itself part of T's linguistic repertoire.

The other seven speakers had productive capacity in TY, some to a greater extent than others. Some of their productive statements were recollected phrases, statements or instructions that an ancestor had repeatedly made and the lexical composition of which they well understood; others were stimulated by current events which provoked comment. The two most able speakers were fluent and confident while observing tonal variation and syntactic orthodoxy. These were L, second generation, and S, third generation. In addition, they had composed short song lyrics in TY. Other song-creators, like second-generation N and K, were less fluent.[4] Third-generation O was initially extremely halting. Third-generation B recalled phrases with fluency but the range of her productive capacity was left largely unexplored because of time constraints. Yet another fluent speaker, third- and fourth-generation Z, produced lengthy creative texts but in a form strongly skewed by English syntactic interference. His comprehension of written Yoruba, however, was good. On the other hand, even the two creative Yoruba users, while able to provide close glosses of parts of their recollected corpus—glosses that showed a recognition of lexical and phrasal segments together with their semantic import—still suffered comprehension lacunae with respect to other sections. Active language users thus could and often did exhibit defective passive skill.

Research Data

The language corpus under study was collected in Trinidad between 1966 and 1972. Oral historical and sociolinguistic data were also gathered there between 1966 and 1991. Translation and reconstruction of the texts, together with dialect identification, were carried out with the aid of Yoruba language speakers in Nigeria, first in 1970 and more intensively in 1975.

The corpus consists of (a) approximately two hundred songs of both a sacred and secular nature, some of them recorded in more than one version,[5] (b) oral and written prose texts, and (c) lexical inventories. The study therefore takes cognizance of *the significance of song and literature in language retention*. By its framed and encapsulated form, the short fixed sequence of thought, word, and image provides a focus for the memory, besides which it may further direct recall to words that highlight designata and themes.

Field Procedures

Since there is no physically demarcated Yoruba-speaking community on the island, informants were located largely through the network system. Having recalled that a now-deceased neighbor had been a Yoruba language speaker,[6] I began by tracking down her surviving relatives and colleagues. Where I was not directed to a specific person, localities indicated by informants as previous Africa-born population centers were visited.

When operating within the latter nonspecific context, potential informants were identified (a) by age, that is, over sixty, and (b) by phenotypicality: height, facial bone structure, eye shape, general resemblance to an earlier informant—indeed, a combination of these impressionistic notions could suggest a specific African ethnicity. These pseudoscientific guesses sometimes proved right. Where they did not, they often served as leads to African language speakers known to the person approached. In a minimal number of cases, however, informants were visibly of mixed African and European descent.

Most of the primary informants were located through direct personal reference within the network frame of operation. Referrals to the heads of shango and *obeah*[7] establishments were largely ignored, though two of these leads proved highly fruitful. This was because some obeah workers were preoccupied with their clientele and this frustrated the interviewer's initial attempts to make contact with them. Furthermore, contact with such practitioners who were in their forties had indicated that their African language skills were rather limited. In any case, primary cultural preservationists such as S, O, and N had had, or still maintained, a close relationship with *orisha* and other Yoruba ceremonial. It was therefore possible to acquire some knowledge of Yoruba ritual, less mystic than descriptive, linguistic, and musical, through these primary culture-bearers. Furthermore, it seemed less troublesome to conduct interviews in private home settings than in public environments, especially since the main Yoruba language component of *orisha* ceremonies—the chanting—took place at night and this was personally inconvenient for the researcher. Also, the high noise element associated with these events—drum accompaniment and spectator remarks and conversation—proved unhelpful for recordings aimed at achieving phonological clarity.

Most of the interviews were conducted in a domestic situation, namely, the homes of the informants. Interviews were largely private, involving only the researcher and the interviewee. Sometimes this privacy was absolute, but on other occasions, some members of the household would intervene with a comment or clarification. The attitude of household members was positive and facilitating. In two or three instances where a knowledge of African culture was known not only by the main informant but also by a visiting familiar or relative, the interviewer incorporated all the knowledgeable parties in the exercise.

Most interviews were conducted in rural locations of southern and central Trinidad among peasant smallholders. Valencia and Manzanilla were the only northern rural areas involved. Other interviews took place in suburban settings of northern Trinidad, such as Tunapuna, Arouca, Diego Martin, St. Anns, Belmont, Barataria, and in Marabella in southern Trinidad. In these localities informants were largely working class but some belonged to the middle strata. Two interviews were conducted in the urban slums of East Dry River and Sea Lots in Port of Spain.

Taped recordings of communal activity were undertaken only on three occasions. Two of these were *orisha* ceremonies in the suburban commercial district of Tunapuna. The other occasion was a farewell function for me put on by T in 1968 on the eve of my departure to take up employment in Nigeria. The social involved drumming and Yoruba songs, performed by male drummers who usually assisted in T's religious rites. Choral singing unaccompanied by drums was performed by a small female group. This function took place in a rural town setting.

Informants were highly receptive to being interviewed, though there were a few cases of initial reluctance towards being tape-recorded. Other reservations were motivated by spiritual factors outside the informant-interviewer relationship.[8] Collection was generally facilitated by the informants' mystical interpretation of the interview experience: the interviewer's unannounced visit was very frequently perceived as the fulfillment of a favorable prescience through dream of a visit from an African lady or one resembling the interviewer.

Extempore methods of language collection and competence testing characterized most of the fieldwork. This was so since the residual nature of Yoruba language facility meant that lexical items, phrases, and songs were recalled largely through association, being stimulated by an immediate or recollected personal sociological context.

Deliberate memory stimulation was used by the interviewer when active recall lapsed. One stimulus tried was the replay of an interview with another informant. This device was largely unsuccessful in that it was time-consuming and distracted the immediate informant from his or her train of thought. In any case, it was an unnecessary device, given that informant attitudes were already highly cooperative. This exercise was, nevertheless, valuable.

In the earliest stages of research, elicitation centered largely on data about family histories and life experiences. Terms and sentences expressing kin relationships and cultural icons such as foods and sacred utterances emerged. Once it was clear from the data collected that informants were, in fact, of Yoruba descent and possessed some level of Yoruba language competence, a formal questionnaire was tried. This comprised a word list of familiar environmental referents, kinship and anatomical terms, and a small number of Standard English sentences. The latter were designed to elicit a variety of Yoruba grammatical structures within the competence of the researcher. However, such structured testing was ill received. Only with Z did word lists and planned sentences work as anticipated. This was so because of his familiarity with formal language learning and teaching techniques.

In fact, this method was better suited to securing data about a living rather than obsolescent language because it further narrowed already narrow linguistic options. The foregrounding of informants' ignorance at the expense of their capacity to display arcane and long-dormant knowledge resulted in their impatience, oversensitivity and demoralization. The formal methodology was also more applicable to an analytically oriented society, whereas the age, peasant background and low formal educational level of many informants predisposed them to the cognitive norms of an oral culture. They needed to fit the ideas in the preframed sentence into real-life contexts or to mentally visualize the actions typical of situations evoked. For example:[9]

S Q. We looked at the house.
A. **Aná mo ń kọjá níbí ulé an.**
Yesterday I PROG pass in place house their.

Q. The children are spoilt.
A. **Ọmọdé wọ̀nyím ọ bá mi jà lóni.**
Children these it ASSOC me fight in today.

Q. He is a bad man.
A. **Ọmakọ̀rẹ̀n yín ọ̀nyà burúkú lo n ṣe.**
Young man this person bad FOC he PROG behave.

Q. He ran quickly to get home in time.
A. **Ó súré súré súré. Ó délé nísìsìyin.**
He run run run. He reach home in now.

Informant continues:

Ọmákọ̀rẹn yín ọ́ jalè ádìẹẹ mi. O ún súré lọ
Young man this he stole fowl my. He PROG ran go

pẹ̀lú adìẹ mi.
with fowl my.

Informant's gloss:
The man thief my fowl and he running going with it.

O Q. We looked at the house.
A. **Mó ri, mó fẹ́ ri úlé lá, mo ri úlé**
I see I wish see house the, I see house

lá... úlé rẹ̀.
the... house your.

Q. How many times a day do we eat?
A. **Mọ́ fẹ́ mà méji... wọ mu jíjẹ... wo jẹ̀un...**
I want know two$_{adj}$... you take food... you eat...

or **wo mu jíjẹ̀... méjí... ọ́kán, meji o mẹtà.**
or you take food... two$_{adj}$... one$_{num}$, two$_{adj}$ or three$_{adj}$

Informant's gloss:
I wants to know how many times per day do you eat, if is once a day, twice a day, or three times per day. I wants to know.

As the informants' reformulations in Creole English and Yoruba signal, the language style selected allowed speakers to approximate the form and manner of the TY language culture and to convey a more holistic impression of the lived context. For instance, an interlocutor needed to be imagined; in some song renditions, it was explained—as an aside, in medias res—that certain segments would be intoned by other, responsorial, voices. Changed pitches by the same singer attempted to replicate this antiphonal effect. Again, remembered domestic discourse was often characterized by the imperative rather than volitive mode, which signaled adult-to-child interaction. Another grammatical index of such utterances was the zero second person pronoun form of familiar address rather than the respectful plural pronominal by which a younger person would address an imperative to a senior. Thus:

lọ	**se**	**oúnjẹ́**	**fún**	**mi**
go	cook	food	give	me

rather than:

SY	**ẹ**	**lọ**	**se**	**oúnjẹ**	**fún**	**mi**
	you$_{pl}$	go	cook	food	give	me
	go and cook for me					

Furthermore, speech was sometimes accompanied by the somatic features of body language and facial expression, song texts would be replaced by ideophonic vocalization meant to replicate percussive musical accompaniment, and feet were tapped or spoons hit rhythmically against tables to convey the pulse of song and dance. This kinesic energy was verbally imparted by the emphatic reduplication and high tone sequence in S's:

O	**súré**	**súré**	**súré.**	**Ó**	**délé**	**nísìsìyin.**
He	run	run	run.	He	reach home	in now.

The vividness of the act is underscored by the historic present signaled in the adverbial 'now'.

As a result of the failure of formal methodological exercises, a return was made to free-form conversation, largely of a self-referential nature, with the interviewee introducing Yoruba words and sentences as recollection prompted, and the interviewer occasionally requesting that ideas under discussion be framed in Yoruba. For instance, S was asked how she spent her days. She was about to reply in English, but was asked to express her thoughts in Yoruba. She laughed drily, suggestive of the difficulty to which she was being put. She expressed this discomfort in her opening idiomatic sentence:

Ori	**ím**	**bá**	**mi**	**jà.**	**Ojojúmọ́**	**na**	**ni**	**mọ**
Head	this	ASSOC	me	fight.	Daily	DEM	FOC	I

n	**dìde.**	**Mi**	**o**	**lé**	**ṣé**	**unkán.**	**Jòko**	**ní**	**mi**
PROG	stand.	I	NEG	can	do	thing.	Sit	FOC	I

n	**jokó**	**nibẹ̀**	**yín**	**ojojúmọ́.**	**Mí**	**ò**	**lé**	**ṣé**
PROG	sit	in there	this	daily.	I	NEG	can	do

unkan	**nisìsìyin.**	**Mí**	**ò**	**léèye,**	**mí**	**ò**	**ní**
thing	in now.	I	NEG	have mother,	I	NEG	have

baba,	**mí**	**ò**	**lẹ́gbàn,**	**mí**	**ò**	**lagbúrò,**
father,	I	NEG	have elder sib,	I	NEG	have younger sib,

ọ́kan...	**ó**	**kù**	**mí**	**nikan**	**ṣóṣó**	**lórí**	**ayé...**
one$_{num}$...	it	remain	mi	one$_{adj}$	alone	in surface	world...

lọ́wọ́	**Olódùmarè.**
in hand	Almighty.

Informant's gloss:
I say, he left me only one in the world in the hands of God, all them dead and gone.

Analytic Procedures

After interview and phonetic transcriptions of conversations with primary informants, the Yoruba language corpus was subjected to a combination of translation and reconstruction. Spoken utterance presented far less difficulty than the poetic language of song and verse. Decoding was based on the knowledge as well as intuition of native speakers.

Knowledge involved recognition of word junctures, morphotactic variables, syntactic units, and of idiomatic and metaphoric expressions. This level of comprehension operated at times throughout an entire text; at others it was limited to disconnected text sequences. But interpretation difficulties arose because hearer cognition varied in degree from decoder to decoder. Decoding depended on the hearer's ability to relax internalized tone rules in the context of the reorganized tonal relations between syllables in TY, on the hearer's comprehension range of Yoruba dialect varieties, and on the hearer's compass of Yoruba culture and history. Meaning proved elusive where there was nonrecognition of personal or place names, of attributive titles for divinities and historical figures, and of occupational practices in dyeing, archery, and smithing, for example.

The researcher's secondary role was aimed at securing *contextually* appropriate meaning based on an understanding of the culture and history of both Yorubaland and the Caribbean, the identification of idiomatic expressions, metaphors, and puns, on relocation of word boundaries, and variable vowel insertion given deletion of one of the segments at Yoruba Vowel + Vowel word juncture.

But interpretive work was jeopardized when presupposition had to proceed in the absence of the physical, social, and psycholinguistic contexts of utterance. On the other hand, the functional contexts or semantic glosses provided by informants, or additionally the discourse frame in which an item was rendered, all proved invaluable.

Where, despite these layers of interpretive labor, a crux presented itself, reconstruction had to replace translation. Reconstruction involved positing phonologically analogous and contextually apt words and phrases.

Linguistic Approach

Trinidad Yoruba (TY) is treated as a dialect of Yoruba, though outside the approximately twenty metropolitan varieties located in Nigeria and neighboring countries.[10] The approach is in the main sociolinguistic, and is supported by largely descriptive presentations of phonology and syntax. Wherever continental Yoruba dialectology has allowed, indications have been given of comparative features shared with TY.

The scope of the lexico-semantic database differs from that for the phonological and syntactic analyses. The lexicon is confined to items of cognitive value for the informants, whereas phonology and syntax have been extrapolated from the twin source of memorized and independently generated texts.

Part One

The Yoruba of Trinidad: Historical Background and Sociolinguistic Behavior

1

The Yoruba and Transatlantic Slavery

The Yoruba Peoples

This chapter outlines the political and cultural history of the Yoruba-speaking peoples and the nature of their involvement in the transatlantic slave trade. These historical outlines are offered to indicate by comparison the subsequent containment and decline of the Yoruba way of life in the Caribbean—a factor that led to narrowing in the lexical, semantic, and grammatical range of TY at the same time that the experience of capture, enslavement, indentureship, and colonial domination produced the conflicting affective responses that led, on the one hand, to voluntary and involuntary language loss, and, on the other, to stubborn attempts at language retention and even revival.

Sociological Background

The Yoruba of West Africa are one of the largest sub-Saharan ethnic groups; their art, their urban-type population concentrations, and the complexity of their religious and divinatory systems have earned them prominence among nonliterate social formations and cultures. The largest Yoruba community, some ten million, is located in the southwest of present-day Nigeria. But there are upwards of some 400,000 who live in Dahomey (now Benin Republic) and Togo (Igue and Yai 1973). Unlike Nigeria, Dahomey and Togo are areas of low population density, and this fact reflects itself in the size of the Yoruba groups there. Despite sometimes wide differences between dialects, the Yoruba are an "association of several sub-groups bound to one another by language and tradition" (Igue and Yai 1973: 9). The Yoruba language itself is classed as genetically related to the extensive Kwa branch of the Niger-Congo languages.[1] These languages are "characterized by the absence—or great reduction—of class systems, typologically similar developments of the verbal system emphasizing serialization and tense-aspect-mood auxiliaries, and a fairly high proportion of shared vocabulary . . . much of it . . . cultural" (Bennet and Sterk 1977: 256).

In the immediate precolonial centuries, Yoruba economy was based on "sedentary hoe farming [and] craft specialization," with "hunting, fishing, animal husbandry, and the gathering of wild foods" also being practiced (Bascom 1969: 18). Trade was originally conducted by barter, but for centuries money transactions took the form of payment in bags of cowrie shells. Amounts were calculated by the Yoruba numeral system which is based on twenty and which involves processes of addition, multiplication, and subtraction (Zaslavsky 1979: 204–12). By the time Europeans gained first-hand knowledge of the area in the eighteenth century, intercity commerce was extremely vibrant, with markets playing a pivotal role in the economic, social, and religious life of each town.[2] Goods traditionally traded included palm oil, salt, shea butter, kola, locust beans, farm produce, cotton, indigo, and woven cloths.

Economic practice initially excluded wage labor, but the prosperity won by certain sectors through trade and war booty produced social differentiation and the resultant use of indentured as well as slave labor by aristocrats, bureaucrats, and warlords. For instance, there existed the institution of pawning, "under which a person could be placed under the authority of another to redeem a debt or other obligation. The pawn, however, remained legally a free man; he enjoyed the normal rights accorded to full members of society and on the redemption of the debt, he was completely free" (Mabogunje and Omer-Cooper 1971: 17–18). But there was also slavery: "Though he might live in his master's household, be entrusted with considerable responsibilities and be trusted as much as a member of the family, [the slave] nevertheless suffered a permanent inferiority of status. He could not easily marry a free-born woman. . . . Even after several generations the family of a slave could not acquire the status of a free man" (Mabogunje and Omer-Cooper 1971: 18). Some persons were perhaps forced into slavery through the intermediate condition of a pawn (Oroge 1975), but by the late eighteenth century the bulk of domestic and agricultural slaves were war captives, a situation fed by the surplus of slaves available for the Atlantic trade.

In their division of labor, farming was largely, though not exclusively, a male province; while the trading of farm products and agricultural by-products and woven cloths fell to women. A wide range of labor specializations brought about the development of internal trade and town markets for the exchange of local produce. This led to the rise of the large urban conglomerations for which the Yoruba are noted. Male work specializations included weaving, iron working, brass casting, wood and calabash carving, bead and leather working, drum making, drumming, circumcising, cicatrizing, divination, and the practice of herbal medicine. Female specializations included midwifery, weaving of certain cloths, dyeing, pottery, and batik printing. Other female activies included cooking, hair plaiting, folktale narration, specialized areas of song performance and musical accompaniment, the preparation of palm oil and palm kernels, and soap making.

Government

Each town was governed by an *ọba* or king, whose person was sacred. He functioned in conjunction with a council of chiefs or elders appointed from among the several clans that comprised the wards into which each town was divided. "The clan or the sub-clan (formed when the clan is too large to be accommodated in a single compound) is a corporate group, owning the compound in which it dwells, and the land on which the compound stands, and the farm land outside of town, as well as intangible property such as titles to political and religious offices. It is a self-perpetuating unit, as it includes the dead who may be reborn into the clan, as well as the living. Internally its members are stratified in terms of seniority, sex, and achieved status" (Bascom 1969: 43). The clan was based on patrilineal descent from a remote common ancestor and marriage was ideally patrilocal. Yoruba men practiced polygyny.

At a macro level, the Yoruba states had been organized for centuries around a large number of kingdoms. These kingdoms had a subethnic identity, brought about by ethnic admixture with aboriginal peoples in various locales, and reflected in variations in the common language, in customs, deities, and so forth. This subethnic identity was a primary focus of affiliation recognized by the people themselves.[3] All the Yoruba-speaking people never at any one time constituted a single political entity, nor did these subgroups refer to one another by a common name (Mercier 1950; Post 1969; Biobaku 1973; Igue and Yai 1973). It was the nineteenth-century European missionaries who categorized all members of this linguistic entity by the term *Yoruba,* a loanword incorporated into the language of the Ọyọ people as their self-definition, along with 'Ọyọ'. The term *Yoruba* was in fact borrowed from the Hausa xenonym *Yarba* ~ *Yaraba*. The application by Europeans of the terms *Yoruba, Yaraba,* or *Yarriba* to Ọyọ-related dialects and their speakers is therefore an instance of semantic extension. In the diaspora, other nomenclatures for the entire ethnolinguistic group are to be found: *Nago, Lucumi,* and *Aku. Anago* is one name for the Ifọnyin and Ahori ~ Awori subgroups based astride the present-day Nigerian-Benin (Dahomey) border on the coastal southwest boundary of Yorubaland, and *Nago* ~ *Anago* is the general designation for the Yoruba in Benin Republic, Brazil, and Jamaica. *Aku* is the term for the Yoruba in the Krio language of Sierra Leone, and *Aku* ~ *Oku* was also used in British Guiana; *Lucumí* is the traditional term for the Yoruba in Cuba.[4]

It appears that the northern savanna-based Yoruba were the object of harrassment by the neighboring Nupe (Tapa) in the fifteenth and sixteenth centuries. These raids were the Nupe's means of securing slaves for the trans-Saharan slave trade conducted by Arabs. After being devastated by Nupe in the early sixteenth century, the northern Yoruba responded by consolidating themselves around the Ọyọ subgroup and developing a defensive war machinery. By the mid-sixteenth century, they had established a formidable cavalry through trans-Saharan imports of stock and accoutrements. These strategies led to the rise of their complex state administration, as well as to a policy of military expansionism. The sixteenth century thus saw the rise to prominence of the Ọyọ which, in a series of wars, came to dominate "most of northern and western Yorubaland as well as . . . parts of the territories of non-Yoruba neighbours—the Nupe, the Ibariba and the Aja of Dahomey. . . . Furthermore, [the Ọyọ kingdom] established relationships with most other Yoruba kingdoms, and its influence considerably curtailed the frequency and severity of the conflicts among them" (Akintoye 1971: xvi).

Ọyọ political dominance was counterbalanced by the spiritual and dynastic leadership universally acknowledged among the Yoruba to reside with the city-state of Ifẹ. The King of Ọyọ—the Alafin—recognized the seniority of the king of Ifẹ and received from Ifẹ his insignia of office. Internal Ọyọ political organization was itself complex, with actual or potential *loci* of power, or both, diffused throughout.

> Around Oyo itself, there was an area, often referred to as Yoruba proper, habited by people who regarded themselves as Oyos. Much of

> this area was administered directly from the capital though it contained some towns large enough to have dynasties of their own. Outside this area, there were towns which were governed indirectly from Oyo, through residents (*Ajele*). These were members of the Alafin's palace staff appointed to reside in vassal towns to watch over the Alafin's interests. Such towns possessed their own royal families and exercised considerable autonomy in their domestic affairs though the Ajeles could intervene when they felt it necessary. Other towns again remained almost completely autonomous merely giving formal recognition to the authority of their more powerful neighbour by informing the Oyo ruler of the accession of their kings and sending formal presents. . . . The Oyo empire thus shaded off into a loosely defined sphere of influence (Mabogunje and Omer-Cooper 1971: 12–13).

Such an extensive imperial administration reflected itself, at the Alafin's court, in "a complex bureaucracy of palace servants, consisting of male and female slaves, the king's wives and eunuchs. Altogether, they constituted a considerable community and the palace was virtually a town in itself." On the other hand, the king's

> political power in Oyo itself was counterbalanced by that of the seven hereditary chiefs known as the Oyomesi. Of these, the leader, the Basorun, was by far the most important and always took the initiative in the name of the group. . . . The Basorun . . . had a "civil service" staff of his own similar to that of the king, if on a smaller scale, and the Oyomesi could call in military forces of their own which were largely independent of that of the king. . . . Military matters were delegated to a number of palace servants of whom the most important was the chief commander of the Alafin's forces known as the Are-Ona-Kakanfo. . . . As the Alafin's position was as much religious as secular, spiritual power was as important as military in maintaining his authority (Mabogunje and Omer-Cooper 1971: 15–17).

The Alafin was a divine king, representative of his deified ancestor, Shango, the *orisha* controlling lightning. When he died, he was believed to ascend into the sky like Shango to join his divine predecessors. A successor was chosen by the palace chiefs from candidates among competing royal patrilineal clans.

For reasons of political control, links existed between religious organizations and the secular administrative system but "in particular, the Shango cult played a vital role in state administration. The Alafin's position as representative of Shango was exploited to the full as a means of supporting his authority. The Shango cult was spread to every town under Ọyọ influence and organised in a hierarchy centred in the palace at Ọyọ. The Alafin's Ajeles were often themselves Shango priests" (Mabogunje and Omer-Cooper 1971: 17). The widespread and influential nature of the Shango cult in areas under Ọyọ control no doubt accounts for the prominence of this deity in overseas Yoruba culture areas,[5] and for the application of their deity's name to *orisha* observance in general in Trinidad.

Yoruba Entry into Transatlantic Slavery

By the late seventeenth century, one of the economic supports of Ọyọ's might came to be the exploitation of the Atlantic slave market. The sources from which the Ọyọ procured their slaves is still uncertain, but it appears that, apart from adjacent peoples like the Nupe, Ibariba (Borgu), and Hausa, some northeastern Yoruba subgroups that were outside Ọyọ's jurisdiction also fell victims to its depredations. Among these subgroups were the Yagba, the Ekiti, and the Akoko. Yoruba-speaking peoples therefore formed some portion of the seven to ten thousand slaves exported annually by Ọyọ from the late seventeenth to the late eighteenth centuries. These slaves exited through ports in the Bight of Benin to the west of Ọyọ—ports like Whydah, Porto Novo (Hogbonu ~ Ajasẹ ~ Assem ~ Ardrah), and Anecho (Little Popo). These ports were used because until the late eighteenth century there was no international sea port within Yoruba territory. Porto Novo, a self-governing kingdom over which both Dahomey and Ọyọ contended, had in fact eventually come under the protection of Ọyọ. Porto Novo lay on the extreme southwestern Yoruba language boundary.

The establishment of Lagos (Eko ~ Awonlin) as a major British slaving outlet toward the end of the eighteenth century was to serve as an impetus for several Yoruba kingdoms to participate in slave capture and trading as a vibrant economic activity. This new opportunity would effect a massive increase in the numbers of Yoruba-speaking slaves shipped to the New World in the nineteenth century. The population of Lagos itself would rocket from five thousand to twenty thousand within two decades around the beginning of the nineteenth century. Most of its inhabitants were slaves captured inland.

The shift in trading activity eastward from Whydah to Lagos was occasioned by several factors. One factor was that Dahomey had assumed a state monopoly on slave exports from the outlets it controlled, chief of which was Whydah, and this forced up the price of slaves, to the displeasure of slave traders. In addition, the spillover from hostilities engendered by the Napoleonic Wars endangered European shipping at multinational slave ports. The British therefore saw merit in transferring their operations to the swampy Lagos inlet which hitherto had been considered unattractive for regular navigation.

The presence of a slave port immediately south of Yorubaland acted as a powerful external stimulus to widespread intra-Yoruba slave trading. But there was also an internal stimulus, partially but not wholly a result of the external factor. Toward the close of the eighteenth century, the Ọyọ empire was witness to a sequence of decisive internal upheavals. Despite—or perhaps because of—its prosperity, its development of social and professional differentiation, and its subtle political organization, a number of factors combined in the second half of the eighteenth century to precipitate the disintegration of Ọyọ. There were a series of constitutional crises: the Bashorun, Gaha, made a bid for power; the southerly Ẹgba kingdom revolted; an unfortunate punitive military raid undertaken in pique against the important city of Apomu ended by estranging the revered Ifẹ. In addition, an attempted palace coup by Afọnja, a pretender to the throne, took place in the final decade of the eighteenth century. This led to the head-on collision between Islam and polytheism because, to unseat the Alafin, Afọnja made an alliance with the Fulani jihadists under Usman dan Fodio.[6] When this happened the Muslim Hausa and Nupe slaves of the Ọyọ fled en masse to the more northerly town of Ilọrin from which they launched an effective holy war against Ọyọ. They sacked Ọyọ City [Ọyọ Ile] around 1812.

Civil Wars and Social Disruption

Both the northern Ọyọ and the southeastern Ijẹbu—another Yoruba subgroup—had been marginally connected with the slave trade from about the sixteenth century. The northeastern and southwestern Yoruba were particularly vulnerable slave-raiding targets because they were relatively disorganized, not having consolidated themselves into powerful city-states. By the late eighteenth century, the Ijẹbu seized the advantage of their previous slave trading experience, their control of hinterland trade routes, and their geographical position slightly north of Lagos to consolidate their economy on the basis of bartering slaves for guns. But it was the decline and fall of Ọyọ as political and administrative capital of Yorubaland that catalyzed widespread political upheavals and re-alignments in the entire Yoruba-speaking area. These developments led to the decay of several kingdoms and, in the 1820s, the creation of new centers of power, notably Abẹokuta and Ibadan. In order to succeed to Ọyọ political hegemony, Ibadan armies began to penetrate into eastern Yorubaland towards the end of the forties. For about three decades afterwards, their raids "resulted in widespread insecurity, while the migrations, the flights and the forcible seizures of people led to the desertion of homes and means of livelihood, the breaking up of families and the scattering of their members in different directions. Whole towns and villages became deserted and large areas of farmland were reclaimed by jungles." As a result, "probably more than ever before, the nineteenth century witnessed a great deal of mixing of Yoruba peoples. Fragments of the various Yoruba subgroups were thrown all over the Yoruba homeland, most getting absorbed into their new homes" (Akintoye 1971: xviii).

This demographic dislocation was the environment in which, for the first time, the Yoruba-speaking people came to experience transatlantic slavery on a large scale. This nineteenth-century dating is important since a synchronous linking of the Yoruba slave trade and the earliest such trading out of the Congo and Senegambia basins has led some pioneering scholars of New World Yoruba to question glottochronological methodology largely on the erroneous premise that Cuban Lucumí has been separated from mainstream Yoruba by a time-differential of between three to five hundred years.[7]

The Yoruba-speaking subgroups recalled by Trinidad oral sources are the Ijẹbu, Ijẹsha, Ẹgba, Ẹgbado, and Yaraba or Yooba or Yoruba—these latter meaning, in indigenous, pre-European terms, the Ọyọ. Towns of origin were another focus of identification, and among those named were Owu and Ọyọle (Ọyọ Ile ~ Old Ọyọ ~ Katunga) to the north; Ado, Arigidi, Igosi, Ikọle, Ọyẹ—in the easterly Ekiti region; nearby Ondo, and Yagba further east; Abẹokuta and Ibadan in Ẹgba country to the south; and Ọta in coastal Ẹgbado.[8]

Anthropological data of a religious nature provides supporting evidence that the earliest Yoruba-speaking migrants, who probably arrived during slavery, derived from scattered populations outside the jurisdiction of imperial Ọyọ. Among these were apparently Yagba and Ekiti as well as Nago, Ajasẹ, and Ẹgbado from the southwestern border of Yorubaland contiguous with Dahomey. A ceremony of reverence for family ancestors, *saraka,* was the main religious ritual among this earlier wave.

On the other hand, the Yaraba ~ Ọyọ and Yoruba peoples like the Igbomina, Ogbomọṣọ, Owu, Ọfa, Isẹyin, Ikoyi, and Ilọrin from within the centralized government of the Ọyọ Empire figured heavily in the later exodus. This exodus must have begun early in the nineteenth century, thus pre-dating but also including the post-Emancipation migrations. This periodization is reflected in the fact that the cult worship of Shango that was institutionalized throughout the Yoruba Empire came, in Trinidad and Grenada, to supercede the observance of *saraka.*[9] In addition, Ọyọ preeminence dictated that the deities whose worship has continued in Trinidad are those whose worship constituted a cultural denominator throughout Yorubaland—such as Ogun, Ọya, Ọshun, Shokpọnnọ, Ọsanyin, Ọrunmila, Yemọja, and those of Ọyọ origin like Shango, Dada, and Bayanni. An Ijẹbu deity adopted by Ọyọ is Erinlẹ, but his name is rendered in Trinidad in accordance with the Ọyọ phonological rule of intervocalic *r-* deletion, thus /ɛilɛ/. By comparison, the specifically Ifẹ deities or the Ifẹ nomenclatures of Ọyọ divine counterparts are less well known, so that Oduduwa, Olokun, Ọranyan, and Oramfẹ or Jakuta do not survive in the generally recognized Trinidad *orisha* pantheon.[10] The Ifẹ term 'Yemoo' for 'Yemọja' appears unknown. Similarly, local deities worshipped in the Ẹgba, Ẹgbado, Ekiti, and Akoko areas declined into oblivion.

In its turn, analysis of the Yoruba dialects most dominant in TY suggests that the northern Yoruba—Ọyọ, Ijẹsha and Ekiti—were numerically dominant among slave captives: the Ọyọ, on the one hand, because they were in flight from their traditional homes and attempting to relocate further south in uninhabited areas; the Ijẹsha and Ekiti, on the other, because their presence in the earlier phase was supplemented by later victims of warfare—for Ibadan in the nineteenth century, in attempting to incorporate the area, partially depopulated it. Numerical strength alone would have ensured greater linguistic influence for these groups. Both these factors could in turn have bestowed on them higher social status than that enjoyed by other subethnic groups. Although numerical dominance is not inevitably consistent with social prestige, it appears plausible that in this case it might have been. In general though, the Ọyọ had the greater social advantage. This rested not only on their numerical profile, but rather on the political power they had until so lately wielded in Yorubaland itself. This direction was sealed when the Church Missionary Society, though based in Abẹokuta in Ẹgba territory, commissioned Bishop Ajayi Crowther, the first African Anglican prelate, to devise an orthography for Yoruba. The ultimate aim was to effect translation of the Bible and other evangelical material. Crowther, himself an Ọyọ, chose to work with the Ọyọ dialect from among all the Yoruba regional forms. He did, all the same, include a few Ẹgba elements.[11]

Slaves, Soldiers and Indentured Laborers

The synthesis of peoples that took place among the Yoruba whose destiny kept them in Yorubaland had its parallel among those whose fortune bore them overseas. One ingredient of this mingling was interdialectal contact. For those like Bishop Ajayi Crowther who did not proceed directly to the sea after initial removal from their village, there was no doubt a gradual accommodation towards their host dialect.[12] Host locations were in fact several when, as in the case of Crowther, the subject was bartered several times over. The attempt to approximate to the phonology and idiom of the host dialect was likely to have been easier in the case of young captives than among the mature. This conclusion, though, is qualified by the fact that sojourns with buyers along the internal trade routes were in some cases prolonged and in other instances brief.[13] Interdialectal contact would have been further fostered among those who fell into the transatlantic trade. There would have been dialect interaction during the period of waiting at the slave barracoons, and then on the sea journey. In the case of those slaves who were liberated before arriving at their New World destinations, there was in addition the intensive interdialectal and interlingual contact fostered by settlement in Sierra Leone.[14]

Mention of Sierra Leone is relevant here because the Africans who landed in Trinidad between 1840 and 1867 arrived not as slaves, but with the legal status of immigrant indentured laborers. This statement is not only based on documentary evidence, but is also orally supported. Some informants were aware of the difference between indentured and slave Africans. Where this was so, the informants specifically stated that some people came to the island "bound," that is, in chains as slaves, or, on the other hand, that they "did not come bound." Some expressed this by saying that slavery had been abolished when their forebear "was coming on the sea," and that on arrival in the island these predecessors were able to see the cuts and abrasions that the former slaves still carried as relics of their miserable condition.[15]

Other oral evidence of indentureship was provided by the approximate dates given in informants' biographies. Significant popular dates in nineteenth-century Trinidad are events such as the cholera epidemic of 1854, the Venezuelan civil disturbances of the 1850s that caused a flood of Venezuelan immigration into the island, the 1837 revolt in a local militia by dissident African soldiers led by Daaga, as well as the Ashanti Wars of the 1870s and the Boer War of 1899–1902 (in both of which the West India Regiment battalions took part).[16]

Another helpful guide was information that some arriving mothers had been accompanied by children. One concludes that such partial family units had enjoyed a period of settled existence at some intermediate stage between capture in West Africa and arrival in the West Indies. A more definite indication of indentured status was an informant's recall or display of artifacts brought by an ancestor from Africa. The existence of these items indicates that their owners had arrived under travel conditions differing from those of the slaveship holds in which fettered humans could claim little more possession than their bare selves, if as much. In this regard there was mention of books of a religious nature and books dealing with African languages. These latter were probably rudimentary African-English glossaries or evangelical material possibly given to the migrants by missionaries or civil authorities in Sierra Leone. Most of these books had been lost by the time of this research. However, one informant still possessed a very old copy of the Koran brought by his grandfather. Another African had brought along his *banja* (< *mbanja* ~ *mbanza* (KiMbundu): a thumb piano) which had been thrown away after the old man's death. At another residence a glazed clay bowl with its cover survived from a pair used as food containers.

Furthermore, direct inquiry as to whether Africans had stayed in Sierra Leone or whether the informant had heard the older people speaking about Sierra Leone generally elicited a positive reply, though informants knew this place-name as /sa liɔn/.

History of the African Indentureship Scheme

The British Parliament, having in 1807 passed the Prohibition of the Slave Trade Act, instituted a British Naval Preventitive Squadron to police the transatlantic trade run beginning in 1808. These warships patrolled particularly in the seas off the Guinea Coast, though some also carried out maneuvers close to well-known slave ports in South America and the Caribbean, such as Rio de Janeiro and Havana. This blockade had the rather reluctant and lukewarm support of other slave-trading nations, among them the United States, Spain, and France. Courts of Mixed Commissions with representatives from the supporting countries sat at Freetown in Sierra Leone, Luanda in Angola, Boa Vista and Rio de Janeiro in Brazil, Havana in Cuba, and at St. Helena island in the mid-Atlantic. All these were ports to which the condemned vessels were brought. These courts were empowered to "condemn captured slave vessels, sell the ships so taken, punish the owners and masters, and set free the slaves found within them" (Asiegbu 1969: 23).

The chief of these courts was the Vice-Admiralty Court at Freetown, a settlement established in 1787 by British philantropists of the Sierra Leone Company to host the free Blacks of England and Nova Scotia—originally soldiers fighting for the British in the American War of Independence and exiled Maroons from Jamaica.[17] In 1808 jurisdiction over the Sierra Leone Colony passed from the Company to the British government, which then used the colony as a settlement for slaves liberated from impounded slavers and later also as a depot for slave recaptive transhipment.[18] Most of the data concerning the fate of these Africans concerns those who landed at Sierra Leone.

They were housed in the African Liberated Yard, also called the King's or Queen's Yard, until their ship was confiscated. Those who were ill were first hospitalized. Once declared free, they were given English names and registered. Some were then sent to settle villages on the outskirts of Freetown, peasant agriculture and market trading being the main activities. A subsistence of two pence per day was available to the old and incapacitated. Children were either sent to the villages or placed in households where they worked for their masters during time off from school. Some adults were apprenticed to worthy Freetown residents. "Unmarried women were granted rations for three months, by which time they were expected to have gained employment or a husband" (Asiegbu 1969: 28). A large number of men were recruited, voluntarily and forcibly, into the military, of which by 1837, "the whole of the African Corps and a large part of the West India Regiments serving in the West Indies were supplied from the liberated Africans at Sierra Leone."[19] It was from among both the new arrivals to Sierra Leone—the recaptives—and the earlier colonists that Britain tried to satisfy the labor needs of the West Indian planters in the immediate post-Apprenticeship period.[20]

Emancipation of the slaves in British colonies was proclaimed in 1834, but to allow the planters some respite from the consequences of labor outflow, a four-year transitional period, euphemistically called "apprenticeship," was attached to the conditions under which the slaves would eventually be liberated. This prolongation of slavery caused the effective date of liberation to be 1 August 1838, which is why oral history in the West Indies continues to favor Queen Victoria with credit for liberating the slaves from their shackles, although the British monarch in 1834 was William IV.

Once free, the slaves deserted the plantations in large numbers, setting up in free villages on the outskirts of the plantations. From these locations they were able to engage in independent small farming as well as to hire out their labor for seasonal tasks on the large estates. This pattern, however, did not recommend itself to the plantation owners, who had become habituated to a steady, captive, and unpaid labor force to produce their wealth. The planters therefore proposed to the British Government the importation of laborers under an indentureship system as the best short-term method of regulating their labor supply and lowering labor costs. (The latter would result from a depression of the free laborers' wages because of job competition.)

Although later attempts were made to secure laborers of other nationalities, such as Chinese and Madeira Portuguese, to fill this perceived gap, it was to the African liberated slaves that the British Government and planter interests first looked. However, since such economic motives savored too much of the discredited slave trade, philanthropic interests were invoked: "[E]migration of free Africans to the West Indies would help Africa itself. The West Indies provided a much closer approximation to the ways of Europe than did West Africa, and the emigrant would be able to acquire 'civilization'" (Laurence 1958: 111). To allay opposition from several administrative and missionary quarters in Sierra Leone, the British Government, in acquiescing to the emigration scheme in 1840, laid down the condition that "all emigrants must have been at least six weeks in the colony and be allowed twenty-one days to consider the matter before embarking" (Laurence 1958: 112). This proviso had been intended both to ensure that newly liberated Africans would not emigrate while still debilitated by their slave ship experience, and that Sierra Leone did not become an entrepot for the embarkation of slaves culled from surrounding areas. But economic interests increasingly held sway over humanitarianism. By 1842 a new plan was adopted to speed up the flow of labor, thus meeting the pressures of the London-based West India Committee formed of wealthy sugar barons. The six-week residence qualification was reduced to four weeks in January 1843, and to one week in April 1844. The sex proportion law of one female to two males and "the passport fees, which tended to hinder recruiting, were also modified, and then scrapped" (Laurence 1958: 119). By now, the potential African indentured labor force was comprised largely of recaptives rather than of liberated Africans settled in the Sierra Leone villages.

On arrival in the West Indies, the immigrants were subjected to medical inspection. Smallpox, dysentery, dropsy, and debility, all brought on by overloading, poor ventilation, and malnutrition, were the chief causes of a sometimes alarmingly high mortality rate. The ill were hospitalized. Since Colonial Office policy during 1838–46 forbade emigration officials from making the emigrants sign contracts, the allocation of the laborers took place only on their arrival at destination. "Orphaned children were committed to the care of adult immigrants whom they liked or were placed with 'respectable' town-dwellers" (Laurence 1958: 165).[21] Adults in sound health were divided by the Agent General for Emigration into lots of ten, fifteen, twenty, or even fifty later on, and distributed—or rather "advised" to place themselves at the disposal of certain estates. The immigrants, however, "often ignored official advice and chose employment on the advice of Africans already settled—often with those employers who offered a cash incentive" (Laurence 1958: 164). But this freedom of choice was minimized in 1845–46 when West Indian planters privately financed the transportation of emigrants, so that arrivals during that period were given out "to the estates of persons responsible for any particular shipload, provided wages and accommodation were up to standard, as some compensation for the risk involved in sending ships to Sierra Leone" (Laurence 1958: 164).

In 1842 indenture was authorized for one year, or until the age of eighteen, but by 1850 "new Ordinances authorised the compulsory indenture of captured Africans for two years, while providing security for their good treatment. But the Africans did not take kindly to indentures; they would enter none unless compelled, and took every opportunity of leaving the estates on which they were located" (Laurence 1958: 172) since the contract to remain with one estate suggested a form of slavery. Feeling that their purpose was being frustrated, the planters sought to bind the immigrants for even longer periods. They succeeded. By 1852 indentureship was extended to three years, and by 1863 to five.

Clearly, the whole emigration scheme was plagued by a host of administrative difficulties and corrupt practices. Furthermore, some of the problems were precipitated by the attitude of the Africans themselves. After their experience of enslavement and forcible removal from their homelands, both the recaptives and Freetown settlers were reluctant to uproot themselves once more. Not uncommonly, Sierra Leone residents who came to look over the recaptives discovered in the Yard relatives or townsfolk whom they had last seen in their homelands or in the barracoons. Kinship discovered in a foreign land acted as a deterrent to further removal, and with kinship and language ties reinforced by alien status in a new society, Africans opted for a reestablishment of normalcy in Sierra Leone rather than in an unknown overseas territory.

These and other factors militated against large-scale emigration, so that over the period 1841–1867 only an estimated 36,120 Africans had landed in the British West Indian territories including British Guiana.[22] For this twenty-six-year period, only about nine thousand Africans are known to have landed in Trinidad.[23] Some others, certainly, arrived from other sources, as, for example, directly from slavers headed for Cuba and Brazil that were captured in Caribbean seas. Furthermore, oral sources indicate that Africans originally indentured in Grenada, St. Lucia, Guadeloupe, Tobago, and Montserrat eventually joined the heavy flow of nineteenth-century interisland migrants who found their way to Trinidad, which was being cleared for development but which was underpopulated. Their movement signaled a sense of individual freedom and wage bargaining power on the part of ex-slaves and ex-indenturees. They journeyed to Trinidad, "attracted . . . by prospects of higher wages." Initially, they emigrated "at their own cost, but they soon found that the planters were ready to advance the passage-money, only provided they would engage their services as a compensation." Furthermore, the Trinidad Legislature, "having been induced to make the introduction of labourers a public enterprise, a 'regular trade in immigrants' was established between

Trinidad and the neighbouring islands, but especially Grenada, Montserrat, Nevis and St. Christopher. The captains who introduced them were entitled to a bounty" (de Verteuil 1858: 370). Although these operations were resisted by the plantocracy and the Legislative Councils in the negatively affected islands, the Trinidad government would again, later in the century, actively institute a policy of encouraging migration from English-speaking territories; this time the motive was primarily linked to language policy.[24]

Repatriation

Relatively few immigrants returned to Africa, particularly after regular boat trips ceased (Schuler 1980: 89–93). "Return passages were offered only to residents of Sierra Leone between 1843 and 1848, and of the Kroo Coast between 1843 and 1852" (Laurence 1958: 155, n. 1), never to recaptives, except for a few sent back as delegates.[25] Passages were available after a five-year stay in the West Indies, and by 1857 the governor of Trinidad asserted that no further Africans were entitled to this gratuity (Laurence 1958: 160). However, if one could extrapolate for Trinidad from the evidence of Cuba and Brazil, it is highly likely that there were individuals and families who financed return passages to Africa out of their savings. Some of these voyages took them to England in transit to the African west coast. Other voyages—by the brigantines, *goletas,* and merchant ships, including the steamship *Growler,* all of which brought indentured laborers and merchandise across the Atlantic—took the repatriates to West African ports where British consuls were stationed after 1849—Lagos, Badagry and the Niger Delta, apart from Freetown. Even earlier, in 1837, "two Hausa, emancipated in Trinidad" are reported to have "arrived in Freetown on their way to Badagry . . . whence they meant to return to their homeland. Their inspiring story stirred many recaptives."[26]

There is even, fortuitously, a glimmering of oral evidence that Africans in Trinidad did indeed return home. It is not clear whether the individuals in question had been former Sierrra Leone residents or recaptives. The information, retailed by Adeniyi Williams of Ibadan, Nigeria, revealed that a native of Ọyẹ Ekiti known in Trinidad as Henry Williams, a laborer, was one such person. He returned to Yorubaland, with his wife, formerly Betsy Davis. She was from Ilesha, chief town of Ijẹsha, and wore Ijẹsha facial marks. Henry and Betsy "were married under a Registrar of Marriage certificate dated 1st June 1869, and issued by Mr. John Herbert Trollope, District Registrar of Marriages for the Couva Ward Union in the island of Trinidad." Their Trinidad-born son, Philip Henryson Williams—later to become a "Merchant Prince" of Lagos, and grandfather of the informant—was about seven years old at the time he was taken by his parents to Yoruba country.[27]

On the other hand, there were those who lacked the means or decisiveness to rejoin their relatives across the Middle Passage. Correspondence from Sierra Leone residents to British administrators and missionaries in the colony, on the one hand, and on the other from immigrants desirous of returning all betray a sense of anxiety, frustration, and desperation at a bureaucracy unconcerned with human needs and conniving at its own financial convenience.[28] But the desire for return was real and the motives clear: unfulfilled financial expectations, oppressive working conditions, a longing for reintegration with relatives. Two letters from Trinidad-based immigrants addressed to their former Church Missionary Society teachers forcibly reflect both these concrete and emotional conditions.[29] A letter by Thomas Peter Norman was eloquently couched in Biblical imagery: "To you our Teachers, and Ministers, I do write this most importance, to inform you the Gentlemen, that I your scholar left my native country for only vain glory and come to Trinidad but afterward I am repented—as the prodigal son, would have return to his father and will say unto him father I have sinned against heaven and before thee and am no more worthy to be called thy son make me as one of thy hired servant." John Gammon's conclusion to his letter was also dramatically metaphoric: "We went an inquire the Governor of Trinidad and the agent for our return passage back to Sierra Leone they told us there is no returning passage for us. From the time that we was in Trinidad we suffer much by the Planters . . . through our own foolishness cause us to left our native country for Trinidad, but we are very sorry to state to you that we have repented for the day that we left Sierra Leone. . . . We are in distress and in darkness and under the shadow of death."

2

First-Generation Trinidad Yoruba Society

The African Ethnicities in Trinidad

No census lists the relative numerical strength of post-Emancipation (1838) African nationalities, but the 1813 Register of Slaves does provide such evidence for the first decade and a half of the nineteenth century.[1] This shows 41.2 percent coming from the Bight of Biafra, an outlet for peoples such as the Igbo, Ibibio, Efik, Calabari, Itsekri, and Sobo[2] from the Niger Delta, along with Chamba and other northwestern Bantu of the Cameroons. Some among these peoples were referred to as Moko.[3] The next largest group (19.1 percent) were from Central Africa, peoples from the Congo Basin and the Central African Atlantic coast as well as the peoples from present-day Angola. Another 12.2 percent derived from the Senegambia—the Malinke or Mandingo, Wolof, and Kanga.[4] Both the Gold Coast and the Bight of Benin provided just marginally more than 8 percent, the Windward Coast 6.6 percent, and Sierra Leone 4.5 percent.

For the post-Emancipation (1838) period one surmises an increase in the numbers from Central Africa and the Bight of Benin, though it is unclear which other groups proportionately declined. It is interesting to note that in 1844, only three years after the traffic of indentured laborers out of Sierra Leone commenced, the proportions on one shipment of 154 laborers show one-fifth being Creoles of Sierra Leone, another fifth Yoruba, and a similar amount being Moko.[5] The Congo were a negligible amount. In any case, Congo are not mentioned as comprising the population of Sierra Leone at this stage.[6] Perhaps their numbers out of St. Helena, given its geographical location, might have been more, and since the Congo and Angola traffic to Brazil and Cuba was high, slavers bearing Central Africans might more often have been captured in waters at the approach to Caribbean and South American ports. Certainly, documentary and oral sources indicate the numerical and cultural strength of the Congo from West Central Africa. All the same, *Congo* emerged as an umbrella term for an array of peoples from the vast Congo River Basin and did not signify the Bakongo alone. Oral sources, however, distinguish broadly between the Congo and the Chimbundu or Angoles, Umbundu-speaking Ovimbundu (Ochimbundu, sg.) located in the Portuguese colony of Angola.

The Congo, Igbo, and Yoruba were consistently noted as among the African peoples in mid- and late-nineteenth-century Trinidad. Speaking about the 1840s, Thomas James St. Hill indicated that Belmont, then known as Freetown Valley, was populated by "Mandingoe, Eboe, Kramanti, Kroomen, Congo and Yarraba." (quoted in Franklin 1910: 76) J. J. Thomas, writing in 1888, indicated "Mandingoes, Foulahs, Houssas, Calvers, Gallahs, Karamenties, Yorubas, Aradas, Cangas, Kroos, Timnehs, Veis, Eboes, Mokoes, Bibis, and Congoes, as the most numerous and important of the tribal contribution of Africa to the population of these Colonies" (1969: 142).[7] And Joseph Lewis, testifying during the Royal Franchise Commission of 1888, declared "the chief tribal groupings in Trinidad were the Congos, 'Yarribas', and Eboes" (1888: 287).

The salience of Congo and Yoruba in contemporary literature as well as in twentieth-century recall may be a testimony less singularly to their numbers than to the distinctiveness of their way of life or their social cohesion or both.[8] It is to be noted that more than one written account of the African presence in Trinidad begins by naming the Mandingo. This might have to do with force of numbers, but it might just as well have had to do with the cohesion wrought by their Moslem faith, the favorable rating of their monotheism, the Arabic literacy of their spokesmen, and their repeated written petitions to the colonial authorities.[9] In the same way, the Yoruba attracted attention from the intelligentsia because of their internal social organization, their dedication to commerce, independent occupations, and land acquisition, and their capacity for integration into civil society—all likely products of a populous, urbanized, and trade-oriented society. Their embrace of Catholicism also recommended them highly. The Congo tended consistently to attract negative comments relating to lack of industry and honesty, and a fondness for entertainment, factors which appear to reflect, on the one hand, an unwillingness to cooperate with the civil and religious authorities and, on the other, the less urbanized social structure of small, isolated, hinterland peoples.

Of course, a distinctive life-style, whether perceived negatively or positively by outsiders, indicated cultural self-assurance. This in turn was enhanced by overall numerical strength or micro patterns of social cohesiveness. The same enabling factor (or factors) need not have applied in the case of every ethnic group. But to judge from the results of these complex and varied processes, we may see the retention into the second half of the twentieth century of languages such as Yoruba and KiKongo, and more tenuously of Umbundu, Hausa, Fon, and Arabic, as one pointer in assessing the relative cultural, if not numerical, strength of African communities in the previous century.

Apart from the Congo and Yoruba, other post-Emancipation African culture-groups named by oral sources were the Wolof,[10] Mandingo and Kanga, Kisi, Susu, Kru and Bassa[11] from the the Windward or Grain Coast and its Upper Guinea or Senegambia interior; Hausa, Fula, Gwari, Chamba, and Gurunsi[12] from the West African savanna belt stretching from its Atlantic Coast to the Cameroon Highlands; Igbo, Efik, Ibibio, Calabari, Ijo, Sobo, Hona and "Moko" generally, from the hinterland of the Bight of Biafra and the Cameroon; Fanti and Ashanti from the Gold Coast, given the blanket name "Koromanti" after their port of exit; Popo[13] and Rada or Allada from the Mina Coast, also called the Slave Coast in the Bight of Benin.

Ascriptive Roles of Africans in a Creole Society

African-born Trinidad residents numbered 8,010 in 1851, 6,035 in 1861, 4,250 in 1871, and by 1891 "only 2,055 remained . . . , more than half of whom were over sixty years of age" (Stark 1897: 72). By 1861 when the total population of the island was calculated at 84,438, some 46,936 were Trinidad-born, Blacks and Whites; 13,488 were of Indian ethnicity, both India- and Trinidad-born; 11,716 were from British colonies, largely Caribbean; only 1,040 were from the United Kingdom; and just 6,035 or 7.15 percent of the population had been born in Africa.[14] It is therefore clear that in mid century, first generation Trinidad Africans were a minority in relation to other culture-groups such as Indians, Europeans, and African Creoles.

Like other African-born peoples, the Yoruba entered a polity that was a construct of European colonialism and imperialism, and one in which superior and inferior roles had long since been assigned on the basis of skin color and its graduated shades. Color was the visible and popularly accepted manifestation of the economic and political power that created the society and that shaped the goals and values of the colony. Although wealth was not always the collateral of whiteness, whiteness was a passport to privilege.[15] With privilege lay the potential for wealth or social success or both. This schema formed the target ethos, the "positive" social and cultural underpinning of the colony; by the reverse, blackness meant lack of privilege, poverty, victimization. The norm in force was therefore not the "norm," given the ethnic composition of the population, but it was a norm imposed by economic power and cultural domination, and integrated into the cultural values of the society as a whole. Indeed, the values and institutions that held together this "divided society" were, firstly, "the act of metropolitan control through the Crown Colony system.[16] Everyone . . . whatever his race, class, or colour, was affected by this fact. . . . Secondly, nearly everyone accepted the white elite as the legitimate upper class. Thirdly, most people accepted and subscribed to the colour stratification." From this it followed that "European culture, and especially all things British, were considered superior to all other cultural forms in the island" (Brereton 1972: 346–47).

The African immigrants joined nonwhites in the position of inferiority which had already been assigned to them. In socioeconomic terms, they were tools of the planter class that organized their immigration. They worked on sugarcane and cacao estates, cutting, hoeing, axing, trenching, planting, weeding, and driving carts. Some males were artisan carpenters, masons, and smiths. Many of the young women were hired by Europeans as domestic servants. After indenture, some in Port of Spain "worked for the Government as free labourers—on the roads, the Savannah and in the Public Gardens" (St. Hill quoted in Franklin 1910: 76). In rural areas, many became small peasant cultivators, and some combined this with higglering. Some sold their produce, confectionery, or herbs in the market, others at their doorstep or on sidewalks of the city and larger towns. In forested areas men were hunters. Further means of self-employment were provided by cottage industries such as drum making, pottery, and the practice of divination and herbal medication.

But the Africans were at a further disadvantage. According to the accepted "norm" they not only "defaulted" as to color; they also lacked Eurocentric cultural values and mannerisms. "They were pagans retaining the full vigour of their tribal customs; they could not speak English. . . . No one like them had been seen in Trinidad since the Capitulation [1797]; and with their 'country marks' or tattoos, their unfamiliarity with European clothes and the bizarre hairstyles of their women, and their behaviour which was truculent or cowed in turn, they were quite unlike the Creoles, with their Sunday muslins and taffetas, their stove-pipe hats and frock coats" (Wood 1968: 74). The kaftans worn by the Moslem men were thought of as "night-gowns"; some African men wore an earring, some had their hair and beards in plaits. The voice of Creole upper class consensus considered them "generally speaking, industrious and laborious, but avaricious, passionate, prejudiced, suspicious . . . many of them still adhering to heathenish practices" (de Verteuil 1858: 46). They were "no higher than semi-barbarians" (de Verteuil 1858: 46). One island governor went further in endorsing this view by disparaging reference to "savages who go by the name of liberated Africans."[17] A Presbyterian missionary, Reverend Alexander Kennedy, described them as "wild-looking or ill-habited . . . ignorant beyond what you could possibly conceive. . . . The majority . . . make no profession of religion at all—are absolute heathens, having no idea of a God, living scarcely elevated above the brute creation" (Kennedy quoted in Franklin 1910: 33).

The eventual integration of the Africans into the broad black masses is reflected in a change over time in official attitudes towards them. There was a sense in which the government treated them as distinct from other social groups. This differentiation was fairly pronounced in the immediate post-Emancipation period when there was need to make a public distinction between slave codes and indenture. Special provisions were made regarding African indenture and there was even a proposal that homogeneous African communities be encouraged, along the lines found workable in Sierra Leone.[18] In 1845 a Kru settlement was proposed in the Port of Spain vicinity, though Wood doubts its eventual establishment. On the other hand, the immigrants' own herd instinct produced "as late as the 1870s . . . a squatter settlement . . . called Krooman Village . . . in South Naparima" (Wood 1981: 278).[19]

However, the authorities apparently came to feel that a distinction between the African immigrants and the earlier African and African-derived population was spurious. African defectors from indenture were sufficiently common and served to point to the existence within the established population of culturally sympathetic persons and groups. These supportive elements already formed an integral part of the society—a society that culturally was a European-African symbiotic product. Since the newcomers were clearly being integrated into a creole life-style, no official obstacle was placed in their way. This was in contradistinction to official policy regarding Indians. The latter were demographically isolated on sugar estates, particularly in central Trinidad: segregated health facilities served them, specific labor codes were designed for their indenture, while religious and educational disincentives to wider social integration served as a means of retaining them as a large and cohesive labor force.

The low profile of the African immigrants in the official consciousness is reflected in the general silence regarding the post-Emancipation African phenomenon in both the official and nonfictional accounts of late-nineteenth-century Trinidad.

In the 1850s the Anglican bishop of Trinidad, Richard Rawle, proposed that although the Chinese and Africans were more amenable to Christian teaching than the Indians, no separate missionary work should be undertaken for them. (Cuffie 1963: 148) The less established Scots Presbyterians, however, opened up a special mission to the Africans in suburban Belmont or Freetown Valley (Gamble 1866; Franklin 1910). Native Africans were noticeably absent, either as ethnic group representatives or as individuals, in the hearings of the 1888 Royal Franchise Commission. Even where, as the evidence of the Reverend O. W. Darling leads one to perceive, it was highly possible that his pastoral work brought him into contact with African groups, their presence was sidestepped by the investigators. Only Lionel Fraser, Stipendary Justice for the Eastern District of the County of St. George, and author of a history of Trinidad, specially mentioned that the votes of "numbers of old African proprietors" were "worth having," since they were "very shrewd men, like the peasantry of Normandy and other places," even though they could "only write their name, if even they [could] do that" (Royal Franchise Commission, 20 April 1888: 37). In the courts no interpreters of African languages were provided. In 1869 the Government-employed interpreters numbered nineteen for French, nine for Spanish, one for German, and only one for Hindustani.[20] By comparison, in 1852 at least, of the 1,055 prisoners in the Colony, liberated Africans accounted for 201 or 19 percent.[21]

Clearly, the white elite, who were the Government officials and the writers, could easily "ignore the existence of non-whites, except as domestics or labourers" (Brereton 1979: 62). Furthermore, post-Emancipation African immigration was overshadowed by Indian immigration and Caribbean-derived population influxes that were massive in comparison.

African Cultural Responses

One of the earliest sociocultural reactions to alienation and class oppression was solidarity. The cultural distance between the Africans on the one hand and the Europeans, Creoles, and Indians on the other led Africans to seek the protection and security of members of their own linguistic group. This brought about the spontaneous formation of ethnically demarcated settlements.[22]

Some of these settlements represented attempts at a maroon[23] existence in the hilly Central Range of the island. The people hunted wild game and farmed. They grew sesame for its oil, useful in cooking. Sesame also served for ritual purposes along with guinea pepper.[24] They dyed cloth with the indigo which grew "wild almost everywhere along the roadsides" (de Verteuil 1858: 271) and wove cotton to make lamp wicks and cloths, but the availability of imported cottons acted to suppress this art by making its products redundant.

A parallel infringement on the self-reliance of those who attempted this maroonage was that they were diligently sought out, relocated, and supervised by the colonial authorities. This was because colonial land policy in the West Indies during the latter part of the nineteenth century was geared towards a harnessing and control of the labor power that remained unavailable to the plantocracy in the persons of "squatters." This policy was particularly operative in underpopulated territories like Trinidad and British Guiana where the labor supply was short. During the 1850s and '60s "squatters" were evicted from Crown [government] lands and selected plots subsequently sold to them. De Verteuil, himself one of the plantocracy, advocated that "squatters" should be grouped together in order "to serve the needs of the surrounding cocoa . . . or . . . sugar estates . . . actual or prospective." A subordinate rationalization was that "by the purchase of Crown land, in convenient localities, the squatters could be given a chance to become a peasant class, officially integrated into the society" (1858: 386). These localities indeed needed to be "convenient" since the planters "saw the Montserrat district as fertile cocoa country, and fertile sugar lands too" and so wanted lands here for "internal colonization for the unemployed and poorer sons" of the plantocracy. Therefore the land in Montserrat Ward which was offered to the "squatters" was the worst agricultural land in the area (Campbell 1976: 436–37).

But it was a civilizing cultural zeal that was often the Establishment's stated purpose for resettlement of the Maroon communities.

"The great mass of these unsettled settlers is composed of Africans" who, "more than any other class, require the lessons of civilisation and the watchful eye of the law" (de Verteuil 1858: 383). Governor Manners Sutton considered the loss of Crown land revenue as the least of "the harmful results of squatting . . . while the lawless habits, and the tendency to relapse into barbarism—are the greatest" (Manners Sutton quoted in Chapman 1964: 70).

Some of these officially organized communities still reflected African ethnic biases. Among these and other less officially organized communities there were those that showed a predominant Yoruba composition. These were districts or "blocks"—a street or contiguous streets— within larger cosmopolitan communities.

By the late 1830s "Belmont was, to a large extent, peopled by African settlers, brought . . . after . . . 1807 when the African slave trade was prohibited by Great Britain." Many of these free Africans were "Mandigoe, Eboe, Kramanti, Kroomen, Congo and Yarraba— this latter settled in that part now known as Sorzanoville" (St. Hill quoted in Franklin 1910: 76). Elsewhere it is recorded that Dry River in the lower Belmont/east Port of Spain area was also called "Yarriba Village" or "Yarraba Town."[25] Part of Diego Martin district was called Sierra Leone Village, "owing its name to the fact that a number of freed slaves from Sierra Leone were located here" (Collens 1888: 185).[26] One of the primary informants, Z, lived in Sierra Leone Village and in 1973 was buried in the "Congo" or "African" Cemetery nearby. The existence of this cemetery substantiates the presence in this locality of a large and distinctive African population. The land for the cemetery was donated to the community by a first-generation Yoruba, Mr. Vanderpool, "for the burial of all African descendants"[27] since Africans who were known by Catholic clergy to have practiced African religions and whose burial included related rituals[28] were churched by laymen, not ordained priests, and were denied burial in church cemeteries.

In Tunapuna, the main "block" of Yoruba extended along the narrow belt between Back Street and the Eastern Main Road. There was a spillover into the portions of Balthazar and Bazilon streets and El Dorado Road nearest the Eastern Main Road. Some Yoruba were also located in Fairley Street. Gasparillo and Caratal had strong Yoruba concentrations and one song even boasted Caratal's particular fame: "Caratal which possesses drums that ring like bells."[29] A sizeable Yoruba community was also located at St. Margaret's in Claxton Bay, and northward of St. Margaret's Junction in Carapichima there was a settlement known as "Yarraba Wood." This covered the site of today's Chase and Macdonald villages. Beyond

St. Mary's Junction in Oropuche there were two African villages, "Yarraba and Krooman" (Collens 1888: 202); one of these must have been either in the Avocat or Bois Macaque districts. There were also Yoruba "blocks" in New Town outside of Port of Spain, in Cocorite, Carenage, Petit Valley, St. Joseph, Arouca, Princes Town, Freeport, Couva, and the Third and Fifth Company villages.

The earliest "Company" villages established in the south of the island were created for slaves who had been coopted by their British masters to fight on the colonial side in the 1776–1783 American War of Independence. Later Company villages were established in the Valencia and Manzanilla districts in north Trinidad for soldiers recruited in Sierra Leone from among slave recaptives and demobilized after the 1793–1815 Napoleonic Wars between France and Britain. From early 1817 to October 1818 and again in 1825 these soldiers and their families were continuously settled on Crown lands in the Caribbean, particularly in Trinidad. "Settlements were located on several sites about two miles from each other and located eight to twelve miles east of Arima" (Buckley 1979: 136). So substantial were these settlements that it has been estimated that "in 1862 one-eighth the population was composed of discharged soldiers" (Buckley 1979: 137). While documentary evidence does not indicate the settlement of demobilized troops in the southern Company villages, oral evidence suggests that this might well have been the case, since it is still recalled that Yoruba, Congo, Hausa, and Mandingo constituted part of the population of these villages and they thus formed part of the African social networking of the late nineteenth century.

Social Life

According to Yury Zhluktenko, "even when a cohesive group is numerically small but lives compactly, it has a far greater chance of maintaining its language than does the group which, though larger in number, is dispersed among a population which speaks another language."[30] Ethnic cohesion created Yoruba language islands in nineteenth-century Trinidad, but because the Yoruba population was comparatively small, these islands were simply "blocks." For all that, Zhluktenko describes "the position of the minority language" in language islands as "rather strong." The language "is used not only in the family but also between neighbors, at social gatherings, particularly in business transactions, and at times in the schools" (quoted in Shaffer 1979: 372). While use of Yoruba in the school domain would hardly have obtained in the colonial context of Trinidad, except as a surreptitious code among pupils of Yoruba descent, its function in the other contexts specified has been orally verified.

It was clear that neighborhood solidarity within and between Yoruba language islands was intense. Family and neighborly social inter-relationships and evening social visits provided occasions for mother-tongue usage. So too did work routines. Weekly trips to buy and sell at the large neighboring towns allowed for sociolinguistic interaction at meeting-places such as markets.[31] In addition, there were special secular and religious occasions that brought together Yoruba from several scattered communities. These were ceremonies which marked rites of passage. Certainly, there were Christian christenings soon after birth, but it is not known if Yoruba traditional naming ceremonies were held. There seem to have been no formalized puberty rites, but marriage was celebrated with the firing of guns, and feasts involving drumming, dancing and songs of veiled sexual reference as well as songs expressive of good wishes for the bride and groom. There could also be a pseudo-masquerade procession of women displaying sexual and fertility symbols such as stuffed busts and buttocks. A great deal of attention was paid to burial rites: wakes held up to nine nights after death featured the singing of dirges that bewailed the loss of the beloved, others that defied death, and some that expressed a belief in the return of the "shadow" or ghost of the dead one.

Apart from these functions, there were religious ceremonies to the *orisha* or deities. These ceremonies were hosted by families who had strong religious dedication and by individuals who had some training in the Yoruba priesthood. Ceremonies were held over a number of days to commemorate the annual festivals of the *orisha,* or for the purpose of special intercessions—for health, for success in financial undertakings, and litigation. Each *orisha* festival had its thanksgiving celebration two weeks later. Further religious rituals centered around religious initiations such as those to celebrate the first possession seizure by a devotee and the induction of a neophyte into priestly functions.

Saraka were yet another religious form of expression. These were annual communal feasts sponsored by families and involving animal sacrifice, prayers and offerings to family ancestors, but not possession. Their purpose was to placate and honor the ancestral dead as a means of ensuring material good fortune and psychic wholeness for the coming year. *Saraka* were also held for Emancipation Day anniversaries, and *la bòn fèt* took place at Easter time.

Secular entertainment took the form of story-telling, games such as *ayò*,[32] and dances that featured singing and the playing of percussive instruments like the drum and the beaded calabash.[33] The intimate details of this intense network of activity among Yoruba communities have not been documented, however, and the skeletal reconstruction of this social life has had to depend almost solely on oral evidence.[34]

All the same, Yoruba communal cohesion attracted the specific attention of several nineteenth-century social commentators. One of them observed that the Yoruba were "guided, in a marked degree, by the sense of association; and . . . the principle of combination for the common weal has been fully sustained where-ever they have settled in any numbers; in fact, the whole Yaraba race of the colony may be said to form a sort of social league for mutual support and protection" (de Verteuil 1858: 175). Similarly Cruickshank, writing of British Guiana, commented: "The Yoruba is more than sociable; he is clannish" (1917: 75). There was an internal social hierarchy whose pinnacle was occupied by an individual known as a "headman" or *capitaine* (Fr. Cr.) who was the spokesman for the group in its formal dealings with other Yoruba units and also with the outer society. He arbitrated disputes within the group.[35] This internal system of arbitration accounted for the fact that "the cases [were] rare in which a Yarraba [was] brought before a magistrate for theft, breach of contract or other misdemeanour" (de Verteuil 1858: 175). The headman also acted as banker, being the collector of monies for the traditional *èsúsú* subscriptions towards personal, communal and inter-communal events, and for joint transactions such as communal land purchase.[36]

Family Life

Neither the average size nor the stability of family units is known for certain. However, a study of slave family organization in Trinidad shows that African adults were more often to be found in unitary man-woman households than were Creoles. This was particularly so on slave plantations with small holdings.[37] The same seems to have applied in small and isolated post-Emancipation communities, considering that unattached nubile women from outside the community would hardly go to settle or remain for any length of time in such an environment.[38] With respect to nubile women within these closed communities, oral evidence suggests that parental control over the sexual relationships of unmarried daughters was strict, and where marriage did not materialize, these women maintained coparental residence. At another level, Yoruba wives in one community are reported to have acted to counter sexual promiscuity in the wider Creole society among married women and permanently attached females. Their action took the form of ostracizing delinquent members from their social dances. Delinquency was detected through divination performed by one of the seniors in the sorority. No such detection or censure of male conduct is reported. It was probably not thought promiscuous in a male-dominated society with optional, but unofficially recognized, polygyny.

The rationale for the nuclear family structure was that it provided "the essential building-block of extended or polygynous family types rooted in lineage and locality" (Higman 1978: 171). The mayor of San Fernando, Robert Guppy, spoke approvingly of the slave family "up to and during the time of the apprenticeship" (1834–1838). The fact that on the majority of estates "each family had its own detached cottage" meant that households had "privacy, decency, and virtually, morality. And although seldom lawfully married (in fact the means of being lawfully married scarcely existed for them), the relation of husband and wife, and family ties in each household, were recognized and seldom violated" (Royal Franchise Commission, 14 July 1888: 29).

When the slaves became freedmen and established villages, the pattern was adopted that married sons were given portions of land contiguous to the parental home. Thus the framework of an African family compound was established.[39] Married daughters moved away from the parental residence, but in communities where Africans of the same nationality lived in close proximity, social cohesion was still maintained.

The ideal adult male-female relationship among the Africans was one that united members of the same African nationality. This ideal is plainly articulated in oral evidence and is supported by mutually antagonistic songs. Each group conceptualized itself at the top of a caste-like hierarchy. Moslems were offended by the physical and spiritual pollution of non-Moslems and it appears that the Moslem faith formed a bond across ethnic divisions. The Hausa considered the Yoruba polytheistic infidels, and the Yoruba in turn applied to the Hausa their own Hausa term for foreigners, *Gàmbàrí*.

The Yoruba, while favoring the Rada as cultural affines, were very dismissive of the Congo and Koromanti, whom they saw as fit only for domestic work. Both the Hausa and Yoruba thought of the Congo as sorcerers, but the Congo held a very poor opinion of the "Chimbundu."

Pragmatically, tribal cohesion promoted through marital links was favorable to cultural retention. "Those who belonged to the largest contingents were likely to have more success in finding partners" among "those who shared a common culture and language" (Higman 1978: 172), whereas members of smaller contingents were more readily forced into national exogamy.

But the nuclear family was not the only marital pattern. "Large plantations were relatively favourable to extended and polygynous family formations because they provided a larger population from which to choose mates (without breaking the rules of exogamy), because they tended to be isolated (making cross-plantation mating more difficult), and because the slaves tended to be less subject to separation through sale than on small holdings" (Higman 1978: 168). Similarly it may be surmised that in the post-Emancipation period, in fairly well-populated areas within and near large towns and plantations, more women were available for marriage and concubinage. This meant that extended and polygynous family arrangements were effected. Since such arrangements were not necessarily confined to plantations, but operated in the more extended society, many of these would not have involved the polygynous partners in coresidence.

This was one of the new environmental factors that gave rise to matrifocal households. Another factor was the relative isolation of females in domestic service because of the small number of domestics per household. This circumstance made for the high incidence of mother-children units, particularly in urban areas. Socioeconomic circumstances in other parts of the colony also led to this lifestyle. Robert Guppy spoke in highly critical terms of the quality of life provided for Indian and African immigrant labor in the estate barracks. One effect of the overcrowding and lack of privacy in these tenements was sexual "immorality." Such license, he felt, was promoted in part by the "greater force and independence of character of the black woman" when compared with her Indian counterpart (Royal Franchise Commission, 14 July 1888: 30). The mother- and grandmother-centered family unit was to emerge out of these conditions as a prominent pattern in black Creole society, and explains the significance in this context of mothers and maternal grandmothers as transmitters of African language and culture.[40] By contrast, those African males who practiced polygyny were unable to disseminate African cultural behaviors among their offspring to the same extent as their female cultural counterparts. This is because polygynous African men included Creoles among their mates and these partnerships were largely extraresidential.

Creolization

One powerful agent of creolization came by way of intermarriage. Intermarriage led either (a) directly to creolization, or (b) indirectly to it by way of inter-African cultural contact.

The demographic profile of the island meant that it was difficult for Africans to escape social and sexual relationships with Creoles. During slavery, "although there [had been] a preponderance of African-born males in the population, Creole men [had been] able to compete successfully for African women" (Higman 1978: 172). This may have been due as much to the greater domesticity of African women—a factor which would have appealed to the male—as to the passive courtship role traditionally assigned females. This latter factor meant that women would eventually marry or liaise permanently with males who approached them rather than with men whom they would actively prefer. In this case, if there was a higher proportion of male Creole than male African suitors for African females, the chances of African female–Creole male alliances were stronger. The fact that children more readily acquire the maternal language than the paternal acted favorably in the transmission of African languages from mother to offspring. This must have been so particularly where the Creole father was nonresident in the mother-child household, and where the African female was resident in an African-speaking locality. Where the Creole male and African female shared a coresidential household, the chances of African language transmission to the children were somewhat mitigated, particularly where such a family was sited in a predominantly Creole community. In both cases, however, individual variables operated, such as the fierceness or apathy of mother-tongue loyalty in the African partners, and the aptitude of the Creole partner in the language learning process.

Apart from African-Creole mating, the incidence of inter-African conjugal relationships appears to have taken place with greater frequency than originally thought desirable. The oral biographies of informants in general reveal that alliances occurred, for example, between the following nationalities: Congo and Chimbundu, Congo and Yoruba, Congo and Hausa, Yoruba and Rada, Yoruba and Hausa, Yoruba and Igbo, and Yoruba and Gurunsi.

A further stimulus to creolization was the growing class differentiation in sectors of the society that formerly had faced stringent social restrictions. This was brought about by the widening of labor roles and increased class mobility following on slave emancipation in 1838.[41] The introduction of African indentured labor (1841–67) overlapped with the beginning of an era that witnessed the gradual growth of the black middle class—the late nineteenth century. This new Black elite was composed of Africans and Mulattos, "descendants of the Trinidad ex-slaves, or of 'liberated' African immigrants, or of Negroes from the Eastern Caribbean." They acquired their class status "mainly through their command of British culture and their white-collar jobs" (Brereton 1979: 86). A few of these men were sugar and cacao cultivators;[42] some were in business as pharmacists, printers, journalists and editors; some were minor civil servants; a few were in the legal profession as solicitors, lawyers, and clerks; others served as clergy; a few worked in the medical profession. The 'nucleus' of this class was comprised of primary school teachers.

In tandem with this class differentiation went a marked urban drift of the African population toward the closing decades of the nineteenth century. A recurrent feature of the family histories collected in the course of this research was the agricultural base of the African-born generation in local marketable food produce and in cacao for the export trade. By contrast, another motif is the migration of the second-generation Africans to urban centers like Port of Spain or San Fernando. They migrated either because their educations tore them away from the land and they set their sights on clerical employment, or because they sought regular employment in government public works projects or with government institutions. In turn, the fact that aging parents were often taken into the care of their offspring could necessitate their removal from country to town. Such removals, of course, weakened the social network of rural African communities at the same time that a steady decrease in the overall numbers of the African-born necessarily signaled the triumph of the language and ethos of Creole society.

The black middle class, for its part, like the society in general, attached great importance to the concept of "respectability." This referred to "a certain life style and especially to command of European culture and 'manners'" (Brereton 1979: 211). Joseph

Lewis, the black editor of the *New Era* newspaper, applied these value judgments to Africans in Trinidad, whom he described as "a quiet, passive people, settled in Trinidad for 40 or 50 years. They were not Obeah practitioners" but a "most respectable people" (Royal Franchise Commission, 15 March 1888: 11). Their reliance on Victorian virtues was compensatory for their social liabilities "because they had no other valuable and valued possession to hold on to. They were not wealthy. They owned few businesses, and no large ones. . . . They had no vote, no voice in the government, no political influence. They did not control the economy" (Brereton 1979: 94). Clearly, if one could not change one's color, one could change one's culture and become socially acceptable.[43]

Diffused in small "blocks" throughout the island, and, moreover, living in a Crown Colony regime where no group had the right to self-determination, the Yoruba along with other Africans had little option but to follow the precedents shaped for them by British colonial society. Exemplars in their immediate environment tended overwhelmingly to be oppressed individuals and groups who had arrived at an accommodation with the prevailing cultural thrust in varying degrees along a more-to-less European continuum. That the Yoruba in general acceded to the official promotion of Eurocentricity is to be deduced from the favorable comments they drew from other culturally discriminating sources: "The Yarribas or Yarrabas deserve a particular notice. . . . They are a fine race, tall and well-proportioned, some of them with fine features, . . . their houses neat, comfortable and kept in perfect order within. In character they are generally honest, and in disposition proud, and even haughty" (de Verteuil 1858: 175). One English missionary spoke disparagingly of the Congo, only to laud the Yoruba: "The Yarrabas will dwell in clusters, co-operate with one another, becoming small holders of land" (Gamble 1910: 31). He also considered Africans, especially the "Yarriba" as "apt in learning languages" (Gamble 1910: 40).

A significant reason why the Yoruba created such a formidably good impression with Europeans was their acceptance of Christianity. It is clear from nineteenth-century commentaries that the most heinous offence on the part of non-European peoples was ignorance or rejection of Christianity. De Verteuil's comments on the Yoruba are therefore highly meaningful. He described them as "intelligent, reflective and seeming to appreciate the benefit of civilisation and Christianity" (de Verteuil 1858: 175). This gives the impression that, as a community, the Yoruba sought upward social mobility and from early on perceived and acted on the cultural compromises that were deemed necessary. Oral and documentary evidence suggest that they were overwhelmingly Catholic—the dominant Christian persuasion—and that they were active workers in and financial contributors toward parish projects.

The foregoing evidence, both oral and documented, illustrates indirectly another factor that led to the decline of African languages, that is, the need to function in, and therefore to communicate with, the wider society. Church activities, economic necessity, and social interrelationships dictated the need for use of a lingua franca. There were two such tongues in nineteenth-century Trinidad —the French and English creoles.

Given this sociolinguistic framework, most Africans came to acquire a competence in one or both the creoles. Code-switching between the African mother tongue and the creole must have been minimally, and then increasingly, a feature of their idiolects as the Creole cultural ambience impinged more and more on their behaviors. This erosion of African language function must particularly have affected Africans living in urban cosmopolitan areas and those whose business took them frequently to economic centers such as markets. For they had complex and precise communication needs. At least from an economic point of view, if not from a social, they needed to master a lingua franca with sufficient competence to be intelligible and to reduce errors of interpretation on the part of their interlocutors. Even so, the creoles served as vital communication links in a contact situation unifying Africans of widely differing languages and perhaps as well mutually unintelligible dialects of the same language.

Code-switching also involved various African languages. This was because differing ethnic settlements were often contiguous, so there was social and commercial interaction between them. This interaction was based on cultural affinities and more so on shared experience as slaves, shipmates, and indentured aliens.[44] To communicate with each other, Africans in heterogenous areas learned words and phrases—principally greetings and songs—in languages other than their own. Such languages included Mandingo, Twi, KiKongo, Hausa, Kisi, and Umbundu.

African language decline operated in the wider context of changing language roles in Trinidad society—the result of the struggle for language supremacy between English and French. The former was the language of the nineteenth-century English and Scots elite comprised of planters, merchants, officials, and accountants. The latter was the prestigious language of planter settlers from New

Orleans, Haiti, Martinique and Guadeloupe. In 1838 English was so rarely used among the masses that the educationist C. J. Latrobe was able to identify places in the island where English-lexifier dialects were spoken: Manzanilla, where there was a population of disbanded black soldiers of the West India Regiment; Erin; the seven Company villages and Woodfordia (near Chaguanas) where free African Americans were settled; a section of Montserrat populated by Bahamian Blacks; a section of Diego Martin settled by Tortolan Blacks; Tacarigua, Arouca, and Port of Spain—areas settled in part by immigrants from the English-speaking Caribbean territories.

But the language of most Creoles, even by 1866, was still French Creole. It was "the language spoken most widely, the lower orders scarcely using any other, though they can nearly all of them speak English. But among themselves, this patois is the medium of thought. It is, moreover, the language which the African and the Coolie [Indian] and the stranger in general learns first, and of course for the simple reason that he hears it most frequently in use" (Gamble 1866: 39). The psychological insecurity of the masses when addressed in English is manifest from the fact that in the law courts people under cross-examination in English preferred to have a French Creole "interpretation of every question to make up their minds about giving the answer" (Francis Damian, Royal Franchise Commission, 2 February 1888: 17). "Carenage, Santa Cruz, Maraval, Diego Martin, St. Ann's, Caroni, and Arima were all said to be mainly patois speaking areas. All the 'older' people spoke patois and nothing else" (Brereton 1972: 316).[45] In such areas, prayers recited by the priest in English met with a patois antiphonal response (Fr. Brown, Royal Franchise Commission, 2 March 1888: 36).

Nevertheless, towards the close of the century, the government's vigorous English language policy began to bear fruit. Even among the peasantry English began to be used passively. Most people understood English. If a question was put to a peasant in English, he would understand it even if he answered in French Creole. Indeed, by the late 1880s it was evident that English was within the linguistic repertoire of the younger generations, whereas "Fifteen years ago every boy spoke Creole patois" (Felix Lazare, Royal Franchise Commission, 22 March 1888: 40–41). But "we now hear little children of Trinidadian parents running about the streets, nay even in the cocoa woods, chattering English as fluently as their predecessors fifteen years ago did creole."[46] By 1900 both young and old peasants and laborers "spoke and understood English, though they might not use it in their homes" (Brereton 1979: 166).

Two factors were responsible for the swing in favor of English: "public primary education, with instruction in English, and the influx of English-speaking immigrants from the Eastern Caribbean" (Brereton 1979: 165). In the 1840s one of the ways by which Governor Henry MacLeod "hoped to disseminate the English language was by encouraging immigrants from English-speaking countries" (Cuffie 1963: 87).

The Decline of African Mother Tongue Speakers

Just as English and English-lexicon Creole gradually ousted French and French-lexicon Creole, the pervasiveness of both creoles served to weaken the functionality of African languages. This became true even within the domestic context. African languages could hardly hold primacy in a domestic domain where the younger generation outnumbered the older. Even in households where an African language was the child's first, as in the cases of Z and O, it could not hold a unique position once the child was old enough to fall under the socializing influence of its peers.

As a result of this situation, African languages became increasingly hermetic and esoteric. The smaller the number of speakers, the more a language became associated with secrecy of behavior. The association was often a valid one: Yoruba, for example, served as a concealment language for its in-group. One well-remembered secret code was *Ọlọkpa m bọ wa* 'The policeman is coming,' which was issued to warn other Yoruba committing the multiple infringements to which Africans were wont.[47]

But as the African communities declined, not only were law officers, other African nationalities, and Creoles treated as outsiders, but even Creole relatives of the Africans. This sociolinguistic retreat was reinforced by declining age in the immigrant population. Gerontological alienation and isolation became compounded by the uniquely different cultural orientation of the aged. It is also likely that cultural loyalty to Africa became even fiercer when the immigrants had retired from active life and from concerns with survival and material advancement, and as African friends and relatives died off. Thoughts of Africa became more fond as lament for their present alienation and physical condition deepened. T's grandfather died singing in his native language a song of praise to his spiritual father, Shango.

In addition, age brought a more critical attitude towards the mores of the succeeding generations. Since Africans had at their command an otherwise largely dysfunctional linguistic vehicle for these criticisms, the language as well as its users were resented by the second- and third-generation Africans and by Creoles. Under such circumstances, the use of African languages for private communication among the aged in-group was discouraged by younger household members and the phonological peculiarities of these languages came in for abuse. In this way, the older generation was increasingly "denuded into silence,"[48] with its facility in the mother tongue assuming an increasingly nonreciprocal function.[49] As such, speaker and language were so intensely identified that Africans are reported to have expressed sentiments such as: *I sell with the language, so let me dead with it* 'I was sold together with my language, so let me die with it'. Such purposeful withdrawal into self and such nonreciprocal language use were, however, token gestures of defiance by culture-bearers not merely on the defensive, but more so on the retreat.

3

Language Attitudes of Second- and Third-Generation Africans

The African Creole Cultural Ambience

The culture-forms of the second generation were strongly permeated by creolisms. The alienation of first-generation Africans in a creole society produced in them "a certain secretiveness" toward even their own children. Africans therefore regarded their offspring as "implicit threats to privacy and security," capable of divulging "private family matters to strangers," or through childish "idle chatter" bringing about their imprisonment, financial embarrassment, or even death (Schuler 1977: 178–79).[1] First-generation Africans were therefore caught in a vise between the instinct toward cultural perpetuation on the one hand and the need to withhold the vehicle of that information on the other.

This ambivalence produced a situation in which members of the second generation were truly "African Creoles," the term their parents applied to them. They were *ọmọ ìrèké* 'children of (a) sugar (plantation economy)', rather than *ọmọ yorùbá* 'children of Yoruba (nationality)'.

Yoruba Creoles reproduced their parents' culture-forms, but either coopted other names for these cultural expressions or modified them by replacing or integrating elements from other ethnic sources. Such names and cultural elements were non-Yoruba African or European in origin. Thus, in African fashion, they ate *ilá*, a thick, slimy mush made of finely chopped ochro (okra) boiled in water, the antecedent of Louisiana *gumbo*. This meal could also be made from *ọ̀yọ́yọ́* leaves, which when finely chopped became as slimy as ochro. Because of cultural contact, however, they called such meals not only *ilá*, but also *krɛnkrɛn*, a Twi term (Hancock 1971: 412–13). In fact, perhaps because of some other element of culture-contact, they came to combine tannia leaves and okra as the vegetable from which this meal was made. The tannia leaves were shredded, boiled with water or coconut milk and seasonings, and then battered into a mush to which crab segments were added. This seafood component replaced the ground cashew nuts or sesame seeds that their African parents preferred in their *ilá*. No doubt these divergent preferences reflected ecologically conditioned tastes. For their part, many of the Africans originated in areas quite distant from sea coasts and riverain shores. On the other hand, coastal and riverside Africans shared with Creoles a familiarity with sea and swamp, and acquired a taste for salt- and fresh-water foods.

The term by which the ochro-tannia leaf-crab variant of *ilá* was known was *kalalu,* a word of possibly KiMbundu origin, though a native American source is also possible. Like their parents, African Creoles loved *àkàsán* or *àgìdì* tied in water-resistant leaves, but the use of yellow maize rather than white-grained corn and the introduction of highly available sugar and grated coconut into the mixture led to a new designation, the French Creole *pain maïs* 'corn bread' apocopated to *pemi. Obì* 'kolanut' would be dried and parched to reduce the stimulant properties of the fresh kola—which their parents could tolerate. The pounded food they ate was called by the Fanti and Ga generic term *fufu,* a word that in Yoruba "refers specifically to cassava starch and cassava starch porridge" (Bascom 1951b: 132 fn. 1). This semantic extension, like the use of the term *kɛnkrɛn ~ krɛnkrɛn,* reflects inter-African convergence reinforced by a similar process that had taken place in Sierra Leone (Hancock 1978: 58). Some African Creoles avoided boiled cassava, a Creole dish, just as their parents had done. But they preferred rice as the bulky component of their meals in contradistinction to the various pounded and steamed starches their parents held in particular regard. Olive oil replaced palm oil as the fat of choice for their cuisine and for *orisha* ritual.

Male dress was largely European, but female dress combined African and European elements. Both men and women wore the *fula* 'neckcloth', a KiKongo term. Women added to this a *kalande* 'headtie', another KiKongo term. Females wore several skirts, the overskirt going by the French term *douillette.*

Entertainment included the *kalinda,* a Southern KiKongo term for stickfight, and "African dances." These latter occasions featured both African ethnic dance styles and Euro-African syntheses like the *bɛlɛ,* a variant of French courtly dances performed to drum accompaniment. The term *bɛlɛ* even came to replace *saraka* when it was danced for the party and accompanying religious ritual which the Yoruba observed as thanksgiving for recovery from sickness or career advancement and in commemoration of the ancestors. African Creoles also maintained observance of *orisha* ritual.

Language Transmission

Several Congo descendants claimed that the first-generation Yoruba were more assiduous than their Congo counterparts in consciously transmitting their native language skills to the succeeding generation. In general, however, third-generation Africans tended to make blanket reiterations that first-generation Africans did not teach their mother tongues to their offspring.[2] Perhaps these third-generation informants ruled out opportunities for mimesis from the process of education as they had come to understand it.

Despite the barriers to learning the languages of their forebears, empirical evidence shows that succeeding generations did acquire some facility in their ancestral languages. This competence was acquired both by direct and indirect means. Certain circumstances particularly favored language transmission. The eldest child in a family came under the close control and tutelage of parents. In addition, where an African language was the main communicative medium of the parent or parents, that African language was sure to become the child's mother tongue. This situation would have obtained particularly in the early years of an African's arrival in Trinidad, at a stage before he or she became bilingual in the mother tongue and a creole.

Another favorable situation was provided where the youngest child in a family developed a great intimacy with his or her parents because of ill health and disability in the latter, and because older siblings had by this time become independent householders or else wage-earners in or outside of parental residence. Yet another favorable circumstance prevailed where juveniles were unofficially adopted by African fictive and ritual kin. In a situation of social disruption and ethnic dispersal, consanguinity necessarily played a less significant role than it did in a settled polity. Fictive kin were therefore acquired from among favored shipmates on the transatlantic journey and possibly also from among those who had shared other experiences involved in slave capture and indenture. *Ará ilú* 'country folk', that is, individuals belonging to the same ethnolingual group, also qualified for fictive kinship. There was an overlap between fictive and ritual kin in that being a godparent carried more practical responsibilities then than it now does in a less communalistic society, and godparents were chosen from the fictive kin.

In situations in which parents had more children than they could easily manage to rear, and in which a godparent had no children of his or her own, juveniles were placed with ritual kin. This also occurred when the mother and father were separated, as well as when either parent died and children were dispersed. An only child reared with an African-language-speaking adult was thus well placed to acquire a fair language competence.

Grandparents played a significant role in the upbringing of juveniles. As we have seen, by the second generation intermarriage and unions between African Creoles and Creoles were apparently common. These ties served as a cultural factor strengthening the role of the mother to the detriment of the father in parent-child relationships.[3] By and large, then, the third-generation Africans were reared in households headed by maternal grandparents. In some cases, these grandparents were both titular and effective heads. This happened when their daughters, for economic and personal reasons, had permanent or seasonal domicile away from the family. In such a domestic unit, the responsibility for running the household fell largely on the eldest member as long as she was still active. These grandmothers were influential in promoting African-language skills among the juveniles in their care. For instance, grandmothers showed favor toward individual juveniles by giving them special language training during leisure hours. Judging from the recollected data in the corpus under study, learning mechanisms under such conditions are likely to have been songs, the citation of lexemes of concrete rather than abstract categories, as well as simple cognitive and factitive statements. Sentences would avoid complexity of syntax and connective or subordinate clause formations. Phrases with a religious content are also likely to have been taught, given the sacred associations of the language. A formal learning mechanism involved the notation, at the insistence of the grandparents, of words, sentences and phrases. The death of instructors who were native speakers of the ancestral languages weakened the role of that language for both adults and juvenile descendants. Apart from the fact that a grandparent's death removed from the home the physical link with tradition, it was not uncommon for juveniles to be dispersed among other kin at times like these. Such dislocation would only rarely have afforded children closer contact with an African language. Indeed, the passing of the immigrants coincided with a growing awareness of and contact with a wider, more cosmopolitan world on the part of the third generation. Now between five and twelve years of age, such a child was coming into contact with French Creole and English Creole language environments through play, social relations and employer-employee, buyer-seller interaction. Poverty and consequent economic need meant that many among this generation were on the child-labor market. They were rarely schooled for more than five years. In any event, school itself was the domain of English and English Creole in the classroom and French Creole on the playground.

Informal acquisition of the ancestral language was still possible, however, through casual contact with second-generation users. Opportunities for this contact were intermittent, being confined to the domestic setting, African dances, religious ceremonies, and rites of passage, which they attended more often as helpers and observers than as participants. Communal activities like these were the ambience in which the song repertoire of the third generation was spontaneously built up.

Furthermore, when in later life African Creoles began to sense an affective loyalty toward their ancestral language, they, on their own initiative, took steps to rectify their ignorance of it. N's son, F, recounted how he took the opportunity presented by his encounter with an old Yoruba man: "When I finish work at night I make it there (to the man's home), and catch up (learned), buy copy-book and catch up. . . I'll write out these (what the man said)." Later on he would "go down by my decease(d) aunt. She pronounce, (I) hadn't the real accent for the pronunciation, but whenever I speak to her she know (understood)." His last comment indicates a level of tolerance on the part of second-generation Yoruba speakers and sheds some light on the linguistic accommodation enforced by a language situation in which the mother tongue was at once multi-dialectal and obsolescent.

Affective Role of African Languages

That there were obviously instances where second-generation Africans attached heightened emotional significance to their ancestral language is illustrated by the following example. Once when ill in hospital, N's husband was asked by one of his sons—in Yoruba and then in French Creole—"What's the matter?" The father began crying and burst into a song expressive of the joy at being visited by his own children:

Arálé ní	Relatives inquire
Ṣé ni mo mà jí ire	Whether I indeed woke well
Ṣé ni mo mà jí ire	Whether I indeed woke well
Kò ṣé bí abímọ ni	(But) it cannot be the same as if my own children ask

Clearly, at a moment of such intense relief, his emotion could find an appropriate channel only in his ancestral language. Not only were both his parents from the Ekiti region of Yorubaland, but they had stayed in Sierra Leone for some time and it is even likely that he himself had been born there. He had been very assiduous in teaching his ancestral tongue to his wife, N, a non-Yoruba descendant. On other occasions the subject used Yoruba song as a means of maintaining a steady work rhythm and also of distracting his mind from the awareness of arduous physical activity. He always sang the following work song while clearing his farming plot:

Ojónkpéré	We are all together
Ṣáwé ojúdè	Cut the grass outside
Ṣáwé ojúdè	Cut the grass outside

Similarly, another of his generation is known to have liked singing the following song on his way to his cultivation plot:

Mo fẹ́ lọ ní Mayo	I want to go to Mayo[4]
Kori, olówó	Kori, the wealthy man

L recalled a composition she made on a picnic journey by train to the southern town of San Fernando:

Níbo niwa ti ń rè?	Where have we been going?
Ará gbogbo, ho yé!	Everybody, oh listen!
Níbo niwa ti ń rè?	Where have we been going?
Ará gbogbo	Everybody
San Fernando **la ń rè**	San Fernando is where we are going
A ń lọ o, o yé	We are going, oh!

Indeed, L's Yoruba language skill bolstered her not unseemly flair for exhibitionism. She recounted her occasional countrywoman's visits to Port of Spain, the capital, to buy shoes from a Bata shoe store. Having been privileged to see the connection between Yoruba *bàtà* 'shoe' and the Czech name for the store, L seemed to have established a pattern of behavior whenever she visited this particular establishment. There, she would dance to the following song:

Iyá, jáde a wò mí	Mother, come out and look at me
Bàbá, jáde a wò mí o	Father, come out and look at me
Iyá, jáde a wò mí	Mother, come out and look at me
Bàtà idẹ ni mọ wọ̀ lẹ́sẹ̀	It is brass shoes that adorn my feet

Then she would gloss: "Ladies and gentlemen, `Mooma come and see me, father come out and see me. Is the golden boots that I have on my foot. That is the words." The store clerks must have been amused by this display deriving from a culture from which many, but not all of them, had been fractured. But they responded generously: "They say, *every time you come and give we a little tune,*" that is, 'any time you want, come and sing us a little tune'.

Exhibitionism was tempered—ambivalently—by the need for both full and partial concealment of meaning. Full concealment, for instance, was achieved in the following circumstance: L was able to warn her mother, Ọ̀shuntókí, in the presence of a visiting friend, that the friend's little son had urinated in the family's drinking water, which was kept in a container in the yard. L couched her warning in song, as she pretended to cut grass in the yard.

Iyá, ìyá o	Mother, oh Mother
Omi la ò dára	The water isn't good
Omi la ò dára	The water isn't clean
Ọmọdé la ti tọ̀ sí	The child has urinated in it
Omi la ò dára	The water isn't good

On the other hand, partial concealment reflected a semicautious attitude in the speaker and intimated hostile relations. Such partial concealment was possible where customary use of an utterance in analogous affective contexts conveyed to the listener a psycholinguistic meaning, even though the precise semantic content of the utterance was lost to the listener. Abusive and critical messages were thus conveyed publicly by means of song lyrics, which by their proverbial content or metaphoric frame were capable of double entendre. The cat–rat antagonism was transferred to the human plane in:

Ekúté ilé kpara má o	The house-rat hides itself
Ológìní tájò dé	(When) the cat returns from its trip

Resentful feelings against the perceived (sometimes human) source of unhappiness were conveyed by the proverbial:

Bíná bá jò mi	If fire (trouble) burns me
Màá bèrùlé	I will fear the house (where I was burnt)

Bíná bá jò mi	If fire burns me
Màá bèrù iná	I will fear the fire
(?I)kpakúta mẹ́ta	The breaking up of the three stones (of the fireplace)[5]
Màá bèrù láyé o	I will fear throughout life
Bíná bá jò mi	If fire burns me
Màá bèrù iná	I will fear fire

Withdrawal was also an important aspect of speaker response to Yoruba language marginality, particularly as the age of its speaker advanced. Geriatric isolation led the unique language skill of the elderly to function as an intimate and private vehicle of thought and expression. It is clear that O's favorite songs functioned for her in this way. These songs are predominantly laments, which speak of necessary departure from home and a consequent desire to return there.

Ó dẹ̀ mí lọ, o	I have to be going
Ó dẹ̀ mí lọ, é	I have to be going, hear
Ànà irere	Farewell
Má ì lọ	Don't go
Ì yọ (< ì lọ)	Don't go
Ọ̀nà irere	Walk well
Má ì lọ	Don't go
Ó dẹ̀ mí lọ, o	I must be going

The longing to return to the ancestral homeland was a wish of O's, as much as it was a wish of Z, S, and T.

K's songs and statements were dominated by thoughts of kinship ties severed through death and the consequent loneliness of the survivor, who looked toward his own demise. This in fact took place exactly a week after his interview. S liked songs that recalled courtship and a love of dance. One of her songs—a song that betrayed personal romantic notions interwoven with political loyalties—provided one of the very few instances of individually creative use of Yoruba:

Mani Wili[6] **o o**	Mr. Willie, o
Ọlọ́ràn	Leader
Mo fẹ́ bá ọ lọ	I want to go with you
Ènìyàn ò mọ̀	Nobody knows

Like S, N favored songs that reawakened her zest for dance and other modes of entertainment. But after the death of a son who shared her home, N's heartbreak found vent in mournful dirges. Such songs are still sung at wakes and at the graveside by a few families who maintain Yoruba burial traditions. A song still intoned by one extended family at the death of one of its members recalls the names of all the deceased kin of the ancestress, Ma Ika or Mamin:

Àjò, àjò	Traveling, journeying
Àjò nílé	The journey home
Irìn wá ra o[7]	The crowded journey of disappearance and decay
Àjò nílé ~ *Mamin ale*	The journey home ~ Mamin has gone

But nowhere during our research did we uncover evidence that sentence-length Yoruba was currently used for communicative interaction.[8] Active reciprocal language use in the lifetime of the primary informants had been forced into nonreciprocal avenues because of the decrease in language users and because of the speakers' own greater fluency and code flexibility in languages such as the English and French Creoles. Yoruba, on the other hand, had become a language of nonreciprocal display and recollection. It conjured up associations with a Golden Age of youth, gaiety, cultural "authenticity," moral uprightness, and good neighborliness.

A concomitant of this linguistic isolation was that each speaker was convinced of his or her role as the last bastion of an inheritance. The ancestral language therefore functioned as a symbol of self-identity rather than of group identity. Such group loyalty was coincident with childhood. By the time these subjects were adult wage-earners in their twenties, those language pockets had by and large dissolved. In that context, encounters with Yoruba-speaking individuals in the wider community became memorable events recounted with pleasure. Z remembered singing in Yoruba on a work site in Sangre Grande and being overheard with rapture by another workman of Yoruba parentage. N's eldest son recalled meeting an old Yoruba baker on the train platform at Chaguanas. Their conversation began with greetings, then established the young man's lineage, and the two exchanged their home addresses.

Progressively, by the second half of this century, since there was no Yoruba speaking group with which to identify and no sense of shared cultural activity, each inheritor of the linguistic tradition retreated into individualism and self-idealization. These psychological reactions were manifested in several ways. One such reaction was criticism of others who purported to be knowledgeable about Yoruba culture, for each primary informant claimed that province as his or her exclusive domain. If the researcher repeated to informant X a phrase learned from informant Y, it was not unlikely that informant X would offer correction. Reprimands were prompted either by the researcher's tonal inaccuracies, or by disagreement with her syntactic structure or idiomatic choice. Where informant X heard the tape-recorded discourse of informant Y, similar criticism was forthcoming. Disagreement over phonological realizations of the language was pervasive. S was somewhat less than tolerant of what to her judgment were errors, but B good-naturedly despaired of improvement in the linguistic capabilities of a friend who announced his entry into her home by saying *Ago nle* rather than *Ago nile.* Criticism was voiced even by a minor informant whose Yoruba was fragmentary but who deplored the linguistic incompetence displayed by *orisha* devotees!

Similarly, informants with a creditable language competence often expressed reservations about the linguistic purity of chants or songs broadcast via the elctronic media during cultural programs.[9] Furthermore, when the interviewer requested from informant X a song previously contributed by informant Y, informant X would often preface his or her rendition by suggesting that informant Y's version could be faulted in some way. This opinion may have been an allusion to the textual variations that are typical of oral literature. However, the more overt suggestion that informant Y had surely been unable to gloss the meaning of the song in question made it clear that such textual variation was not the main concern of informant X.

These antagonistic attitudes seem, in some measure, to underlie the personal conflicts that developed among the teachers involved in the Yoruba language teaching project of the 1950s (see below). There were necessarily qualitative differences in the Yoruba of Z and Modeste: Z, whose recall of his mother tongue had been actively reinforced by formal grammatical retooling; and Modeste, whose tendency to mysticism induced him to blend what must have been a failing competence with intuitive and subconsciously derived data. As a result, Z criticized Modeste for his inability to "pronounce the language the way it was spelled,"[10] by which Z meant that Modeste's phonetics were faulty. Indeed, among Modeste's students, the coarticulated stop *gb* is, among other things, simplified by the intrusive high front vowel *i,* so that *gbogbo* is rendered as /jibojibo/. It is not unlikely that other such differences would have emerged among the language-teaching personnel, given the lack of a norm-enforcing model. And, to pursue the matter, might there not have been similar conflicts between teachers on the one hand and students with some Yoruba language competence on the other? Such differences would have been a contributory factor to a decline of interest in these classes.

Several reasons can be posited for self-congratulatory attitudes toward language and culture among primary informants. From a contemporaneous point of view, these aggressive postures are a psychological response to a cultural position the informants perceive as embattled. They also reflect genuine idiosyncratic linguistic divergences engendered by the lack of a model language community. In part, such divergences have a historical basis, dating back to the undocumented dialect and cultural variations among the nineteenth-century Yoruba subgroups. These linguistic conflicts, rather than achieving resolution by discussion and mutual interaction, remained unresolved because of the short life of the language as an exclusive means of communication. This impasse meant that each contemporary residual exponent of the Yoruba linguistic culture was now psychologically entrenched within his or her isolated and self-justificatory position.

Africa and Its Languages: Aesthetic and Cultural Perceptions

At one level of lingual aesthetic appeal, there were African Creole informants who expressed mild hostility to African languages. This was an ambivalent hybrid of contempt and tolerance. Such persons offered a notional description that these languages "sounded like singing," and especially like Chinese: the languages went "wá wà gbá." This comparison reflected the tonal structure shared by Chinese and many African languages.[11]

On the other hand, Creoles hostile to African languages used opprobrious terms such as "hog," "pig," and "coarse" as epithets for them. These terms are only in part related to phonaesthetic values and mirror a more fundamental racial and cultural antagonism toward Africa. This attitude is the result of colonial policy: the active promotion of Eurocentric values matched by a parallel demotion of things African as subhuman, savage, and heathen. Such ideas—including on one occasion the ascription of cannibalism[12]—were voiced by a very small number of minor informants.

Given the pervasive negative stereotypes of Africa and Africans in Creole society at large, it was highly significant that these notions were absent from the discussions of Africa with major informants. Instead, their perspective of Africa derived from personal relationships with Africans. Africans had been their close forebears. These relationships were favorably described, and so too was the life-style of these ancestors. Personal descriptions of them were relayed in either enthusiastic or matter-of-fact tones.

Many of the informants identified with at least one (and sometimes two) African heritages, and pride in this knowledge was reflected in statements like the following: that Africans were "a very high high high blood people," that is, aristocratic; that they were "decent," "godly," and "respectable"; that their community solidarity was highly developed; that they shouldered their parental responsibilities; and that they observed a strict moral code.

A number of contemporary factors reinforced these favorable sentiments. Because of their familiarity with a more cohesive African social fabric than now exists, African descendants were sensitive to the contemporary declining economic and social position of Trinidad Blacks vis-à-vis other ethnic groups, particularly Indians. This constitutes the chief sphere of racial antagonism in the society and dates from the mid-nineteenth century when the colonial authorities recruited African, but more so Indian, indentured laborers to depress wages.[13] Indian immigration lasted from 1845 to 1917. By the 1940s, profound social changes in Trinidad society resulted in the demographic diffusion of Indians,[14] as successive generations migrated from sugar estate peripheries to urban and semiurban centers and as their birth rate increased over that of other ethnic sectors.[15] This meant that by the 1970s when fieldwork for this study was conducted, Indians predominated in several rural areas where African settlements had once existed, for example in Gasparillo, Caratal, Mamural, and sections of Tunapuna. The economic drive and prosperity of Indians were perceived as products of their psychological stability derived from retention of ancestral cultural customs, among which were close kinship ties and communal cohesion. These positive attributes were contrasted with the present weakness of Africans as a collective force on the island.

Another factor is the growth of cultural nationalism in Trinidad following on political independence in 1962. As a nation of immigrant peoples, of many ethnicities, and of recent historical formation, political independence precipitated a search for self-definition. This need for self-definition spurred interest in the peasantry, considered the "authentic folk," so to speak, and attempts were made to uncover folkways that had passed from use and to forestall decay of those on the wane. Projects such as the annual folk festival called the Prime Minister's Best Village Competition were official means of cultural restoration and education.[16]

Cultural loyalty to Africa had deeper roots than could be explained by contemporary pressures and awakenings, however. Fundamentally, cultural loyalty to Africa derived from Africa-oriented socialization within the family and an intimate relationship with Africa derived from a knowledge of personal genealogy. This affinity with Africa was forged by these factors despite the drawback that in most cases lineage could only be traced matrilineally and, in addition, for a comparatively shallow generational depth. But this genealogical connection with Africa was remarkable, given the fact that the majority of Creole Africans command no specific knowledge of African ancestry. The uniqueness of this information can only be appreciated against a realization of the shared historical experience of West Atlantic Africans—a dislocating experience of ruptured kinship ties effected by the kidnapping and sale or resale of persons from Africa, repeated migrations and resettlements in alien environments, the loss and recovery of free status, and the substitution of personal names. Notwithstanding all these impediments, the genealogical information given by primary informants included the provenience and profession of known forebears. Further information concerned conditions of slave capture, estate of indenture, and descriptions of personal mannerisms and distinguishing physical features. Information concerning unnamed ancestors in a longer time frame was available only from T.

Family pride was commensurate with ethnic pride: both were associated with cultural activity and the consequent social prestige enjoyed by African forebears. Among the Yoruba such activity was manifest in the celebration of rites for the *orisha* and *saraka,* ceremonies of annual thanksgiving and almsgiving. As was customary in African society, individual wealth and social status were expressed by acts of largesse toward the community.[17]

For the Yoruba, national pride also had religiocultural roots. Their complex pantheon of deities appears to be rivaled only by its Dahomean counterpart, which it closely resembles.[18] The fraternal interrelationship between the Yoruba and Rada in Trinidad is therefore not surprising. But the Rada were evidently a minority in comparison with the size of the Yoruba community. Yoruba religiocultural dominance or influence was further strengthened by the fact that *orisha* devotion was able to attract to itself non-Yoruba participation beginning at least in the nineteenth century.[19]

The Literary Factor in Yoruba Language Retention

Some literate African culture conservationists have sought to concretize their race-consciousness by the acquisition of books in the Yoruba language. Z, David Modeste, and Ebenezer Eliot (popularly known in Trinidad as Papa Neeza) were such conservationists.[20] For all three men, the Holy Bible (or *Bibeli Mimọ*), as well as *Yoruba Composition* by de Gaye and Beecroft, served as documentary symbols of Yoruba language loyalty.

Eliot had acquired his *Bibeli* in the early 1960s, and it was earmarked at page 108 where the Lord's Prayer was to be found. Both Z and Modeste had procured their Bibles since the 1940s. In 1932, Eliot had secured a copy of de Gaye and Beecroft's grammar from a Trinidadian who had come by the book (probably from travel to and work in Nigeria, since the individual in question had not been of Yoruba ancestry). Eliot possessed yet another grammar book; this one he had imported. It was *Iwe Ekini li Ede Yoruba* published by the Christian Missionary Society Bookshop in 1948. Like the *Bibeli,* it was written exclusively in Yoruba. These books must have had a largely symbolic significance for their owner, since Eliot could not read the language. But possession of such books must have satisfied his sense of ethnic identification, and furthermore consolidated that sense of mysticism with which he felt Yoruba was invested. Perhaps these books were kept in his *chapelle* and were used in his more potent *obeah* rites.[21] Knowledge among his clientele that such books were in his possession could have enhanced his prestige.

It was quite probably a copy of de Gaye and Beecroft that Z had assiduously studied and copied from during the 1920s. He spoke of having consulted a grammar book on Sundays at the home of a friend who had possessed a copy. Clearly the owner considered the book precious and had forbidden its removal from his premises.

The only other literature on the Yoruba located during my research was in the hands of T. It was *Yoruba Culture* by Afọlabi Ojo, a gift from a Yoruba friend married to a Trinidadian townswoman of T's.

Apart from reading material, there was residual evidence that literacy had encouraged Yoruba language learners to write down words and phrases in notebooks. This aspect of the Yoruba linguistic presence on the island was most exemplified by Z who had turned exercise books, envelope exteriors, old disused calenders, shirt stiffener cardboard, writing pads, and odd bits of paper into closely written Yoruba language scrapbooks. The writings consisted of lexemes, phrases from grammar books and the *Bibeli,* and phrases of his own composition. There were also letters to individuals, but these must have been drafts that were not meant to be sent to the persons in question, but that allowed their author to vent deep feelings: one such letter was highly accusatory. On the other hand, correspondence in Yoruba between Z and the author had been exchanged during the period of the latter's 1968–70 stay in Nigeria. In addition, he had stenciled wooden plaques with prayers and nationalistic statements. These plaques were artistically decorated with carved borders of flowers and geometric patterns and were either hung on the walls of his house or displayed on tables.

The effect of Z's literacy on his Yoruba expertise was both positive and negative. On the positive side, he has left concrete evidence of his dedication to Yoruba language and culture; on the negative side, his acquaintance with archaic, formal, written Yoruba prevented the development of Yoruba colloquial expression, while his command of Standard English channeled his syntactic and idiomatic structures along an English rather than Yoruba model.

T, too, kept notebooks. These contained commonly used phrases and prayers such as "O Lamb of God," the Apostles' Creed, and the Lord's Prayer. Since, however, she was not familiar with written Yoruba, this corpus was rendered on paper in a spelling that attempted a phonetic reproduction and that followed the erratic conventions of English orthography. Her reading from this written material was extremely halting, in that it involved an effort to recall the correspondences between the English-based orthography she had utilized perhaps in the 1940s and the vaguely familiar sounds she recalled her grandfather using. However, once she had deciphered a phrase by reading, she repeated it more fluently as her memory became refreshed.

Formal Yoruba Language Teaching

From time to time, race-conscious persons in Trinidad have proposed the introduction of African languages in the school curriculum. These appeals either have been ignored by the government and by teachers, or have met with outright hostile responses. Opposition to this proposal seems to be rooted in ethnocentric prejudice against Africa, a prejudice disguised by the argument that the teaching of African languages would promote divisiveness in a cosmopolitan society. This argument is, of course, based on an acceptance of European culture as the target toward which a Creole society should aspire. Furthermore, in the context of the major contemporary ethnic divergence on the island—that is, African-Indian suspicion—European culture acts as a neutralizing factor.[22] On the other hand, a difficulity with the promotion of African languages in schools is the problem of choosing from a multiplicity of African languages. Moreover, the problem of teaching expertise must be considered. And in any case, pragmatism dictates the need to encourage the acquisition of languages with widespread functionality.

Despite these practical problems and in the face of deep-seated Establishment hostility and disinterest, a few individuals and organizations have made brave but not very successful formal efforts at the linguistic rehabilitation of Trinidad's Africans. The examples of two such individuals—Z and David Modeste—will be presented here.

Z was motivated by a fierce racial consciousness, a pride in Yoruba ancestry, an intellectual bent of mind, a scholarly dedication, and a self-taught literacy in Yoruba. In 1927–29 he conducted evening classes in Yoruba twice a week at the old Diego Martin Catholic School on Rivers Estate. Maximum attendance was thirty. Z alleges that the headmaster of the school was pressured by Church authorities into barring him from using the school—a move which led to the termination of the classes. There may be some truth to this allegation, as the Church authorities may have been responding to Z's involvement in the Garvey movement, which the colonial authorities considered seditious.[23] Z also complained of ridicule on the streets from creole Africans contemptuous of his efforts, but mentioned the support and encouragement received from an Indian who was himself involved in attempts to rehabilitate Hindi.

Z based his language-teaching techniques on a knowledge of the alphabet and the current graphemic conventions of Yoruba spelling. Students proceeded from a recitation of the spelling of two-letter words to those of increased length. This emphasis on graphemes and spelling was obviously patterned after the English-language learning techniques applied in primary schools. That methodology had been recommended to the Trinidad Government by the Irish Education Commissioner, Patrick Keenan, in 1869, and had been put into effect in the island's elementary schools.[24] It was based almost exclusively on rote learning; and whereas this had praxis in a living language context, it could hardly have been inspiring in reawakening either interest or verbal skill in a moribund language. Z's students were adults, motivated toward acquisition of a language symbolic of racial pride, whether or not this pride originated in blood kinship with the Yoruba; they were motivated too by a desire for a tool for mystic communication. The mystic need may have been answered in part by the inclusion of Christian prayers and hymns among the texts taught. But it is clear that part of Z's frustrations in the language-teaching experience lay (a) with the difficulty inherent in teaching a nonfunctional language and (b) with the inability of his methodology to sustain the interest of his students.

In pursuing this methodology, Z designed large scrolls, some headed *Diego Martin Ile Ekọ Asalẹ Yoruba* 'Diego Martin Yoruba Evening School'. One such scroll carried the following letters, each in its respective box:

a b c e ẹ f g gb h i j k l m n o ọ p r s ṣ t u v w y

Underneath was the advice that c, q, v, x, and z are omitted in Yoruba. Below this was information regarding the significance of tone—referred to as "accents"—in Yoruba, together with diacritic conventions to signify tonal differentiation on single-mora and double-mora vowels (see chap. 5, sec. 1.1.3, *Apocope*). This material and its wording indicate that Z had at his disposal *Yoruba Composition* by de Gaye and Beecroft, first published in 1914 and revised in 1922. Another scroll carried numbers up to twenty expressed in figures, together with their lexical equivalents. Yet another scroll demonstrated vowel phoneme differentiation in di- and tri-syllabic words. For example:

da	cease	**kà**	count
dà	pour	**ke**	cut
de	wait	**ki**	that
dẹ	set, hunt	**kó**	gather
di	'twas	**kọ́**	teach

One visual aid contained picture cutouts of various animals with their Yoruba lexemes. A less lively aid carried the terms for anatomical data, the compass points, kinship terms, times of the day, and the seasons. Others treated of nominals signifying abstract concepts such as 'wisdom', 'soul', 'study', 'patience', as well as syntactic connectives like 'so that'. Phrases glossed variously in

Standard and Creole English also occupied some of the teaching scrolls:

> **Wakati melo ti mbẹ ninu ọsan kan?**
> How many hours are there in a day?
>
> **Mo ni ologbo kekere kan.**
> I have a small kitten.
>
> **Tal'o fun ọ li orukọ rẹ?**
> Who give you your name? [E: Who gave you your name?]
>
> **Emi ko pe ọ.**
> I did not call you.
>
> **Ago ile ekọ lu.**
> The school bell ring. [E: The school bell rang.]
>
> **Maşe pe bi o ba lọ.**
> Don't delay if you go.

The Apostles' Creed and the Lord's Prayer were also written out in large legible letters. Z's versions were couched in his idiosyncratic Yoruba syntax and idiom.

I never met with David Modeste, so data on his motivation and methodology have been gleaned from indirect sources.[25] Modeste was from Chickland in central Trinidad, and it appears likely that knowledge of his African ethnicity—quite probably Yoruba—may have activated his strong racial consciousness. It is certain that he joined the Garvey movement, which had its heyday in the 1920s and was still influential in the 1930s.[26] It is reported that on the day of Garvey's death, 10 June 1940, Modeste had a dream that inspired him with a mission in life. That mission was to continue the work of raising the racial consciousness of Trinidad Africans with the aim of "gathering the lost race together." The zeal with which Modeste pursued this aim found an outlet largely through non-Establishment religion—in the first instance, the Shouter Baptist faith.[27] But Modeste clearly believed that race consciousness needed a language dimension. In an effort to secure Yoruba language materials, he sought the advice and assistance of the United States-based African Nationalist Movement, a successor to Marcus Garvey's Universal Negro Improvement Association (UNIA). He was referred to their contacts in Nigeria and secured grammar books and probably a *Bibeli*. Thus equipped, he launched Yoruba language classes in 1945 in several areas in south and central Trinidad, probably among remnants of the earlier UNIA divisions. These classes continued in various places and at various intervals until 1950. His presence was recalled at Congo Block (Moruga), St. Margaret's (Claxton Bay), Tortuga, Arouca, Princes Town, and San Fernando. However, obviously aware of his inadequacy for the task, both in terms of initial response, which was good, and his own minimal language skill, Modeste recruited several teachers, among them Garnet Springer and Francis Charles of San Fernando, themselves Yoruba descendants, together with Roy Woodley of Princes Town. Modeste also approached S, who refused to cooperate with him, and Z, who did collaborate for a time. By 1950 Modeste, Springer, and others had engineered the embryonic formation of the Ethiopian Orthodox Church in Trinidad and for this purpose had financed contact and travel between Trinidad, Nigeria, and Ethiopia. Modeste's religious affiliation with this church led to the teaching of Amharic and Geez, in addition to that of Yoruba.

As in the case of Z, Modeste and others demanded rote learning of their students. His former pupils recall original song compositions of a religious and nationalistic flavor. One of the latter goes:

Ìbàdàn	Ibadan
Ilúyá wa	Our mother's town
Ilú wa	Our town
Kó fún mi Ìbàdàn[28]	May you give me Ibadan

But the best-remembered tribute to Modeste's efforts is his students' recall of the Lord's Prayer, chanted in rocking phrases with lengthened vowels, indicating an attempt to compensate for tonal erosion.

In terms of attendance levels at classes, Modeste's experience was similar to Z's: enthusiastic initial support followed by declining numbers. Despite these faltering and apparently failed efforts to inculcate in others a consciousness of Yoruba and other African languages and to raise their level of visibility in the sociocultural fabric of the island, the following chapter will indicate, paradoxically, instances and domains of their unconscious, submerged, and still extant retention in Trinidad's public and private arenas of life.

4

Residual Language Domains: Names and Ritual

Toponyms

"Priority of settlement with accompanying adherence to the land is by far the most powerful factor in determining how long a . . . language will persist."[1] This contention is borne out by the fact that it is native American toponyms that have persisted most vigorously in the island. Indeed, there may exist a correlation between the entry date of a culture-group and its quantitative toponymic imprint. But this correlation can be modified by factors of class and economic power, for it is these latter factors that largely account for the occurrence in Trinidad of Spanish, French, and less often, English place-names. These were the languages and language choices of the large landowners, whose names for their estates remained attached to laborers' settlements on the estates (or, after the plantations had dwindled in size, on their peripheries).[2]

One group that had neither the advantages of prior settlement nor socioeconomic power nevertheless has left a noticeable, though not overwhelming, toponymic legacy. This group comprises the Indian immigrants whose arrival in the island coincided with that of African indentured labor. The Indians' naming of localities stems from several factors: their numerical superiority over the African immigrants; the unbroken character of their immigration from mid-nineteenth century to the end of the second decade of the twentieth (1845–1917); their demographic isolation on or near the estates; the relationship of their enclave culture vis-à-vis a potentially erosive Creole culture; their internal sociolinguistic cohesion—albeit relative, considering the fact that they spoke dialect varieties of Hindi and Urdu;[3] and their longer attachment to the land in their rural conglomerations as distinct from the early urbanization and nuclear family fragmentation of the African experience.

While the Indians were able to legitimize their place-names, the Africans, when they did bestow such labels, do not appear to have won wider than in-group currency for them. Oral sources did, however, indicate use of African place-names. The toponyms fall into various categories: (a) terms that describe the topography. For example: *Abẹokuta* 'under the rock'. A Yoruba woman gave this name to her estate on account of its rocky land;[4] *Hololo* (KiKongo) 'standing alone', a mountain in St. Anns; and *Mayo* (Fula/Fulbe) 'river';[5] (b) terms that indicate the status of a site, such as: *Kambu* (KiKongo) 'compound', near Firebond in the Carapichaima vicinity; *Orí* (Yoruba) 'head', given to Caratal which was demographically and culturally the chief Yoruba stronghold at one point; (c) the transference of personal names to locations. For example, *Hengloe* (Ewe/Fon) given to a lane, and *Mafumbo* (KiKongo), a famous stickfight yard, both in Belmont; and *Ojo* Road (Yoruba) the name of a street and its environs in Sangre Grande; (d) ethnonyms, the most numerous category, were applied to settlements and cemeteries: Kanga Wood in central Trinidad; Yaraba Woods in Freeport; Yaraba Village in Oropoche; Yaraba Alley, Yariba Village or Yariba Town in Belmont; Congo Block in Moruga; Congo Kunukor Congo Konuk or The Kunuk[6] in Buen Intento outside of Princes Town; Congo Village in Diego Martin; Sobo Village in La Brea and Palo Seco; Ibo Hill in Camparo; and the various African ethnic burying sites in the island. Such names are merely residual now.[7] On the other hand, Madinga or Madingo Road, named for the Mandingo, still functions as the place-name of a location in Indian Walk outside of Princes Town.

Personal Names

Colonial authorities did not encourage Africans to retain their native names. Liberated slaves who had settled in Sierra Leone were given European names by civil administrators, employers, and missionaries. The changed circumstances of recaptive indenture are reflected in the fact that records of immigrant arrivals in Trinidad identify individuals by their African names.[8] European names were later allotted them by their masters. Sometimes the master bestowed his own surname on his servants and laborers; in other cases, the servants, in search of a European name, chose their master's. Since there was more missionary activity among the Africans in the postslavery period than during slavery, the rate of conversion to Christianity was fairly rapid and this was yet another means by which European names were acquired. Oral data indicate that some

Africans acquired more than one set of European names: additional names were acquired upon transfer from one country or Christian religious sect to another. Such relocation invariably involved a change in the European language environment. For instance, in the nineteenth century, the language of the Catholic Church in Trinidad was predominantly French, whereas that of the Anglican Church was of course English.

It is probable, then, that from an official standpoint most Africans carried at least one alias. It appears highly unlikely that these personal names were known to the state, unless perhaps as an alias in a court of law. The state, however, did arrive at acknowledging the Africanness of some of its citizens. The identity such a name described was more generalized than the personal names chosen within the family. This official method—used on land titles and court documents—was to postpose a broad ethnic ascription to a European name or names. Thus, John George African, Patrick African, Stephen Houssa, Sanco Houssa, Magdalen Yaraba.[9]

On the other hand, many Africans were known in their communities by an African name.[10] The use of these names served to reinforce a sense of community among the in-group of multinational Africans who used these names to identify each other. These anthroponyms preserved a self-identity, specifying personal-cum-family history and circumstances, lineage, professional affiliation, spiritual patronage, and ethnic or subethnic derivation. The Yoruba names recalled from oral data are set out below, with indications of their gender application and meaning or reference.

Inventory of Yoruba Names

One category of Yoruba names is called *àmútọ̀runwá,* names a child 'brings from heaven'. These describe the physical condition of the baby at delivery or its position in the sequence of siblings.

Name	*Gender Application*	*Meaning*
Àìnà	m. f.	child born with umbilical cord coiled around it
Ajàyí	m. f.	child born in breech position
Alàbá	m. f.	second child born after twins
Ẹdọn	m. f.	one twin
Idòwú	m. f.	first child born after a twin
Káyìndé[11]	m. f.	second-born of a set of twins

Òjó	m.	child born with umbilical cord coiled around it
Ọ̀ké	m.	child born with unbroken 'bag of waters'
Táíwò	m. f.	first-born of a twin
Tàlàbi	m.	child born with head and body covered by ruptured membranes

Names known as *àbísọ* constitute another category. It includes names given on the day the child is named, as well as names acquired subsequently in life. Some of these names describe the emotional response of the parents to the birth, the circumstances of the pregnancy, or the conditions that prevailed in the home or social environment at the time of the birth.

Abílógun	m.	One born in wartime
Adedikẹ <? Adédíkpè	?	One who arrived to fulfill our plea
Agiya <? Agíya	m.	One who demolished suffering
Ajemi	m.	My trial by ordeal
Ajìmí	m.	One who compensates me finally
Alàdé	m.	One whose coming is unexpected
Amanikẹ́	f.	A child to be petted
'Fijabi[12]	m.	This child was born in time of conflict
Mẹẹ̀se	m.	I did not offend
Moróhundíyà	f.	I have found something to reward my suffering
Ọmọkpé < Ọmọkpénínú	f.	This child overstayed its time in the womb
'Ṣéyíbí[12]	m.	This child was easy to bear

Among the *àbísọ* are names for children believed to be *abíkú*—children possessing a spirit that repeatedly enters a mother's womb. They die soon after birth or live only till about nine years old.

Amọ̀ṣà	f.	One who is known repeatedly

Àbísọ may describe observed behavior or express wishes concerning the child's future character or conduct:

Akínbọ̀	m.	The brave one has come
Asàdé	f.	One whose coming is expected
'Gosimawa <? Ogosìnmúọ̀wọ̀	f.	Fame brings honor with it
'Jọba[12]	m.	. . . is kingly
Kúṣìká	m.	May honor surround him
Ọgoyẹ̀	?	Fame befits this child
Oní	f.	One who cries a lot

'Títí[12]	f.	May ... last forever
Akaṣọ <? Akáṣọ́ **? Aákaṣọ́**	m.	One who surrounds and guards The hedgehog watches
Asato <? Asatò	f.	One who is diligent and orderly

A name may also constitute a warning:

Ayégboró	f.	The world accommodates adversity

Some names identify the professional affiliation of the lineage into which the child is born:

Aṣẹ́tólà	f.	Commerce deserves wealth
Afolò < Afólògbà	m.	One who uses money profitably
Atẹ́kùn	m.	One who is worthy of the leopard lineage
Àyàmbísí	f.	Music augments its own numbers
Ẹlẹ́yẹ́bí < **Ẹlẹ́yẹ́bíòkín**	m.	The owner of a bird like a peacock; name used in a family that has achieved fame
'Nàniyà	f.	Art is her characteristic
Olóríkì	m.	The singer of praise songs

Other names commemorate ancestors and express belief in the reincarnation in the newly born of the spirit of deceased elders:

Akínrìndé	m.	Akin [the ancestor's name] has come walking
Ìyábọ̀	f.	Mother [the child's grandmother] comes
Kòsónibéìyé	m.	There is nobody like [the child's parent's] mother

Several names reflect the parents' thanksgiving to deities for the birth of the child. These anthroponyms may also indicate the child's patron deity as ascertained through divination.

Asato < ?Ọ̀ọ̀sàtó	f.	The *orisha* are worthy
Ato	f.	A female initiate into *Egungun*[13]
Ẹfunlabọ̀	f.	Orishanla[14] is the one we worship
Fálóni	m.	Ifa owns this person
Fáródé	m.	Ifa sees everywhere
Fáṣádé	f.	Ifa makes this child a queen
Odùwá	m.	The *odu*[15] has come
Odùfúwà	m.	The *odu* want someone of good character
Ògúnjìmí	m.	Ogun has finally given me this
Òrìṣàbíyì	f.	The *orisha* have caused the birth of this child
Òrìṣàtúyì	f.	The *orisha* are worthy of our pride
Ọ̀ṣunbùmí	f.	Ọshun has given me a gift

Ọ̀ṣuntókí	f.	Ọshun is worthy of praise
Ṣàngódéyì	m.	Shango is responsible for this child's arrival

Names such as these were so important in perpetuating cultural allegiance that African immigrants bestowed African names on children of successive generations. All the primary and some of the secondary informants possessed Yoruba names. A name was given at birth and, in the case of Yoruba society, an additional name was given at the time of an *orisha* initiate's consecration to a deity. (This latter event usually occurred at puberty.) As a result of these naming practices, all the primary informants except B possessed Yoruba personal names. In fact, the primary informants showed pride rather than hesitancy in divulging their African personal names. Only T, who carried two Yoruba names, confessed to disliking one of hers—*Ayégboró*—on phonaesthetic grounds. Perhaps a residual recollection of its unhappy meaning—indicating as it did the harshness of life's experience—led to her resistance to the name and had reinforced this by making her even unsure of its phonetic realization. By contrast, T responded positively to her other name, *Títí,* and knew its meaning. In fact, this name was sometimes used by her familiars to address her.

While African immigrants typically gave their offspring African names, I found that second- and third-generation Trinidad Africans had given African names to their offspring only in a few cases. Moreover, these names did not reflect the ethnic derivation of the family but were the first names of African political figures such as *Kwame* Nkrumah (1909–72, prime minister and first president of Ghana), *Jomo* Kenyatta (1893?–1978, first president of Kenya), and *Seretse* Khama (1921–80, president of Botswana), or were derived from the Greco-Egyptian aspects of African culture, such as *Hannibal.* Another source for names had been provided by the Ethiopian Orthodox Church. Ethiopian names such as *Desta, Demptu,* and *Kandesia* had been given as middle names by a second-generation Congo descendant to his children, who resented these uncommon anthroponyms. Some persons who had joined the Ethiopian Orthodox Church had also unofficially taken Amharic names.

Before 1970, the desire on the part of adults to give African names to children was negligible, and in any case was thwarted by the reaction of Christian ministers of religion and the Creole values of relatives, teachers, midwives, and registrars of births and deaths.

The black cultural renaissance that began in Trinidad in 1970 and that was inspired initially by the Black Power movement in the

United States brought about a new perspective toward the use of African names. This attitude affected both the black working and professional classes. African names were adopted by adults, both officially—by affidavit—or unofficially. In some cases given names and surnames were both changed; in others, the family name was retained. European family names have continued in force, while African given names were used increasingly during the 1970s, then less often in the 80s and 90s.

African given names in Trinidad come from a wide cross section of African languages and are made available to the public by various means: Africans residing in the West Indies and West Indians who have resided in Africa are consulted to offer names and furnish their meanings; and books on African onomastics are available either from private sources, bookshops, libraries, or from African-oriented groups. In addition, the Christian clergy have, in some cases, been furnished with name lists by their churches, in an attempt to respond positively to the demand from a small but significant percentage of their congregations, but also in an attempt to co-opt, outflank, and neutralize the potentially radical political constituency of certain African-oriented organizations (for instance, the National Joint Action Committee, which spearheaded the 1970 demonstrations). But while the churches have officially adopted a compromising stand, individual clergymen occasionally have shown hostility to this new practice, camouflaging their cultural antipathy to Africa behind the argument that the parents are ignorant of the meaning of the names they wish to give their children, as if, for Trinidadians, the meaning of European names has ever been a factor in the matter of choice!

Another source of African names in Trinidad is the Arabic language. The use of Arabic names has been encouraged by the universal recognition accorded Arabic culture, on the one hand, but has also been the result of a post-1970 resurgence of Islam among Africans and the rise of militant Islamic fundamentalism beginning in the late 1970s.

In general, the reintroduction of African and Arabic names in Trinidad has educated the public to the fact that names in all cultures have meanings, and that African cultures lay particular emphasis on the appropriateness of meaning in naming persons. By contrast, Trinidadians of African descent choose European names largely on the basis of phonaesthetic, hereditary, religious, and sentimental factors, with circumstances of birth and parental contextualization playing a lesser role. This area of neglect has now been highlighted by the general awareness that each African name carries a statement about the parents' perception of the child's role in their life and in the lineage, or intimations about the child's personality and destiny.

The favorable attitude towards African names has been prompted either by an outright rejection of Eurocentricity or by its converse—a positive recognition of African ethnicity. In either case, use of these names constitutes an expression of pride in African culture and is seen as redressing the imbalance of exclusive Eurocentricity in the West Indian cultural perspective.

Family Names

A few Ewe and Akan[16] names have persisted in Trinidad as surnames. In part such names have arrived with immigrants from other Caribbean islands but they may be seen as part of the common African patrimony of Caribbean peoples.

Cartey is a Fanti version of *Quartey* (Ga) and is believed to be a phonological reinterpretation of the English name *Carter*. Other names are: *Cudjoe* < *Kodjo* ~ *Kwadwo* 'male born on Monday'; *Cuffy* < *Kofi* 'male born on Friday'; *Quamina* < *Kwabena* ~ *Kobina* 'male born on Tuesday'; *Quashie,* the Ewe form of *Kwasi* ~ *Kwesi* (Twi) 'male born on Sunday'. These four day-names are well known family names on the island. Other possible names from this culture-zone are: *Adu* < *Ado,* and *Beddoe* < *Bedu,* the tenth child. The name of a Senegambian ethnic group, the Susu, occurred as its phonological variant *Soso.*

Yoruba in Ritual Language

Prayers

Primary Yoruba speakers also know prayers in the ancestral tongue. One of the reasons for their language loyalty is the belief that mystic power invests African languages. Such belief inheres universal religious ideas about the creative and generally enabling potency of speech.[17]

In the Caribbean, certain experiences of the African ancestors are interpreted in the light of these beliefs. These experiences have become mythologized. They appear to have originated in slavery and form part of a still-extant oral lore. Most of these myths revolve around resistance to slavery and indenture and the reaction of Africans to abuse of their self-respect. A common belief is that some slaves who were being beaten could have their hurt telepathically transferred to their master's wife.[18] Another is that some Africans, both during the Middle Passage and after arrival in the islands, were able to "fly back" to Africa.[19] All these magical occurrences were said to be induced by incantations. Language was therefore a tool of rebellion against slavery, and the use of African languages incurred the hostility of Europeans. Their overreaction in flogging slaves and also indentured workers for the "offense" of using their native languages in turn confirmed for Africans the spiritual power of these tongues. In the perception of Africans it was the spiritual force of African languages, rather than the political solidarity forged by them, that the Europeans feared.

Notions of language mystique were further encouraged by the increasingly esoteric roles and domains of these languages as the African language communities dwindled. By the late nineteenth century this exclusivity and esotericism were in turn deliberately achieved through the efforts of some elderly Africans to thwart the linguistic curiosity and talent of their offspring. Some of the immigrants are reputed to have made statements like: "The children born under the English law is going to betray us, so not to teach them" and "Don't teach them the language; make them come to you," that is, let the children ask to be taught.

The intrinsic spiritual force still ascribed to African languages is also linked with exoticism. Part of this uniqueness derives from ancestral usage. These ideas underlie the assertion that the Hail Mary recited in mesolectal French Creole is more "powerful" than when said in English.[20] In *orisha* ceremonial, French Creole is treated as a sacred language: mediums usually begin their tranced utterances with a salutation in that language.[21] T's prayers at her *orisha* altars were overwhelmingly in French Creole. Yet she expressed the view that divine response was quicker when the *orisha* had been addressed in their language. She also asserted that the more appellations addressed to an *orisha,* the more flattering to the deity.[22] In fact, an *orisha*'s favor was particularly won by using the deity's own preferred praise name. For instance, *Olúbámbí* was said to be Shango's favorite name: "He would give you anything if you call him by that name," she said. Similarly, knowledge of Yoruba prayers bestowed special protection on the believer. They provided a heightened spiritual armor against evil, persecution, loneliness, and adversity. The following two prayers were part of S's Yoruba linguistic inheritance:

Morning Prayer

Ojú tó maa lóní	Day which is dawning today
Olódùmarè, ọ mọ̀ je kọ̀ maa sí ire	Almighty God, please be favorable
Ire ire báayin náà ni	Goodness, well-being certainly is like oil
A je ki ó bórí mi àdò lórí ayé	Let honey flow on my head, on the fate of the world
Mo jíbà rẹ	I pay my respects to you
Igigun mẹ́ẹ̀rin ayé	The four corners of the earth
Mo jíbà rẹ	I bow to you
Ọlọ́jọ́ òní	Creator of the day
Mo jíbà rẹ	I bow to you
Mọ ń jí bára mọ́ fọ́n òrìṣà gbogbo gbogbo gbogbo	I wake and present a clean body to all all all the *orisha*
Ka ń kpè alósọ̀n, 'lòrun, 'labosùn	(Those) whom we call the Creator of Daylight, Creator of the Sun, patron of the one who possesses the diviner's dust [the *babalawo*]
Ta jí wá	Whom we came into the world to find already there
Má mọ̀ je kọ tẹ̀ lóju irin	Don't let you/him step on a metal edge
Má mọ̀ je ka ń wíkpé "Kì ni olórìsà n kíni ó lè ṣé?"	Don't let others say, "What can the *orisha* devotee do?"
Adumílẹ̀, *mwè* jíbà	Lord, I bow to you

Evening Prayer

Mọ ń jíbà rẹ, Alẹ̀	I pay my respects to you, Evening
Mọ ń jíbà alẹ̀ òní	I pay my respects to you, Evening of today
Alẹ̀ tó le mi lóní	Night that covers me this day
Mọ́ mọ̀ je ko lè mi súkú	Don't let me accompany death
Mọ́ mọ̀ jẹ kọ lè mi sárùn burúku	Don't let me succumb to evil sickness
Mọ́ mọ̀ je kó lè mi séléǹìní	Don't drive me to make a relentless enemy

Ará tó ń róru	He who uses darkness to his advantage
Ará tó ń ròkúkú	He who smells foully
Mọ́ mọ̀ jẹ kọ́n rí mi	Don't let him see me
Mo m bẹ̀	I am here
O sí ire lálẹ́ im	Please be favorable this night
Bàbá, o mọ̀ jẹ kí mí jí ire láùrọ̀	Father, certainly let me wake in health in the morning

Not surprisingly, taboos against the use of ritual language manifested themselves during my interviews with the informants. S divulged a consecration prayer only after several years of our relationship; indeed she initially sang that chant only after the tape recorder had been switched off. T refrained from singing chants to Ogun because her particular reverence for him led her to fear casual invocation of the deity and possession by him in an inappropriate context. Taboo attitudes extended to written texts. T treated her annotations of ritualistic formulae with a degree of religious reverence and secretiveness. She kept these notebooks in her *chapelle.* After first revealing the existence of the notebooks in a 1968 interview and having read from one, it subsequently proved difficult for her to locate them. Some years after her death, a relative showed the researcher the contents of one of these books. The books contained Yoruba-English lexical lists, significant family dates, herbal prescriptions, and Yoruba prayers. The book therefore functioned like the Cuban *libreta* and had been obviously cherished and treated with sacred awe.[23]

Sacred Song

Christian Hymns

Oral evidence indicates that as part of the evangelization process hymns were composed in African languages.[24] But the paucity of hymns collected during research may indicate that the form lacked vitality and authenticity—particularly if the hymns were sung to European melodies—or that their usefulness was quickly superseded by European-language equivalents. Z however had composed several in this Yoruba-European medium, one of which went:

Àwa ó máa yọ̀ tinú-tinú	We will rejoice with all our heart

Nígbà gbogbo	All the time
Ọlọ́run Olúwa	God Supreme
Agbára ìgbàlà wa	Our strength of salvation
Ọwọ́ ọ̀tún rẹ yío si dì wa ni	Your right hand will hold us
Jehofa wa	Our Jehovah
Kpa wa mọ́, Olúwa	Guard us, God
Nitórí ti àánú rẹ li àwa fẹ́	Because your mercy is what we want
Àánú rẹ, Olódùmarè	Your mercy, Almighty
Nitórí ti àánú rẹ dúró láíláí	Because your mercy endureth forever
E Olúwa	O Lord
Olúwa, àwa ti ń retí ìgbàlà rẹ	Lord, we have been expecting your salvation
Gbóhùn wa gẹ́gẹ́bí àánú rẹ	Hear our voice, according to your mercy
Gbọ́ àdúrà wa, Bàbá wa	Hear our prayer, our Father

Orisha *Antiphonies*

In *orisha* worship, the sung liturgy forms the strongest language element of the ritual. The lyrics are generally short, perhaps sometimes fragments of their originals, and are composed of a repeated three- or four-line stanza repeated again and again to drum accompaniment though some require only shac-shac percussion, and others are rendered a capella. Lead singers who start off the antiphonies, whether male or female, are gifted with loud, clear voices, and the singing of a few hints at the microtonality and glottal constriction associated with the traditional Yoruba manner of intoning Ifa and *ẹ̀sọ́* sacred verse. They usually have had a fairly long experience in cult observance and therefore with the lyrics and melodies of chants. Long experience derives, in certain cases though not necessarily in all, from a family tradition of involvement in *orisha* ceremonial. This tradition may be traced to Yoruba ancestry, though the interconnection between *orisha* worship and ethnic heritage has weakened over time. All the female primary informants had been closely connected with lead singing for *orisha* ritual at earlier periods of their life and some were still so involved at the time of interview.

Despite the high degree, in general, of phonological deviation in rendition of the chants and variations in the system of religious ritual, for *orisha* participants the illocutionary force of the chants is that they invoke the deities to come into the presence of their worshippers. They are also perceived as songs of praise and devotion. Their effect is therefore to induce possession in some of the participants. In this trance-like state, the medium is able to deliver divinely inspired messages, perform sacred rites, undergo intense physical discomfort, and exert a high level of emotional as well as physical energy.

Like other mnemonic areas of Yoruba language use, the chant performance is largely xenoglossic. The degree of xenoglossia varies according to the Yoruba comprehension capacities of the speaker/ hearer. Much of the sacred repertoire of S, O, T, and N fall into a xenoglossic category of language performance. During fieldwork, some informants signaled the onset of a xenoglossic sacred text by the caveat: "This is deep Yoruba," *deep* meaning 'esoteric, ancient, beyond comprehension'.

Under possession, devotees have recourse to Yoruba-modeled glossolalia. Such utterances reveal repetitious syllables, but approximate Yoruba (v)cv morphological structure, and instance intermittent occurrence of lexically communicable items. The latter indicates that the language of the chants forms a resource from which phrases can be derived, phrases that are arbitrarily incorporated into idiosyncratic strings of utterance. However, the language of some mediums, particularly older ones, may reflect a degree of cryptomnesia, the resurfacing of subconsciously retained language. Some minor informants expressed a belief that their Yoruba language competence in possession derived, not from acculturation, but through spiritual inspiration, that is, while "in the spirit," or through dreams.[25]

Not surprisingly, there is little correlation between the glossolalic or cryptomnesiac message and the length of its interpretation: the latter mirrors prayers and liturgical phrases known in English.[26] Interpretation appears to be based largely on the devotee's perception of an appropriate meaning, a meaning that intersects with the predominantly Christian cultural ambience of Creole society. The erosion of Yoruba cultural and linguistic comprehension is seen in the interpretation recorded by Simpson (1970: 38) of the reverential praise-song to Eshu. A version recorded in the course of this research goes as follows:

Èṣù Bara[27] gbọ́ o	Eshu, Lord, hear
Mo júbà	I pay homage
A rè, a rè	We are here, we are here
Ọmọdé kọrin kó júbà 'rágbó	(Your) children sing to honor Aragbo
Mo júbà Ẹlẹ́gbára Èṣù	I pay homage to Ẹlẹgbara Eshu
Èṣù Bara 'ná o	Eshu, Lord of Fire[28]

For Simpson's informants, the semantic content of this chant was determined by the ritual act accompanying its rendition—that of dismissing Eshu from the ceremonial precincts:

> Satan go away from here,
> We want nothing to do with you.
> We ask you to run away from here.
> Do not interfere in our business.
> We are going to give you everything we have.
> We have no use for you.
> We compel you to stay outside and not come in.
> We are glad we can keep you away from our ceremony.
> (Simpson 1970: 38)

In terms of Yoruba religious etiquette, the ritualistic process by which Eshu is dismissed necessarily involves his prior placation and praise. On the other hand, the hostility towards Eshu projected here indicates an attitude colored less by traditional Yoruba concepts and behavior than by Christianity, which identifies the morally ambivalent Eshu with the exclusively evil Satan.[29]

In general, *orisha* affiliates understand the contexts appropriate for the use of the chants since they have a notional comprehension that the chants describe the immanent characteristics of the deities. This applies even where a deity's name is not mentioned within the song text; for instance, it is known that the chant which begins with the line *Aja ḿ bẹ̀kùn gbélé* 'Dog was living with Leopard' is intended for Shango. Primary informants, however, had a slightly better understanding of the overall literal meaning of some chants, since they were able to translate isolated lexemes and discrete phrases. Yet such limited literal comprehension fell far short of a grasp of the rich contextual framework out of which the chants had emerged. This framework would have been supplied by mythological and historical data,[30] as well as by a coherent religiophilosophical code like that which inheres in the Ifa corpus.[31] Knowledge of this body of thought and the divinatory system through which it is articulated appears nonexistent in Trinidad. By contrast, a respectable body of myth and knowledge of the Ifa and the "sixteen cowries" divining methods has been retained in Cuba.[32]

Loss of the philosophical and divinatory systems is no doubt linked to the fact that formal mechanisms of language learning have not, until very recently, existed within the *orisha* organization.[33] The language of the chants is acquired by imitation during ceremonies, and Yoruba language competence is not a conscious objective requirement for any office in the organizational hierarchy. But "since language is so important as a signal of difference," it is helpful for those aspiring to leadership roles to "symbolize the integrity and uniqueness" of the religion (Samarin 1970: 270, 271). For this reason, those recognized by the membership as adepts in the language of the religion are treated with high regard and are given pivotal roles in the ritual. S, for example, had an annual duty to grace the *orisha* groups to which she belonged by attending the commencement ceremony of their grand August *orisha* festival. Her main function here was to recite a prayer at the mystical moment when the blood sacrifice was offered up.

However, the rationale for the persistence of *orisha* worship is not linguistic and adherents in no way perceive of it as an activity which unifies a discrete language community. Instead, they perceive *orisha* devotion as primarily answering to religious and psychological needs. The religion's functionality derives largely from the psycho-religious power invested in the devotee during possession, from the highly ritualistic nature of the ceremonial, and from the mystique attaching to its ritual. In all this, the cultural rationale is ancillary. Only practitioners who can trace ancestral ties to Africa view the religious observance as a continuation of African and family culture. However, this particular cultural perspective has received reinforcement since the early 1970s. That period saw a rebirth of African nationalism, and members of the general public—including some of the artistic and intellectual community—now identify with *orisha* as a means of reconnecting with the country's African heritage.[34] All the same, the connection between Africa and *orisha* is not lost on the religion's lay membership. Although of secondary consideration, that link serves to reinforce ideas that mystic strength and ancestral sanction are to be derived from the religion. Thus, in more serious contexts of discourse, *orisha* worship is referred to as "African work" or "Yaraba work."[35]

Religious Terminology

While, as a secular tongue, Trinidad Yoruba has been in the process of gradual extinction since the last decade of the nineteenth century, it still retains active function in the *orisha* religion. Although it is a minor religious persuasion in Trinidad, *orisha* continues to attract adherents and has even, since the 1970s, received a measure of sociocultural legitimacy and public recognition never before enjoyed.[36] Indeed, one may even note a linguistic revival in this arena, fed by growing links with the international *orisha* community in Nigeria, Brazil, and New York. Some *orisha* leaders are learning new prayers and are gaining a deeper philosophical understanding of their faith. In some religious centers structured transmission of religious tenets and ritual language has begun.

During this century, however, Yoruba ritual language has shrunk to a few prayers, lexical items embedded in English and French Creole language matrices, and approximately two hundred chants used in homage to the *orisha*.[37] Since the mother-tongue of *orisha* practitioners is today English Creole—a situation that would have obtained for many persons since the turn of the century—the interchanges that take place within *orisha* ceremonies are in that mother-tongue. In like manner, French Creole has served as the mother-tongue of a large number of *orisha* devotees even since the first generation of African Creoles. In either case, both *orisha* officiants and lay members know the religious vocabulary. However, while there is general consistency regarding the semantic content of this vocabulary, slight variations are to be observed in the *orisha*-Catholic saint correspondences. These correspondences reflect the coexistence of *orisha* worship and Catholicism in the same locale. For *orisha* devotees, the *orisha* have syncretic identities—both as African 'powers' and as Catholic saints. Similar syncretism characterizes Bahía *candomblé,* Recife *shango,* Rio de Janeiro *macumba,* Grenada *shango,* and Cuban *santería*. These localities are all culture-zones where Catholicism has historically been dominant and where there is an overlapping affiliation to both *orisha* religion and Catholicism among sections of the laity.

Deities

Names of Divinities in Trinidad	*Mainland Yoruba Sources*
Abalofa: Eternal Father, King of Kings	**Ọbalufọn**: god who invented weaving; Lord of Speech[38]
Aginju: St. George	**Aganjù**: Shango's knife, one of Shango's insignia
Baba: God	**Bàbá**: father
Banyan: St. Anthony, 'barrister of the heavenly court'	**Banyani**: Shango's sister
Dada: patron of children	**Dàda**: Shango's brother, a lover of children and art
Erinlẹ ~ Eilẹ: water deity	**Erinlẹ̀ ~ Eilẹ̀**: hunter who metamorphosed into a river deity

Eṣu: "a troublesome fellow," an agent of evil contained within God's Providence	**Èṣù**: god of chance, amoral trickster deity
Ẹlẹfọn ~ Ẹlẹfan: Eternal Father; Holy Ghost; appellation for the Supreme God	**Ẹlẹ́fọ̀n**: appellation for the Supreme God
Ẹmilalẹ: Mother of the Earth; **Yeye Ilu**: Mother of the Earth	**Ẹmílálẹ̀**: Spirit in Earth; Earth Mother; **Yèyé Ilú**: Mother of the town/community
Ibeji: Sts. Peter and Paul	**Ibéjì**: patron deity of twins
Ogun: "Ogun gave mankind the cutlass, matchet and hoe on which to found civilization;" "there are 4 Ogun: St. Michael, St. George, Uriel, Raphael;" Archangel Gabriel; St. John	**Ògún**: war deity; patron of blacksmiths and users of metal
Ogun *Bwò*: a woodcutter deity	**Ògún Bois** (Fr.): Ogun of the forest
Onire: an honorific for Ogun	**Oníré**: Lord of Ire town in Ekiti
Ologun: mistress of the sea	**Olókun**: male or female deity of the sea
Olodumare: God, Source of Life	**Olódùmarè**: the Supreme Deity
Oluwa: God, Source of Life	**Olúwa**: Lord; euphemism for Shọnkpọnọn
Oriṣa Oko: mistress of the stars	**Òrìṣà Oko**: patron of the farm and agriculture
Oranyan: St. Gabriel	**Ọ̀rányàn**: Shango's father
Orumila ~ Orumilẹ ~ Erumila: St. Anthony	**Ọ̀rúnmìlà**: deity of divination, also called Ifa
Oṣala: Holy Ghost	**Òrìṣàalá**: Great Orisha ~ **Ọbàtálá**: Exalted King[39]
Osain ~ Osan: heavenly doctor; **Osain Dimolẹ; Osain Kiripiti**: various aspects of Ọsanyin **Old Ọsan**: Ọsanyin as cripple and hermit	**Ọ̀sányìn**: god of herbal medicine
Agbemiji ~ Agbemeje ~ Agbwemiji: honorific of Ọsanyin	**Agbe meji**: two touraco birds, emblem of Ọsanyin's mystical knowledge ~ **a-gbé-ìmí-jí**: supporter of the breath of life[40]
Ọba: St. Elizabeth	**Ọba**: wife of Shango
Ọbatala: Virgin Mary	**Ọbàtálá**: god of purity and patience
Ọgẹrẹ ~ Ọgẹrẹ: St. George	**Ọ̀gẹ́rẹ́**: honorific for Earth
Ọlọrun: God	**Ọlọ́run**: Supreme Deity
Ọṣọsi ~ Oṣosi: St. Raphael	**Ọṣọsi**: a hunter deity; as huntress deity, Ogun's wife

Ọṣun ~ Osọn ~ Oṣun: St. Philomen; mermaid goddess	**Ọ̀ṣun**: name of a river; goddess of the waterway named after her
Ọya: St. Catherine	**Ọya**: the Niger; favorite wife of Shango; goddess of tempestuous winds
Yasan ~ Yansa: Ọya	**Yansan**: mother of nine; honorific of Ọya
Ṣakpana: St. Raphael; St. Jerome; deity who brings and removes "copperpox"	**Ṣọ̀nkpọ̀nọ́n**: smallpox deity
Ṣango ~ Sango: St. John of the Cross; the thunder deity	**Ṣàngó**: god of lightning and thunder
Ayira: honorific of Shango	**Àrìrà**: thunderbolt; honorific of Shango
Olubambi: honorific of Shango	**Olúbámbí**: master who helps me give birth; honorific of Shango
Obakoso ~ Ọbakuso ~ Abakoso ~ Abakuso: honorific of Shango	**Ọbakòsó**: king did not hang; honorific of Shango
Yemanja ~ Emanja ~ Imanja: St. Ann; St. Mary Magdalene	**Yemọnja**: deity of coastal waters and lagoons

The connection between Orisha Oko and stars is that the goddess's birthplace was the town of Irawọ, which means 'star'.

Both Shango and Ọranyan are associated with fire. So also is Osain Zagwe.[41] The latter is apparently a Yoruba-Fon composite. Although Zagwe seems phonologically akin to Agwe, the Fon goddess of water, the link is more likely with Agɛ, Fon hunter god of the bush, whose Catholic counterpart is St. Bernard.[42]

Yemanja is strongly associated in Trinidad memory with the Ẹgbado who used buttons and originally seashells on their calabash drums. The latter were called in Trinidad by the Ewe term *boli,* cognate with Fon *govi*. This music was particularly sacred to Yemanja.

St. Anthony, whether as Ọrunmila or Banyan, appeals to professional persons such as lawyers, teachers, nurses and doctors.

Osain has several manifestations.[43] Some believe Osain to be an Indian priest who travelled from place to place in Africa like a missionary. Another interpretation is that he stayed among the Dahomey people and learned African customs.

Manifestations of Ọgẹrẹ are today rare, but he is associated with the earth and a horse. These connections were recalled in a poem by L which went:

Ọ̀gẹ́rẹ́ wọ̀lẹ̀ toún teṣin	Ọgẹrẹ entered the earth with his horse,
Toún tẹgbọn wọ̀	Both he and his older sister[44]

The names of the *orisha* may be preceded by "Papa," "Mister," or "Mama." Yoruba and Catholic nomenclature are used interchangeably. In keeping with the belief system, a devotee possessed by a deity is referred to as the deity him- or herself, even when reference is self-reflexive. In other words, a devotee may say: "St. Michael took the child. . . ." Background information will alert the listener that St. Michael on that occasion was the speaker in the person of St. Michael during a particular manifestation.

Other Religious Terms

Trinidad Yoruba	*Yoruba Cognates*
abuke ~ **abukẹ**: dwarfed hunchbacks who live on the far side of the sun[45]	**abuké**: hunchback
adura: prayer	**àdúrà**: prayer
ago: make way, stand clear; water[46]	**àgò**: make way, clear the way
atare ~ **ata ire**: guinea pepper	**ataare** ~ **ata ire** (Ketu): Guinea pepper (*Afromomum melegueta*)
babalawo: *orisha* priest	**babaláwo**: diviner priest, i.e., priest of Ifa
dabi cloth: red cloth on which kolanut valves are thrown for divination	**dà obì**: cast kolanut lobes for divination
daromi: solemn a capella hymn sung in preliminary stages of religious ceremony; also called *litany*	**ìdáròò mi**: my lamentation
ekpo: olive oil	**ekpo**: oil; palm oil used in religious rites
edi: trouble, malignant magic	**èdì**: charm to cause irrational behavior
ẹbọ ~ **ẹgbọ**: sacrificial feast for *orisha,* small religious feast	**ẹbọ**: sacrifice, feast involving sacrificial offering
ẹdilogun ~ **mẹẹdologun**: thanksgiving feast given a fortnight after the end of an *ẹbọ*	**ẹẹ́dínlógún**: sixteen (num); **mẹ́ẹ̀dínlógún**: sixteen (adj)
hekpa: exclamation pronounced during divination	**heèkpa** ~ **éékpà**: exclamation of surprise uttered by *babalawo* on recognizing the cabalistic sign made by casting beads or kola lobes; an interjection denoting profound awe and reverence[47]

iwere: wild spirits, spirits of the air, devotee in demonic possession
iwèrè: mad person

juba ~ **mọjuba**: act of reverence; perform ritual to reverence Eshu at beginning of *ẹbọ* and at close of sequence of six days of *orisha* ceremonies
júbà (V): pay reverence; **ijúbà** (N): act of reverence

kabiyesi ~ **kabiyesilẹ**: expression of thanks during divination
ka bì iyé sí ilẹ̀: long live the Earth; we prostrate before Earth

kiriṣa: chants in honor of an *orisha*
oríkì òrìṣà: praise song to *orisha*

konkoto: tray with African foods from which children eat after the food has been offered as sacrifice to an *orisha*; also used as V
konkoto: anything used by children at play to represent the worship of the *orisha*[48]

mamalawo: *orisha* priestess
< *mama* 'mother' + **aláwo** 'possessor of divination secrets'

mọngba ~ **amọngba** ~ **ọmọgba** ~ **magba** ~ **mungwa** ~ **amungwa** ~ **omunga**: *orisha* priest
mọ́ngbà: priest of Shango

obi: kolanut
obì: kolanut

omi: water
omi: water

oriṣa ~ **oreṣa** ~ **ọrisa** ~ **oriṣo** ~ **oreṣo**: deity
òrìṣà: deity

ọkpware: tray
ọkpọn ọrẹ: tray with oblation

ọti: alcohol, "puncheon" (overproof) rum
ọti: alcohol; palmwine (the fermented sap of the raffia palm)

perogun ~ **pray ogun** ~ **orogun**: ground altar, also called *stool*
kpèrègún (SY) ~ **kpòrògún** (Ek): *orisha* altar formed by mound of earth; a type of plant found in sacred groves and used as an enclosure

saraka: religious ceremony to placate ancestors involving unsalted food offerings and charitable distribution of food
sàdákà ~ **sàráa**: charity, alms; ceremony of annual thanksgiving or special supplication involving the distribution of food to children, friends, and the needy

singbere ~ **singbẹrẹ**: ceremony in which tiny incisions are made on the scalp and ritual ointments rubbed in
sín gbéré: cut incisions

Ṣango: god of lightning and the thunderbolt; the system of Yoruba-derived worship
Ṣàngó: god of lightning and the thunderbolt, once a king of Ọyọ

ṣẹṣẹrẹ: broom made of *cocoyea* /kokoye/ 'coconut leaf ribs', and used as insignia of certain *orisha*, particularly Shakpana and Ọsanyin	**ṣẹṣẹrẹ**: broom
ṣugudu: image of clay and sticks	**sìgìdì**: image used as an avenging agent, but capable of taking revenge on its master if displeased
were ~ rere: messenger of the *orisha* who behaves in a childish manner; (adj) **were** spirit	**wèrè**: madness, folly

Lexical Loans

Terms	*Cognates*
ababo ~ lababo: yodel made to welcome advent of *orisha*; used also as V	**awóbóbó** (Fon): ululation to welcome or express joy
Adangbe ~ Adangwe: serpent god	**Dãgbwe** (Fon): serpent god, associated with the source of energy, movement, life. Christian counterpart: God Almighty
Adosoji: Banyan, St. Anthony	**Da Zoji** (Fon): god of smallpox. Catholic counterpart in Trinidad: St. Anthony
Aflɛgɛdɛ ~ Aflegede: Ọya	**Avlekete** (Fon): goddess of wind and lightning. Catholic counterpart in Trinidad: St. Catherine
akakũ: Guinea pepper	**àtákṹ** (Fon): Guinea pepper (*Afromomum melegueta*)
Awoyo: honorific for Yemanja	**Awoyo** (Fon): honorific of the sea
Bo Zewɔ̃ ~ Bɔ̃ Zewa: a healing deity, rarely manifesting in contemporary times; Shakpana, St. Jerome	**Bo Zuõ** (Fon): a deity with control over sickness and evil spirits
desunu ~ desuni ~ deshɔne: sacred ceremony in which priest makes incisions on devotee's head and body, and anoints head with olive oil, and with leaves and celts steeped in water. Cognate with *singbere* above	**désùnu** (Fon) < **désù** 'atonement or purification ceremony'; **-nu** 'matters pertaining to'
Dɔmbala: St. Dominic	**Dambala**: serpent god. Catholic equivalent: St. Dominic

drazɔ: vigil to start *orisha* ceremonies, during which prayers are said and a capella chants are sung	**dró zã** (Fon): keep [the] night; to keep a vigil
hubunu: divinely appointed slayer of sacrificial animals	**hobonu** (Fon): sacred slayer of animal to be sacrificed
hũsi ~ ũsi ~ osi: devotee	**hũsi** (Fon): an initiate able to assist in priestly functions
huto: lead drummer in *ẹbọ* ceremony	**hũto** (Fon): lead drummer in *vodũ* ceremony
kobabo: ululate to welcome deity	**?kọ ababo**: sing *ababo*; **?kí ababo**: greet with ululation
kwe: earthen *orisha* altar	**kpè** (Fon): earthen *vodu* altar
Mama Laté ~ Mama Late ~ Mama Leta: Earth; Oshala	***Maman La Terre*** (Fr.): Mother Earth
Naite: Virgin Mary	**Naetɛ** (Fon): a water goddess; St. Philomen in Trinidad *vodũ*
Ologbo: a healing deity	**Oloko** (Fon): god of trees
Osokbo: Shango	**Sogbo** (Fon): thunder deity
Parada: Ọrunmila, St. Joseph	**Parada** (Fon): god of smallpox and disease. Catholic counterpart in Trinidad: St. Joseph
sababo: yodel, ululate	**sẹ̀ ababo**: yodel, ululate
-si: indicator of spiritual affiliation, cf. *Ogunsi* 'devotee of Ogun'	**-si** (Fon): wife of
vudunu: *ẹbọ*, worship ceremony for the *orisha*	**vudunu** (Fon): ceremony in which the *vudũ ~ vodũ* are worshipped
vudũsi: person possessed by *vodũ ~ orisha*	**vudũsi** (Fon): person possessed by *vodũ ~ orisha*

Loan Translations

The practice of *orisha* ceremonial is commonly referred to as *Yaraba work, orisha work, work,* a translation of *iṣẹ́* 'work', which in Yoruba embraces both secular and spiritual tasks.

The possessed devotee is referred to as a "saint horse" or "vessel." The former phrase is a calque of *elégùn* 'the one stung, pricked, or ridden'. The deity is said to "mount" the devotee's head, the head being the seat of consciousness and, in Yoruba cosmogony, the focus of realized and potential experience, i.e. fate, luck, destiny. As a "vessel," the devotee is perceived as being a recipient of the deity, as being filled by a spiritual force.

The *orisha* are commonly called "powers" or "saints." 'Power' translates *aṣẹ,* energizing force. The term *saints* captures the subsidiary but important role which the *orisha* occupy in relation to the Supreme Divinity, that is, Olodumare, Ọlọrun, or Ẹlẹfọn, who created the *orisha*. Another term borrowed from Catholic culture is *feast,* which translates or is used appositively with the synonyms *ẹbọ* and *shango*.

'Stool' is used as a synonym of *perogun,* the locus of the *orisha*'s *aṣhẹ* or power. It is interesting that a combination of metathesis (*perogun* > *preogun*) and folk etymology have been born of the association between the stool as altar and the purpose of that location—prayer, thus *pray* /pre/ > *pray Ogun* /preogun/. Insignia of the *orisha* and other symbolically powerful substances are embedded in the mound of earth that forms the *perogun,* and as such the *orisha* and life-enabling forces are seated there. Stools as seats—even thrones—are themselves important status symbols in many African cultures.

Oríkí òrìṣà, attributive chant to the *orisha,* is rendered as *kirisha* by S, but as 'salutation' by T. Generally known as 'chant', 'sing', or 'song', it states the lineage, achievements, and qualities of the person or object described.

Ẹdùn, meteoric stone celts symbolic of Shango, has not survived in the sacred vocabulary but its substitute is the term 'thunderstones'.

The following chapters will explore the intrinsic properties of TY beyond its lexical inventory of ritual terminology and place and personal names. The structures of a diasporan language will be observed—its amalgamation of phonological, grammatical, and semantic aspects from its own diverse regional sources as well as its absorption of features from the languages with which it coexists in its new locus of operation.

Part Two

Trinidad Yoruba: Linguistic Structures of Second- and Third-Generation Speakers

5

Phonology

1.0.0. The phonological structure of TY morphemes is either v or (v)cv. Nasals are nonsyllabic as well as syllabic.

1.0.1. The phonemic inventory of TY consists of:

Vowels

Oral	i	e	ɛ	a	ɔ	o	u
Nasal	ĩ			ã			ũ

Consonants

Sonorants

Nasals

Labial	Alveolar	Velar
m	n	ŋ

Glides

Palatal	Labio-Velar	Laryngeal
y	w	h

Liquids

Alveolar
l r

Obstruents

	Labial	Alveolar	Palato-Alveolar	Velar
Stops	p b	t d		k g
Fricatives	f	s	š	
Affricates			j	

1.1.0. ***Vowels***

1.1.1. **Free Variation**

1.1.11. Free variation affects the front and back low vowels [a] and [ɔ], oral and nasal. This variation reflects a difference in their phonemic distribution in various regional dialects of Y. [a], oral and nasal, enjoys wider distribution in the Ọyọ dialect than in many others. The extent of this free variation in TY is evidence of "incomplete and competing" sound change in TY.[1] The following are a few of the TY variants noted:

ɔtɛfa	atɛfa	'suppression'
ɔwa	awa	'respect'

ɔmɔ̃ ~ ɔmã	ama	'child'
jɔgba	jagba	'strong'
yemɔ̃nja	yemanja	'Yemọja'
wɔ	wa	'enter'
lɔ	la	'go'

In some cases, SY and Ọyọ [a] corresponds with EY [ɔ]. In TY there were the following variants:

ara	ɔra	'people'
anĩ	ɔnĩ	'person'
mã	mɔ̃	preverbal NEG

In TY, [ɔ̃] sometimes varies with [ɑ̃], both low retracted vowels.

ɛgbɔ̃	ɛgbɑ̃	'elder brother'
ɔ̃	ɑ̃ɑ̃	'they'
ɔkɔ̃	ɔkɑ̃	'one'

1.1.12. In TY, [i] is often in variation with [u], whether word-initially or -medially. Word-initial occurrence of [u] is characteristic of EY. In Y, generally, the differentiation between word-medial [i] and [u] distinguishes the dialect affiliation of such words. The following occurred in TY:

igba	ugba	'time'
ilu	ulu	'town'
ijo	ujo	'dance'
atikɔ ~ akikɔ	akukɔ	'cock'
nĩka	nũka	'only'
jiba	juba	'pay respect to'

1.1.13. Similar front/back cross-height opposition affects word-initial [e ~ o].

ekute	okute	'rat'

and [ɛ ~ ɔ]:

ɛsɛ	ɔsɛ	'foot'

Other potential variants are:

(èkùrɔ́)[2]	okurɔ	'palm kernel'
(èlùbɔ́)	olubɔ	'cassava flour'
(kpɛkpɛyɛ)	pɔkpɔyɛ	'duck'

though the parenthetical forms did not occur in the TY corpus.

1.1.14. Low/high oppositions produce [a ~ ɛ] variation. Northeastern and northwestern Y dialects such as Ifẹ̀ (Togo), Igala, Yàgbà,

Idsumu, Owọ̀rọ̀, and Ìgbómìnà use the [a] forms. TY examples of such oppositions are:

ɛnĩ	anĩ	'person'
bɛɛ	bahi	'thus'
kɛhĩ	kayi	'follow'

[i ~ e] variation occurs in the word-final position and reflects Y dialect differences:

bi	be	'be born'
ibi	ibe[3]	'place'

1.1.15. Oral and nasal [i] may be cognate with oral and nasal [ɛ] or [a] in other dialects. The main dialects so differentiated are SY and EY. TY variants include:

ije	ɛjɛ	'blood'
iwa	ɛwa	'beans'
ilɛ	alɛ	'ground'

1.1.16. Cross-dialect [ĩ ~ ɛ̃] cognation also occurs. The phonemic status of [ɛ̃] characterizes the Ijẹbu dialect. TY variants of this type are:

ɔnĩ	ɔnɛ̃	'person'
ologĩnĩ	ologɛ̃nɛ̃	'cat'
obirĩ	obirɛ̃	'girl'

1.1.17. Another tense-lax opposition accounts for [e ~ ɛ], yet a further differentiation between SY and EY. TY examples of this cognation are:

eru	ɛru	'slave'
ešĩ	ɛsĩ	'horse'
kpelu	kpɛlu	'with'
je	jɛ	'eat'

1.1.18. Low-high oppositions also affect back vowels and are again among the bases of differentiation between southern and eastern Y dialects. In TY there is considerable evidence of alternation between [ɔ] and [u], both oral and nasal:

kɔrɔ	kuro	'leave'
sɔ̃mɔ̃	sumã	'sky'
ɔkɔre	ɔkũrĩ	'man'

word-initially between [o ~ ɔ]:

ogiri	ɔgiri	'bean-sauce'
okuta	ɔkuta	'stone'
orukɔ	ɔrukɔ	'name'
oriša	ɔriša	'deity'
oũ	ɔũn	'he'

and between [o ~ u], mainly word-finally but also -initially:

umẽle	omẽle	type of drum
ɛrũ	ɛro	'mouth'
ɔrũ	aro	'neck'
su	so	'tie'
ilɛkũ	ilɛko	'door'

1.1.19. Tense/lax variation affects the high back vowels [u ~ ʊ], both word-initial and -final, a distinction between SY, which favors the tense form, and EY, which favors the lax. TY repeats this variation:

ulu	ʊlu	'town'
ʊ̃ŋkã	ʊŋkɑ̃	'thing'
oju	ojʊ	'face, dawn'
ɛnʊ̃	ɛnʊ[4]	'mouth'
sũ	sʊ̃	'sleep'
a yulɔ ru	ɛ nlɛ rʊ̃	a greeting
ɔlɔru	ɔlɔrʊ̃	'God'

1.1.2. **Denasalization**

In TY there is free variation between nasalized and denasalized vowels, another instance of dialectal differentiation in Y.[5] TY variant citations listed below are illustrative of a direction towards phonemic nondistinctiveness between nasal and oral vowels, with the probable eventual elimination of nasal vowels, as in the Igala dialect of Y. This process is already advanced in some southern Y dialects.

sũ	su	'sleep'
didũ	dudu	'black'
arũ	aru	'five'
sĩ	si	'follow'
fɛrã	fɛra	'love'
ogũ	ogu	'Ogún'
dukpɛ̃	dukpɛ	'thank'
ibɛ̃mbɛ̃	ibɛ̃mbɛ	type of drum
ɔkɔrĩ	ɔkɔrɛ	'man'
irĩ	ɛrɛ	'iron'

1.1.3. **Apocope**

In Y and TY double-mora vowels may be reduced, so that a "sequence that ordinarily occupies two moras is pronounced with the length of only one" (Stevick and Aremu 1963: xxi).

nãã	nã	DEF
daa	da	'good'
oo	o	'cowrie'
(o)fuu	ofu	'expanse'
mẽẽji	mẽji	'two'

1.1.4. **Vowel Co-occurrence and Euphony**

The application of vowel harmony in nouns and verbs is observed to a greater or lesser degree in all dialects of Yorùbá. It is least operational in SY, is more strikingly observed in the Ọyọ́, Ìbàdàn, Ọ̀ṣun and Ẹ̀gbádò dialects, and is most extensive in the Èkìtì and Akurẹ́ dialects.[6]

Vowel euphony is produced by tenseness assimilation and cross-height harmony. Thus in nouns the tongue root position of the initial vowel corresponds with that of the first vowel following, and the vowels of pronouns and of certain preverb markers assimilate to the tongue root resonance of the first vowel of the verb they precede.

Both cross-height harmony and combined height and tongue-root harmony are in evidence in the TY corpus. At the same time, some TY morpheme sequences violate vowel co-occurrence constraints. The defective application of these vowel harmonies, or its reverse—their partial avoidance—is indicative of a degree of nonsystematization in this aspect of TY. Thus, tense and height characterize the vowel sequences in:

owo	'money'
oju	'eye'
ešĩ	'horse'
ekute	'rat'
mõ de	'I arrived'
o šubu	'he fell'
e kpe	'she called'

but not in:

mɔ̃ nĩ	'I say'
mɔ̃ dukpwɛ	'I thank'
ɔ bere	'you ask'

Laxness and low height harmony are observed in:

ɔjɔ	'day'
ɔgɛdɛ ~ ɛgɛdɛ	'plantain'
ɛnʊ̃	'mouth'
ɛjɛ	'blood'
mɔ̃ pašɔ	'I'm washing'
kɔ tɔ < kí ọ tọ	COMPL 'you follow'

but not in:

o lɔ	'he goes'
mõ mʊ̃	'I took'
mõ mẹ̃rĩ < mo mọ erin	'I know song'

1.2.0. *Consonants*

1.2.1. **Obstruents**

1.2.11. *Fricatives*

A phonemic differentiation between [s] and [š] characterizes SY and several regional dialects. However, this differentiation is not observed in the Ọyọ́, Ogbómọ̀ṣọ́, and Ìbàdàn dialects, in which [s] alone occurs. In TY the stronger tendency appeared to be in the direction of maintaining a phonemic distinction between the two, perhaps under pressure from languages like French and English which maintain such a difference, and at the expense of an influential dialect in TY like Ọyọ. All the same, free variation between these segments occurred within the same TY idiolect:

še	se	'be, make'
šango	saŋgo	'Shango'
išonšo	isonso	'tip'
ajašɛ	ajasɛ	'Ajasẹ'
šare	sare	'run'
šɔ	sɔ	'say'

1.2.12. *Coarticulated Stops*

Historically, processes of labialization, velarization and segmentation affect labial, velar and labiovelar stops in African languages.[7] These processes affect cognates in languages on the periphery of Yorubaland.[8] Similarly, TY displays a phlethora of variant articulations of the Y coarticulated stops [kp] and [gb]. Whether in word-initial, intervocalic, or post-velar positions, the following variants occurred: [gb ~ ɓ ~ gbʷ ~ gbw ~ b ~ g], and [kp ~ pʷ ~ pw ~ p' ~ k]. Thus:

gbe ~ ɓe ~ gbwe	'carry'
gbʷagbwe	'forget'
baguda	'cassava'
bobo ~ gogo	'all'

agbɔ̃	'coconut'
ɛgbwa	'Ẹ̀gbá'
ɔgbʷɔ̃	'wise'
baŋgba	'open space'
ikeŋge	type of calabash
kpe	'call'
kpade	'meet'
mõ ŋ kpe	'I PROG call'
pa	'kill'
p'ɛluu	'with it'
kuro	'break word/tell a lie'
kwariwo	'shatter noise/make noise'
ɔlɔkpa	'policeman'
irekpɔ	'friendship'
opele	'divination rosary'
pikpʷɔ	'much'
dukpʷɛ ~ dukpwɛ	'thank'
ɔkpwɛ	'oil-palm'
ɔkpɔlɔp'ɔ	'many'

The combination of contact with other languages and a perception of the bilabial element in the articulation of the labiovelar stops has led to the simplification of these stops, largely in favor of their bilabial components, though there is a marginal tendency toward the velar option. This change signals a partial rephonologization process in TY, in that it demonstrates the suppression of the Y phonemic distinction between the labiovelar and bilabial stops. The latter exist in French, English, and Spanish, for example, but the voiceless bilabial stop [p] is absent from the Y phoneme inventory.

The partial restructuring of the Y phoneme inventory in TY can effect segmentation of the dual components of the original labiovelar stops. The fact that this process occurs only in an intervocalic environment militates against consonant clustering, the latter being atypical of Y. Instead, a syllable boundary is created between the two consonant segments.

ɛg=bã	'big brother'
ag=bo	'ram'
hek=p'a	sacred exclamation
sɔk=p'e	'speak to'

The insertion of a syllable boundary between the segmented elements of the voiced labiovelar stop can lead to dissimilation between the components. This [gb > kb] dissimilation attempts to approximate the absence of aspiration perceived in the pristine articulation of the coarticulated stops. Thus:

ɛk=bã	'Ẹ̀gbá'
jak=bo	'eat ram'

In opposition to these analytic processes, there was hypercorrection involving a reinterpretation of the voiced bilabial stop as the voiced labio-velar stop and its variants:

aɓuro ~ agburo	'younger brother'
oiɓo	'European'
tak=bata	'beat the *bàtá* drum'
ig=bada	'Ìbàdàn'

1.2.13. ***Nasals***

1.2.131. *Nonsyllabic Nasals*

Nasals may follow nasal vowels in intervocalic and preconsonantal positions, as well as in the sentence-final position:

kɔrĩ^{m}	'sing'
wɔ̃ĩ^{m}#	'these'
ɔšũŋkɛyɛ	'Ọ̀ṣunkẹ́yẹ'
lɔrũŋ ɔba	'at neck king/around the king's neck'
ɔrĩn fũ	'song(s) give/songs for'
ogũn ti	'war which'
mɛrim# < mọ̀ erin	'know song(s)'

1.2.132. The variation in morpheme-final between bilabial and alveolar nasal is to be noted. While use of the latter characterizes SY and related dialects, the bilabial occurs in western dialects such as Icha, Idaisa, Dahomey (Bénin), and Togo.

Denasalization generally affects the alveo-palatal nasal glide which occurred only rarely in TY. Thus:

ɲũɲũ	'delicious'

But there were variant articulations of:

ĩɲã ~ iyã	'pounded yam'
wɔ̃ɲĩ wãyi	'these'

while realizations of the following used only the palatal glide:

yu	'go'
iyĩ	'praise'
ayĩ	'oil'
oyĩ	'honey'

An increase in syllable quantity results from a reconstitution of the palatalized alveolar into alveolar nasal + high front vowel + palatal glide.

e=ɲã ~ e=nĩ=yã	'people'
o=ra=nĩ=yã	'Ọ̀ránỳàn'

1.2.133. *Syllabic Nasals*

In TY, as in Y, nasals can function as syllabics:

ŋ̩=kɑ̃ ~ ŋ̩=kã	'thing'
kpe=ŋ̩=kpe	'neat'
ka=ka=m̩=fu	'military title'

But in TY the nasal syllabic may be deleted:

baba la < baba ńlá	'father big/grandfather'

or replaced by a high vowel that is front or back depending on phonetic environment:

mã ĩ še	'not CONT be'
ke i kpe	'which CONT call'
o ũ sɔ̃ũnjɛ	'you CONT cook food'
ɛ ilɛ[9] rʊ̃ ~ a ilɔ rũ ~ a yulɔ rũ	'you gently support' [a greeting (EY)]

Nasals generally assimilate to their surrounding phonetic environment. As in SY, progressive assimilation affects the allophonic realization of the nasal. The nasal may thus be subject to full or partial assimilation to a preceding vowel:

inɔ̃ mɔ̃ ɔ̃ rele	'they CONT CONT go home/they keep on dying'
mɔ̃ ɔ̃ lɔ̃	'I PROG go'
fuʔula < òfù ńlá	'expanse big/wide expanse'

Nasals may also lose syllabicity by epenthetically acquiring a syllable-initial vowel that is phonetically conditioned by the anteriority either of the anticipated nasal or the vowel it follows. And in thus losing syllabicity, it constitutes itself into a consonant-final:

un=do	Oǹdó

ba=ba=	la=	gaŋ=o=			pe=	ri=	rɛ #	<
ba=ba=	n̩=la=	gã=	ŋ=o=		kpe=	ri=	rɛ #	
baba	ńlá	gan	ng	ò	kpa	erí	rẹ	
'father	great	INTENS	I	NEG	shatter	head	your	/

great father, I did not speak ill of you'

a=ra=le=	ĩŋ=kɔ #	
'members of home	INTERROG/	how is everyone at home?'

ɔ=lɔ=kpa= ĩm= bɔ= wa #
police PROG approach come

1.2.14. [n ~ l] *Relationship*

There is allophonic relationship between [n] and [l] in certain morphosyntactic and phonotactic collocations in Y. For example, in some dialects, the only vowel that [n] may precede is [i], while [l] occurs before vowels other than [i]. In Ẹ̀gbá, on the other hand, [l] may precede [i]. Both these rules appear in TY. Thus:

lɔnã < ní ọ̀nà 'in road'
loke < ní okè 'in mountain'
lanã < ní aàná 'in yesterday'
nĩle ~ lile < ní ilé 'in house'
onĩšaŋgo ~ olišaŋgo < o- ní Ṣàngó 'person possess Shango/ Shango devotee'

Similarly [n], like [l], can precede back vowels.[10]

nũle ~ lile < ní ilé 'in home'
nĩmɔ̃lɛ ~ lumɔ̃lɛ < ní ìmọ́lẹ̀ 'have light'
ɔnɔ̃r̃ũ ~ ɔlɔr̃ũ < o- ní ọ̀run 'person possess sky/ God Above'

The close relationship between [n] and [l] is further evidenced in the following occurrences, brought about by regressive assimilation of [n] to [l] in the first case and by regressive dissimilation in the second:

lɛlu < lẹ́nu < ní ẹnu 'in mouth'
lɛnã < lẹ́la < ní ẹla 'in fragment'

1.2.15. ***Glides, Liquids***

1.2.151. *Sonorant Variation*

Free variation particularly affects intervocalic glides and liquids. There is considerable alternation between these two categories of consonants, but less often their variant may be a stop. The following free variants occur:

[y] ~ [h]
iyi ihi 'praise'
ɛyi ɛhi 'you'
eyi ɛhi 'back'
niyi nihi 'here'
bayi bahi 'like this'

The [y] forms are typical of Ìjẹ̀ṣà and Ọ̀yọ́.

[y] ~ [r]		
ayira	arira	'Àrìrà'
[y] ~ [l]		
demaye	(démɔ̃lɛ)	'cover'
[y] ~ [w]		
ayo	awo	'darling'
yɔ	wɔ	'favor'
[y] ~ [g]		
ayo	ago	'darling'
[y] ~ [ʔ]		
eyi	eʔi	'tooth'
[w] ~ [r]		
awe	ɔrɛ ~ arɛ	'friend'
jawe	šare	'pick leaves/cut grass'
we	rɛ	'his'
[w] ~ [h]		
aworo	ahoro	'sacred bell'
awoyo	ahoyo	'expanse'
awo	aho	'cult member'
[w] ~ [g][11]		
ɔwurɔ	agurɔ	'morning'
awo	ago	'guinea bird'
awɔ̃ okũ	agu ruka	'turtle'
[r] ~ [l]		
rare	lare	'see misery'
aforo	afolo	'Afoólò(gbà)'
oɾukɔ	olukɔ ~ ɔlukɔ	'name'
orogũ	ologũ	'warrior'
ɔrɔkpa	ɔlɔkpa	'policeman'
eregede	alekadɛ ~ alɛkadɛ	'pumpkin'

1.2.152. *Intervocalic Sonorant Elision*

Another process affecting intervocalic sonorants is elision. Most of the sonorants in question are glides. This type of elision affects Ọ̀yọ́, Èkìtì, and Oǹdó among other dialects.[12] Elision is more frequent in connected speech than in lexically discrete utterance.[13] Nevertheless, it is the elided variants that are the norm in some dialects. This elision is reflected in particular idiolects of TY.

[r] elision

erilɛ	eĩlɛ	'Erinlẹ̀'
okurɔ	okuɔ	'palm nut'
ɔlɔrũ	ɔlɔũ	'God'
yoroba	yooba	'Yorùbá'
kuro	kuo	'leave'
bere	bɛɛ	'thus'
rɛ	ɛ	'his'

[y] elision

bayi	bai	'thus'
oyibo	oibo	'European'
nisisiyi	nisisĩ	'now'
ɛyĩ	ɛi	'tooth'
oyi	oi	'honey'

[n] elision

nĩ	ĩ	'is'
nĩ	i	'in, at'

[h] elision

nĩhĩ	nĩʔĩ	'here'
ɛhĩkule	ɛi	'backyard/back'

[w] elision

owo	oo	'money'
ɔwurɔ̃	aurɔ ~ aurɔ	'morning'

1.2.153. *Syncope*

Elision of a sonorant may lead to deletion of the syllable in which it occurs. Thus:

kuro	ko	'leave'
mĩrã	mĩ	'another'
dara	da	'good'
daradara	daada	'very good'
ɛhĩkule	ɛkule	'backyard'

Syncope also affects polysyllabic words with a reduplicated consonant (Oyelaran 1971: 19; Abimbọla and Oyelaran 1975: 45 ff.). The word-medial syllable containing the reduplicated consonant is deleted. The last four examples below show that in TY this syncope also operates across word boundaries.

berere	bere	'ask'
ofofo	ofo	'a tell-tale'

akoko	oko	'time'
emĩmã	e=m̩=ã ~ emõ	'disaster'
adodo ɔndawa	ado ɔndawa	a military title
omĩ gbigbonã	omĩ bɔnɛ̃	'hot water; hot breakfast drink'
(awó kpɛkpɛ́yɛ)	ago pwɛ̃yɛ̃	'guinea bird'
(ò gbɔ́dɔ̀ dojú)	ɔgbɔ doju	'you have to face'

Syncope did not, however, occur in the following:

ɔdɛdɛ	'drawing room'
otitɔ	'truth'
ɔyɔyɔ	type of leaf
afɛfɛ	'wind'
ešiši	'fly'
ajoji	'stranger'
ikakare	'spoon'
eyiya[13]	'comb'

1.2.154. *Epenthesis*

The glides [r] and [y] are sometimes inserted intervocalically at word- and morpheme-juncture.

Intrusive [r]

orisa roko		'Òrìṣà Oko'
ila roge	< ilà oge	'face marks (of) beauty'
ata romĩ	< ọta omi	'pebble water/pebble of ~ in water'
alari šɔmɔ̃	< a ní ài ṣe ọmọ	'person have PRIV be have child/one who is not a child'

Intrusive [y]

ɔmã yelumĩ	< ọmọ elomin	'child another/another's child'
bi yeru	< bí erú	'like slave'
ɔrɛ yɛlɛdɛ	< ọrá ẹlẹdẹ	'fat pig/pig's fat; lard'

Intrusive [h]

[h] tends to be epenthetic in postjunctural positions, signaling stress at the onset of breath.

agido heko	< Agìdó Èkó	a place name
a ho ku	< a ò kú	'we NEG die'
hɛyɛ		'bird'
hĩnɔ̃		'they'

1.2.6. *Metathesis*

(ɛ́gbádarígí)	> ɛgbaragidi ~ ɛgbawaridi	'Ẹ̀gbá of Badagry'
1 2 3	2 3 1 3 2 1	
yaraba	> rayaba	'Yorùbá'
1 2 3	2 1 3	
(kpašaŋga)	> p'anšaga	'prostitute'
1 2 3 4	1 3 2 4	
kuro	> koru	'leave'
1 2	2 1	

1.2.7. *Suprasegmental Features*

1.2.71. **Secondary Nasalization**

Certain Y dialects "display nasal assimilation over *r, w, y, h,* as well as over a preceding vowel, unless it is *e* or *o*." On the other hand, nasalization in Kétu affects as well, "whatever its height, within the word" the vowel immediately preceding the nasalized liquid or glide. Regressive nasalization does not, however, appear to condition word-initial nasalization in vowels (Fresco 1970: 86, 89).

TY examples show that [r] and [y] are affected by regressive nasal assimilation, and [e] and [o] are among the vowels capable of nasalization. In addition, nasal assimilation can extend progressively and regressively across morphosyntactic boundaries. Such secondary nasalization invites comparison with nasalization processes in Kétu as well as in languages within the repertoire of TY speakers. Of these, nasalization is most prominent in Fr. Cr. And in the comparative case of Haitian Creole (since no phonological description of Trinidad Fr. Cr. is available), Tinelli (1974: 347, 348, 353) analyzes nasalization across syntactic boundaries as a general rule, so much so that although "*e* and *o* are always oral in the lexicon, even when followed by a nasal . . . any vowel can be nasalized across morpheme boundaries." TY gives similar evidence:

ɛ̃ mɔ̃ buru < ẹ́ mọ̀ bọrọ	'it certainly glistens'
mõ ŋ̩ kpe	'I CONT call'
õ n̩ sõnjɛ	'you CONT cook'
gbẽ n̩ sa	'carry CONT run'

1.2.72. **Tone**

Tone is lexical in Yoruba, inhering in the phonetic realization of each syllable without regard to the formation of tone patterns in word- or phrase-length utterance.

Yoruba has three level tones: high, low, and mid. These level tones yield rising and falling glides, noticeably on vowels. But glides also occur as allotones of level tones in certain phonetic environments (Hyman and Schuh 1974: 88; La Velle 1974: 185). Tonal register is not absolute but relative, being objectively perceived in the tonal relationship of one syllable to another. Rowlands's comments (1955: 334) on the Yoruba midtone illustrate the convergence or narrowing of register intervals in utterances that are semantically nonambiguous. Register frequency in such cases is influenced by the "emotional state of the speaker and the desire to ensure audibility."

Most TY primary speakers retained notions of tone, whereas the speech of secondary speakers reflected no such approximations.[14] Where vestigial tone remained, speech was syllable-timed with syllables displaying pitch variations.[15] However, a reduced lexical inventory and functional domain must be among factors that have led to an absence of lexico-semantic contrasts dependent on tonal differentiation. Tonal patterns on the same word in the same idiolect were therefore inconsistent.

The following variants may be noted. Each set is taken from the same informant. These data have been extracted from the texts given at the end of this section:

kúò ~ kuro	'leave, come out of'
lúlú ~ nilu	'in (the) town'
mó ~ mo	'I'
lọ́ ~ lọ	'go'
ko ~ kò	'not'
dàrà ~ dára	'good'

On the other hand, consistency is maintained in:

iyá	'mother'
Ọyẹ́	placename
dára	'good'
kò sí	'there is not'

No doubt because of contact with Fr. Cr. and Eng. Cr. intonations, there was a fairly even distribution of rising and falling intonation contours in prejunctural position in complete declarative sentences.[16] This contravenes the English intonation contour for declarative sentences where S-final is signaled by a fall in pitch, as distinct from a rising contour in interrogative sentences. It also contravenes Y tone rules: not being a restricted tone language, Y sentences bear no overall tonal contours. Downdrift of utterance-final level tones does occur, but only slightly in the case of high and mid tones, the downdrift interval not being sufficient to merge high tone with mid or mid tone with low (Hombert 1974: 178–79). Where utterance final is preceded by a sequence of low tones, the final low drifts downwards considerably, there being no lower tonal differentiation to impose a constraint (La Velle 1974: 190–91).

In TY, apart from S-final intonation rises, the frequent occurrence of high pitch may have resulted from hesitant articulation. This means that tone height was not accurately related to the previous syllabic pitch. High tones may also have been associated with the excitement involved in language use and the emphatic quality of certain statements. For example, stress on the first personal pronoun *mo* at S-initial appears to account for its heightened pitch in several instances of its use.

A further area of contrast with Y is the negligible use of tonal glides. There was zero occurrence of the glides produced by progressive assimilation of low tone in Y disyllabic words, for example LH > LR, cf. *ọ̀rẹ̀'* 'friend'. However, there was occasional tonal differentiation of double-length vowels:

nã́ã̀	DEF
màlúù	'cattle'
mɛ̃́ɛ̃̀ta	'three'
láàná	'yesterday'
ĩ̀ĩ́	'this'

At the same time, a double mora vowel could be sustained without concomitant tonal differentiation:

mɛ̃́ɛ̃́ta	'three'

In Y, coalescence of a tonally differentiated double-mora vowel into a single-mora vowel involves the assimilation by the remaining vowel of the tone of the deleted vowel, e.g., *dádá* < *dára-dára* 'good-good'. This results in a tonal glide, *dáadá*. However, this glide allotone does not occur in the apocopated forms listed in *Apocope* above.

In Y, the third person singular Object is indicated in a lengthened vowel-final of the verb, accompanied by tonal differentiation. This syllabic lengthening and tonal differentiation occurs only rarely:

mã ã́	'know it'
ka á	'read it'

The tonal syntactic marker of possession in Noun + Poss. phrases in Y involves vowel-final lengthening of the noun, accompanied by tonal differentiation of the first mora from the second. This vestigial lengthening or differentiation (or both) is found in:

ɔ̃mɔ̃ɔ̃̀ rɛ̀	'child her'
ɔrukɔ́ ɛ̀	'name her'
ɔkɔ́ɔ̀ mĩ́	'husband my'
iyáà mĩ	'mother my'
ɔrɛ́ɛ́ mĩ	'friend my'
adiɛ́ɛ̀ mĩ	'fowl my'

On the other hand, this associative tone is deleted in:

ɔrúkɔ́ ìyá mĩ́	'name mother my'
ɔ̀rɛ mĩ	'friend my'
ɔkɔ̀ rɛ	'husband your'

A selection of comparative sentences bearing TY and SY tones is taken from two informants' texts. In the first, the main difference from the SY tonal pattern lies in the lowering of SY high tones to mid; in the second selection, the main pattern that emerges is that SY lower tones tend to be raised; a minor pattern is that SY higher tones tend to be lowered.

S	*SY*
ìyáà mĩ kúò lúlú ɔyɛ́	ìyáà mĩ kúrò nĩ́lú ɔ̀yɛ
ìyá mĩ́ kuro nĩlu ɔyé	
ɔlɔ́kpàá ĩ́m bɔ̀ wá	ɔlɔ́ɔ̀kpá ḿ̩ bɔ̀ wá
ɔ̀mɔ̃dé wɔ̃̀ yĩ́ ɔ́ bá	àwɔ̃ ɔ̃mɔ̃dé wɔ̃ yĩ́ ḿ̩ bá
mĩ jà lonĩ̀ĩ́	mĩ jà lónĩ̀ĩ́
mṍ fɛrà ĩỹ́ã́	mo fɛ́rã iɲã́

O	
mṍ gbàgbé èdéé mĩ	mo gbàgbé èdèè mĩ́
mõ ń̩ kpè ɔ́	mõ̀ ŋ̩ kpè
owo kò sí	owó kò sí
mõ kɔ́rĩ́ kpúkpɔ́	mõ kɔrĩ kpúkpɔ̀
ó lɔ lúlé ɛja	ó lɔ sílé ɛja
ká lɔ́	ká lɔ
ó dàrà	ó dára
ko dára	kò dára
ɔ́kɔ̀re lá kò dára	okũ̀r̃ĩ nã́ã̀ kò dára

6

Syntax

1.0.0. **The Simple Declarative Sentence**

1.1.1. ***Affirmative***

Like Y, the TY sentence has an SVO sequence.

Emi	bi	meji.
I	gave birth to	two

'I had two children.'

1.1.11. *Negative*

The negative marker precedes the VP aspect markers. Negatives attested in TY were the punctual *ko ~ o* and habitual *ko i ~ ki i*. The completive and future negators *kò ì ti ì* and *kò ní* respectively, were not attested.

owo	o	si
money	NEG	exist

'there is no money'

ko	sebi	
kò	se	ibi
NEG	be	place

'it is not the place'

awo	ki	i	ku
devotee	NEG	CONT	die

'devotees cannot ever die'

Emphatic negation is expressed by a pre-V intensifier which may replace *ko ~ o* or follow it. *ma ~ mọ ~ mẹ* are dialect variants:

emi	o	mẹ	n	ṣani		odi
èmi	ò	mà	ń	ṣe	ẹni	odi
I	NEG	NEG_{emph}	CONT	be	person	city wall

'I am certainly not a guardsman'

1.2.0. **The Noun Phrase**

1.2.1. The NP may consist of a noun. A noun may designate:

1.2.11. a personal or place name:

Ọyẹ
[name of a town]

When polymorphemic, a personal or place name follows normative SVO order:

Ọṣuntoki
Ọ̀ṣun tó kí
Ọshun be enough be praised
[a female name]

1.2.12. a person, thing or mass referent: [1]

ọmọde	'child, children'
owo	'money'
enya	'people'

1.2.2. ***Plurality***

Plurality is contextually inferred, but may be formally indicated by preposing $\mathrm{Pr}_{\mathrm{emph3}}$ pl *awọn* to the noun. As such, the plural carries semantic overtones of specificity:

awọn ọmọ
they child
'those children'

in contrast to the nonspecificity of

ilu naa
drums DEF

1.2.3. ***Nominal Qualifiers***

These are postposed to the nominal.

1.2.31. The numeral *kan* 'one' emphasizes nonspecificity of reference:

kini kan
thing one
'something'

ibi kan
place one
'somewhere'

1.2.32. A definer particle specifies reference.

The Y definer *náà* occurred only in one TY idiolect, that of Z, but the specificity signaled by its use does not always appear contextually warranted. Its overuse may be attributable to hypercorrection caused by word-for-word translation from English.

nigba	ti	awọn	lo	agbado	naa	iwọn	fi	sinu	ewe
in time	REL	they	grind	corn	DEF	they	put	to inside	leaf

'after they have ground the corn, they put it into a leaf'

The TY definer was *la,* which may appear an instance of [n ~ l] allophonic substitution. But since such variation does not occur in Y in the syntagmatic environment of N + DEF, and since *la* is articulated with stable tone rather than a glide, the reasons for this *náà* > *la* replacement may more readily be ascribed to concatenation of the Y DEF with that of Fr. Cr. *la* which is similarly postposed to the noun. Indeed, the form of the Fr. Cr. DEF may in turn represent a concatenation of the Fr. DEF_{fem} *la* with the form-meaning of the Fr. adverb *là,* there. This coalescence was enabled by the specificity and emphasis imparted by the DEF in both Y and Fr. Cr.

omi	la
water	DEF

ọkọri	la
man	DEF

1.2.33. Adjectives specify some qualitative aspect of the noun.

ọmọ	wẹwẹ
child	small

enya	didu
people	black

1.2.34. Deictics indicate distance between speaker and reference. In TY the distal deictics were rare.

Singular Proximate

ibe	yi
place	this

alẹ	im
evening	this

Plural Proximate

ọmọde	wọnyim
children	these

1.2.35. Possessive pronouns in the TY corpus were:

	Sg	*Pl*
Pr_1	mi	wa, riwa
Pr_2	rẹ	[unattested]
Pr_3	rẹ, ẹ	wọn, an

Intervocalic *w* and a concatenation of Ek $Pr_{1\,pl}$ *la* and Poss $_{1\,pl}$ *ra* account for *riwa*. *ẹ* shows *r*-deletion.[2]

ọrẹẹ mi
friend my

ara mi
body my

ara wa
bodies our
'ourselves'

orịṣa riwa
divinities our

ọwọ rẹ
hand your

ọwọ rẹ
hand his

eṣin ẹ
horse his

ara wọn
bodies their
'themselves'

ule an
house their

1.2.4. ***The Independent NP***

The NP may also comprise:

1.2.41. an independent Demonstrative.

Proximate Demonstrative

Sg.	eyi	'this'
	iyẹn	'that'
Pl.	wọn-yi	'these'
	wọn-yẹn	'those'

1.2.42. an independent Possessive.

Sg. Possessive

Pr_1 temi 'mine'
Pr_2 tirẹ ~ tẹrẹ 'yours'

Pl. Possessive

Pr_3 tiwọn 'theirs'

1.2.43. a Personal Pronoun.

Subj

	Sg	*Pl*
Pr_1	mo ~ mọ, ma, me ~ mẹ, mi ~ emi, ng, *mwè*[3]	a, awa
Pr_2	o ~ ọ, wo ~ wọ ~ wa ~ iwọ, irẹ	ẹ, in ~ ẹyi ~ ẹnyin
Pr_3	o ~ ọ, e ~ ẹ, oun, Ø	ọn ~ an, wọn, inọn, awọn ~ iwọn

Obj

	Sg	*Pl*
Pr_1	mi	wa
Pr_2	ọ, rẹ	i, ẹnyi
Pr_3	v replicating V v final, un, rẹ, *họ*, Ø	wọn

1.2.431. Pr_1

mo ~ *mọ* are Y dialect variants dictated by the operation (or nonoperation) of vowel harmony in differing dialects.[4] *me* ~ *mẹ* are EY cognates.

ma precedes *a,* the pre-verbal marker of future tense.

emi belongs in the Y emphatic pronoun set.

mi is used in embedded sentences in the Ijẹsha dialect following:

jẹ 'let'

jẹ	mi	o	sun
let	I	FUT	sleep

dẹ 'be necessary'

owo	dẹ	mi	ṣe	laye
money	be necessary	I	perform	in world

'I need money to make a mark in life'

the complementizer *ki* 'that, so that, until', which is sometimes used after *jẹ* and *dẹ*:

jẹ	ki	mi	wa
let	COMPL	I	come

o	dẹ	ki	mi	wa
it	be necessary	COMPL	I	come

mi also precedes the pre-V negator *ko* ~ *o*:

mi	ko	mọ
I	NEG	know

In some dialects *ng* is the morphotactic nasal variant in the environment of back segments.

ng ko mọ
I NEG know

ng lo sale
ng ni ó se alè
I FOC it be lover
'*I* am the lover'

ng also occurs before the pre-V future marker *o*:

ng o bere
I FUT ask

mwè, Fr. Cr. $Pr_{1\ sg\ Subj/Obj}$, is a loan.

a occurs:
(i) as majestic plural in song:

a a sale
we FUT be lover

(ii) as dummy impersonal Subj:

a bi mi
one give birth to me
'I was born'

1.2.432. Pr_2
o ~ *ọ* is produced by *w*- elision from *wo* ~ *wọ*, forms phonotactically conditioned by EY and Ọyọ vowel harmony demands.
wa is a phonological variant of *wọ*.
iwọ derives from the Y emphatic pronoun set.
irẹ is an archaic emphatic form in the Ọyọ and Ogbomọṣọ dialects.[5]
ẹ ~ *in* are dialect variants of the Y nonemphatic pronoun paradigm.
in belongs to EY, *ẹ* to SY, Ọyọ, and Ẹgba, among others.
ẹyin belongs to the Y emphatic pronoun set.

1.2.433. Pr_3
o ~ *ọ* and *e* ~ *ẹ* are conditioned by vowel harmony rules operating differentially in Y dialects. *e* ~ *ẹ* are EY variants of *o* ~ *ọ*.
oun belongs to the emphatic pronoun paradigm and was contextually appropriate in TY:

toun teṣin
ti oún ti eṣin
CONN $Pr_{3\ emph}$ CONN horse
'both he and the horse'

un is a contraction of *oun*:

ko	i	mọ	ko		ṣi	ma	pwa	un	jẹ
kò	ì	mọ̀	ki	ó	ṣì	máa	kpa	oún	jẹ
NEG	CONT	know	COMPL	he	still	FUT	kill	him	eat

'he did not know that the other would still kill him and eat him'

$Pr_{3\ sg}$ has zero expression before the pre-V negator *ko ~ o*:

ko ye
NEG be fitting
'it isn't fitting'

There was optional deletion of the V-final vowel-lengthening signifying $Pr_{3\ sg}$ and which in Y carries contrastive tone.
rẹ occurred after disyllabic verbs:

mo kpade rẹ
I met him

mo le sọran rẹ
I can speak it

họ represents E 'her'.

1.2.5. ***The Appositive NP***
Nouns in apposition may indicate

1.2.51. a functional or conceptual association between the nouns, with N_2 elaborating N_1 descriptively:

ikoko taba
pipe tobacco
'tobacco pipe'

oko ireke
farm sugar
'sugar estate'

ọmọ ibeji
children twin
'twin children'

ule Ufẹ
home Ifẹ
'Ifẹ hometown'

Ọlọrun Baba Olodumare
God Father Olodumare
'Olodumare (the Almighty), God the Father'

1.2.52. a possessive construction in which
(i) N_1 alludes to the whole or part of N_2:

oju ọna
face road
'surface of the road'

gbogbo wa
all us
'all of us'

(ii) N_2 is the source or possessor of N_1:

eṣin ọba
horse king
'the king's horse'

ara ilu
members town
'townsfolk'

ọmọ ọlọja
children owner of market
'the king's children ~ subjects'

1.2.53. NP apposition can involve reduplicated Sentence Subjects comprising $NP_1 + NP_2$, in which NP_2 is a pleonastic pronoun. It is realized as invariant $Pr_{3\,sg}$ for singular or plural distal reference, and $Pr_{1\,sg}$ for self reference.

onjẹ yi o nyun-nyun
food this it delicious-delicious

ọmọde yi ṣubu ~ ọmọde yi ọ ṣubu
child this fell ~ child this it fell

ọmọde wọnyi o ba mi ja
children these it ASSOC me fight
'these children gave me trouble (to control)'

ọgẹdẹ o wuwo
plantain it heavy

emi ọmọbọrẹn yi mo fẹran ijo ajeni
I_{emph} woman this I like dance Guinea
'This here woman, I love African dances'

This resumptive Subject also occurred in the volitive:

Ọlọrun ko bukun fun ọ
Ọlọ́rùn kí ó bùkún fún ọ
God VOL he bless give you
'May God bless you'

One instance of reduplicated Object NPs was observed:

ede	naa	mo	mọ	ọ
language	DEF	I	know	it

The pronoun that constitutes Subject$_2$ is, in fact, the overt syntactic particle indicating Subject + Verb Phrase juncture in Y. There, it manifests as a high-tone syllablic extension of the final vowel of the Subject, which represents an underlying pronoun. In TY, however, perhaps because of tonal instability and readjustment, the underlying pronoun surfaces. However, there appear to be Y dialects in which the Subject + Verb Phrase Pronoun juncture is similarly overt. In Ekiti negative sentences, "the negative seems to consist of an old concord pronoun *é* before the negative particle *ò*" (Armstrong, Ọlayemi, and Adu 1969: 92). Thus Ekiti:

ọba	é	ò	lọ
king	he	NEG	go

'the king did not go'

1.2.6. ***Conjoined NP***

As a nominal conjunction, TY utilizes Y *ati,* the more formal and archaic Y *oun,* the "semantically subordinating" conjunction *kpẹlu* (which carries a prepositional function also), and *epi* < *et puis* (Fr.) 'and then'. *epi* is the Fr. Cr. nominal coordinator and subordinating associative.

iya	ati	iya	agba	ati	baba	agba
mother	and	mother	old	and	father	old

emi	oun	ọmọbọrẹn	yii
I	and	girl	this

Ẹdọn	kpelu	Taiwo
Edun	and	Taiwo

ọka	kpelu	ọbẹ
kuku	and	gravy

ẹko	epi	ọka
ẹkọ	and	*kuku*

1.3.0. **The Verb Phrase**

The VP may contain

1.3.1. Single Verbs:

wọ	wu	mi
you	attract	me

gbogbo wọn ku
all they died
'all of them died'

1.3.2. Contiguous Serial Verbs that place Vs in apposition in order to particularize direction, intention, and action:

ma ṣe binu
NEG_{imp} behave be annoyed
'don't be annoyed'

mo fẹ lọ ṣe ẹbọ la
I wish go perform sacrifice DEF

wa ba mi
come accompany me
'come with me'

ile Ifa mo ti wa
house/family Ifa I originate come
'I descend from a family dedicated to Ifa'

iya mi kuro nilu Ọyẹ
ìyáà mi kúro nílú Ọyẹ̀
ìyáà mi kúro ní ilú Ọyẹ̀
mother my leave originate town Ọyẹ
'my mother comes from the town of Ọyẹ'

1.3.21. Split Serial Verbs, in which a NP Complement interrupts the verb sequence:

domi nu
dà omi nù
pour water waste
'pour out the water'

maa tẹ o kpa
I FUT crush you kill
'will crush you to death'

pa lẹkun la ma
shut door DEF connect
'shut the door'

lọ mumi fun mi wa
lọ mú omi fún mi wá
go take water give me come
'go get water and bring for me'

ko		ba	mi	tọju	oleyi
ki	o	bá	mi	tọ́jú	eléyìí
VOL	you	assist	me	take care of	this thing

'help me take care of this'

Ọlọrun	a	tun	temi	ṣe
God	FUT	renew	mine	perform

'God will restore my affairs'

iya	mi	oun	babaa	mi	lo		kọ	mi	lede	
ìyáà	mi	oun	babaà	mi	ni	ó	kọ́	mi	ní	èdè
mother	my	and	father	my	FOC	it	taught	me	speak	language

'it is my mother and father who taught me to speak the language'

Interference from English accounted for the neglect of serial verb use in sentences in which it would be normative in Y:

TY	mo	sare	titi	Ø	ule
Y	mo	sáré	titi	dé	ulé
	I	ran	quickly	reach	home

'I ran home quickly'

TY	fun	mi	Ø	omi
Y	fún	mi	ní	omi
	give	me	have	water

'give me water'

TY	wọn	fi	Ø	jẹ ẹ
Y	wọn	fi	i	jẹ
	they	take	it	eat

In the last sentence, Y suppresses overt expression of the $Pr_{3\ sg\ COMPL}$ after *fi* 'take, use', which would be the normative location of the COMPL rather than after V_2 of the TY serial verb sequence.[6]

1.3.3. ***Tense/Mood/Aspect System***

1.3.31. The present and anterior punctual tenses are not formally signaled within the VP. Context and/or adverbials convey tense information.

mo	mọ
I	know

ojo	rọ
rain	fell

iya	mi	ku
mother	my	died

o	tete	ṣilẹkun	naa
he	just	shut door	DEF

1.3.32. The CONT/PROG/HAB aspect marker is conveyed by pre-V nasals before the unique V or before V_1 in a serial verb sequence.
1.3.321. The nasal consonant is environmentally conditioned:

ẹṣẹ mi n dun mi
foot my CONT pain me

mo m bọ
I CONT come

mo ng kpe o
I CONT call you

1.3.322. The marker may also be realized as environmentally conditioned high front and back vowels, as in Ọyọ and EY:

San Fernando la i re
San Fernando ni a í rè
San Fernando FOC we PROG travel
'it is San Fernando we are traveling to'

o un sonjẹ
o ń se onjẹ
you HAB cook food

1.3.323. The marker may be realized as high front and back vowels, following negators:

Pọjumi ki i ṣe ọnikan to biri
Pọ̀jùmí kì í ṣe ọnikan ti ó búrú
Pọjumi NEG CONT behave person REL he bad
'Pọjumi is not a bad person'

o mo i rajo
o mò í rè àjò
you NEG_{emph} HAB travel journey

1.3.324. The marker may be realized as Nasal + high front vowel:

emi ni ṣiṣẹ
I PROG work

ifu lele ni dagi
ifúù lèlè ní dá igi
wind mighty PROG break tree

1.3.33. Y also allows for occurrence of the nasal progressive marker before either or both verbs in a contiguous serial construction. TY examples of this option preceded V_2:

ọlọkpwa wa m bọ
police come PROG come
'police are coming'

nibi	Ọya	gbe	n	sa
in place	Ọya	happen	PROG	run

'where Ọya was running'

1.3.34.The aspect marker was, however, a zero element in several TY instances:

emi	Ø	ṣiṣe	ni
èmi	ń	ṣiṣe	ni
I	PROG	work	FOC

o	Ø	muti		pupọ
ó	ń	mu	ọti	kpúkpọ̀
he	PROG	drink	alcohol	much

'he drinks alcohol excessively'

mo	Ø	jo	kpikpọ
mo	ń	jó	kpíkpọ̀
I	HAB	dance	much

'I used to dance a lot'

1.3.35. The completive aspect marker is *ti,* which also carries semantic overtones of anterior time.

ọmọ	rẹ	ti	ku
child	your	ANT	die

o	ti	ṣilekun	naa
he	COMPL	shut door	DEF

1.3.36. Continuous aspect in the past is conveyed by *ti n.*

San Fernando	la		ti	n	re
San Fernando	ni	a	ti	ń	rè
San Fernando	FOC	we	ANT	CONT	travel

awọn	si	ti	n	gbe	nibẹ
they	still	ANT	CONT	live	in there

1.3.37. The pre-V marker of conjecture or probability is *ba.*
1.3.371. It occurs in the VP following a noun semantically inferring nonspecificity:

nigba	ti	iwọ	ba	ji
in time	which	you	HYP	wake

'when you awake'

A nonspecific noun may initiate a sentence derived from an underlying relative structure:

ẹni	ba	dele
person	HYP	reach home

'the person who goes home'

1.3.372. *ba* may also occur when preceded by the clause initiator *bi* ~ *ti* ~ *di*.

bi	mo	ba	ma	lọ
if	I	HYP	NEG	go

tỌlọrun	ba	gbe	mi
if God	HYP	support	me

do		ba	rohun	
dí	o	bá	rí	ohun
if	you	HYP	see	thing

1.3.373. *ba* is deleted where "the two alternatives in a situation are stated" (Rowlands 1969: 167) or where the outcome is predictable:

bi	mo	ku	o[7]	bi	mo	ye
if	I	die	or	if	I	live

bo		le	ya,	ko		ya
bí	ó	lè	yá,	kí	ó	yá
if	it	can	burst,	VOL	it	burst

bi	o	si	Onire
if	it	lack	Ogun

1.3.374. Before *ba* $Pr_{1\ sg\ Subj}$ may contract to the nasal consonant, which in Y carries low tone. Tonal leveling in TY eradicates the low tone feature, but the nasal segment functions as syllable final. Thus:

i=jọ	m=	ba=	ku
day	I	HYP	die

a=ra	m=	ba=	da
wonders	I	HYP	exploded

'I would have performed wonders'

1.3.38. The markers of intention and of future time are *yo* ~ *o* and *maa* ~ *a*.

iwọ	yo	lọ
you	FUT	go

yọ[8]	ọ	lọle
you	FUT	go home

Ọlọrun	a	fun	ọ
God	FUT	give	you

In TY *a* is segmentally assimilated to the vowel in the $\text{Pr}_{1\ \text{sg Subj}}$, though not, as in Y, also consistently realized as as a double mora vowel, the second bearing high tone. Thus TY:

ma	a	jẹ	ọyọyọ	loni
I	FUT	eat	*ọ̀yọ́yọ́*	in today

ma	a	yọ	ṣẹṣẹ	~ ma yọ ṣẹṣẹ
I	FUT	rejoice	greatly	

1.3.381. Sometimes, however, there is failure to indicate futurity or intention by the use of the pre-V markers. Similarly, there is optional surface expression of futurity in the embedded sentence after the volitional clause initiators *jẹ ki* ~ *ki* 'may, permit' and *fẹ* 'want, wish', or an underlying semantic presupposition of desire:

jẹ	mi	o	sun
let	me	FUT	sleep

mo	fẹ	maa	jaja	lọ
mo	fẹ́	máa	jọjọ	lọ
I	want	FUT	intensively	go

mọ	mọ	jẹ	ki	mi	o	rubi	
mọ	mọ̀	jẹ	kí	mi	ó	rí	ubi
NEG_{imp}	EMPH	let	COMPL	I	FUT	see	evil

'let me certainly not experience evil'

1.3.382. As in Y, the pre-V marker of continuation expresses intention uniquely with *lọ* 'go':[9]

mo	n	lọ	sule
I	CONT	go	to house

Informant's gloss: 'I will go home. I'm going home.'

1.4.0. **The Prepositional Phrase**

Four prepositions occurred at the head of prepositional phrases: *ni, si, kpẹlu, lati.*

1.4.1. Following the verbs *lọ* 'go' and *wa* 'come', *si* 'to', varied with *ni* 'in' according to Y dialect-influenced choices.[10] Thus:

wa	nihin
come	in here

wa	sibe	yi
come	to place	this

mo	n	lọ	lule
I	PROG	go	in home

ọmọ	mi	lọ	suluṣẹ		
ọmọọ̀	mi	lọ	sí	ulú	uṣẹ́
child	my	went	to	house	work

'my child went to his workplace'

1.4.11. And like Y, *ni* was also deleted after *lọ*:

mo	lọ	Ibadan
I	went	Ibadan

o	lọle
he	went home

1.4.12. *ni* was also optional before a NP of place in topicalized sentences. For example:

nibo	la		ti	wa?
níbo	ni	ẹ[11]	ti	wá?
in place	FOC	you	originate	come?

'where do you come from?'

ibo	lo		n	lọ?
ibo	ni	o	ń	lọ?
place	FOC	you	PROG	go?

1.4.2. *kpẹlu* 'with' conveyed subordinate association in:

o	n	sure	lọ	kpẹlu	adiẹẹ	mi
he	PROG	run	go	with	fowl	my

1.4.3. *lati* 'from' occurred prepositionally in:

latauro	
láti	àúrọ̀
since	morning

latori		ẹbọ
láti	orí	ẹbọ
for purpose of	occasion	religious feast

1.5.0. **The Equative Sentence**

1.5.1. *ni* is the Equative or Identificatory Verb.

Abẹkita	lile		iya	mi
Abẹ̀okúta	ni	ilé	ìyáà	mi
Abẹokuta	be	home	mother	my

emi	ni	ọkọ	rẹ
I	be	husband	your

ọmọ	dudan	ni	ọ
child	young	be	you

1.5.2. However the Equative is deleted in statements of lineage identity:

olukọ	iyaa	mi	Orişabiyi
name	mother	my	Orishabiyi

emi	ọmọ	Ọyẹ
I	progeny	Ọyẹ

emi	ọmọ	rẹ
I	child	her

1.6.0. **The Topicalized Sentence**

1.6.1. Noun and Adverb Phrases can be topicalized by preposing them to the identifier verb *ni,* which now functions as the focusing particle:

emi	ni
I	FOC

otitọ	ni
truth	FOC

1.6.2. Two appositive NPs may be focused:

emi	ọmọ	rẹ	ni
I	child	her	FOC

'I am her child'

ọkọnrin	yi	arugbo	ni
man	this	old person	FOC

'this man is an old person'

1.6.3. Complex topicalized sentences contain two clauses. Either the Subj or Obj of S_2 may be focused. The focused Subj of S_1 is redundantly expressed in S_2 as $Pr_{3\ sg}$.

1.6.31. S_2 Subject Focusing

ọba	oyinbo	lo		ko	a	wa
ọba	oyìnbó	ni	ó	kó	a	wá
king	European	FOC	he	gathered	us	come

'the European king captured us and brought us'

iya	mi	oun	babaa	mi	lo		kọ	mi	lede	
ìyáà	mi	oun	bàbáà	mi	ni	ó	kọ́	mi	ní	èdè
mother	my	and	father	my	FOC	it	taught	me	speak	language

1.6.32. S_2 Object Focusing

ira	Eko	no		n	ṣe	wi
irá	Èkó	ni	o	ń	ṣe	wí
person	Lagos	FOC	you	PROG	act	speak

'you are speaking with a Lagos person'

bẹẹ	la		ti	n	ṣẹrẹ		wa
bẹ́ẹ̀	ni	a	ti	n	ṣẹ	ọ̀rẹ́ẹ̀	wa
thus	FOC	we	PERF	PROG	behave towards	friends	our

1.6.33. The Focus Verb may be deleted after a focused S_2:

ile	Ifa	Ø	mo	ti	wa
ilé	Ifá	ni	mo	ti	wá
house	Ifa	FOC	I	originate	come

'my lineage is from practitioners of Ifa'

ara	Ø	m	ba	daye	
àrà	Ø	m	bá	dá	ayé
wonders	Ø FOC	I	HYP	shock world	

'I would have dazzled the world with astounding deeds'

1.6.34. Specificity and additional emphasis are achieved by postposing the definer *naa* to the focused phrase:

bẹẹ	naa	ni	ṣe	laye
thus	DEF	FOC	occurs	in world

'that's the way of the world'

ire	ire	bayin		naa	ni
ire	ire	bí	ayin	náà	ni
goodness	goodness	like	honey	DEF	FOC

1.6.35. A sentence can be focused:

Ọlọrun	fọ	fọye
God	breathed	uttered life

o	ma	biku		ni
ó	mà	bì	ikú	ni
it	EMPH	repelled	death	FOC

'It ~ He [Life ~ God] surely repelled Death'

Ọshun, the river goddess, is addressed as 'The river that flows continually':

emi	a	maa	i	da	ni
emi	a	maa	í	dà	ni
river	CONT	CONT	CONT	flow	FOC

1.6.36. Topicalized Negation

A topicalized NP or AdvP can be negated by postposed *ko* ~ *kọ*.

bẹẹ	kọ
thus	NEG_{foc}

Ado	ko
Ado	NEG_{foc}

2.0.0. **The Complex Declarative Sentence**

2.0.1. The Relative Clause

The relative clause is introduced by *ti* or EY *ki*.

ibi	ti	ẹgbọn	mi	lọ	si
place	REL	elder brother	my	go	to

ede	yi	ti	mo	sọ	fun	ọ
language	this	REL	I	speak	give	you

dide	ti	mo	de
arrival	REL	I	arrive

'[when] I did arrive'

bata	fifun	ki	mọ	wọ	lẹsẹ	
bàtà	fífún	kí	mọ	wọ̀	ní	ẹ̀sẹ̀
shoes	white	REL	I	wear	on	foot

Where the Subject of the embedded clause is coreferential with the relativized NP, the Subject is expressed by invariant $Pr_{3\ sg}$.

ọkọre	kan	to		lọgbọn	
ọkùnrin	kan	tí	ó	ní	ọgbọ́n
man	INDEF	REL	he	has	wisdom

gbogbo	won	to		kere
gbogbo	wọn	tí	ó	kéré
all	them	REL	he	small

2.0.11. But the relativizer, which is sometimes omitted in Y,[12] is deleted in:

mi	o	ni	enya	Ø	maa	sọrọ	si
I	NEG	have	people	Ø	I FUT	speak	to

ata	Ø	o	fi	sikoko
pepper	Ø	you	put	to pot

2.0.2. Clause and Sentence Connectives

2.0.21. The conditional clause initiator *bi* is often deleted. This may be attributed to its suppression at the onset of breath, since most examples occur at the beginning of song lines. But the clause initiator may also have been reckoned as redundant, given the use of the pre-V hypothetical marker *ba* ~ *baa*:

ojo	baa	de
rain	HYP	comes

aye	ba	toro
world	HYP	peaceful

ara	ba	ti	le?
body	HYP	ANT	firm?

'are you well?'[13]

In the following song lines, the presentation of two alternatives appears to obviate the need for the overt hypothetical markers, either clause-initial or pre-V:

o	he,	o	hemimọ		o
o	he	o	he	èmìmọ̀	o
you	pick up,	you	pick up	trouble	EMPH

On the other hand, O opts for the clause initiator rather than the pre-V hypothetical marker in the following sentence which suggests English relexification, more so because the Y 'either . . . or' structure, *tabi . . . tabi,* is vacuous and [o] substitutes for English 'or':

bi	mo	ku	o	bi	mo	ye
if	I	die	or	if	I	live

2.0.22. Volitional clauses are initiated by *ki jẹ* ~ *je ki*:

ka		lọ
ki	a	lọ
VOL	we	go

'let's go'

dide	ko		duro
dídé	kí	o	dúró
rise	VOL	you	stand

'will you please stand up'

sa	jẹ	i[14]	lọ
[dismissive]	allow	I	go

'just let me go'

mọ	mọ	jẹ	ki	mi	o	rubi	
mọ̀	mọ̀	jẹ	kí	mí	ó	rí	ubi
NEG	EMPH	let	VOL	I	FUT	see	evil

'let me certainly not see evil'

2.0.23. The complementizer following verbs of speech or cognition is *kpe* ~ *ki* (EY):

mẹ	sọ	kọ		dun	ni
mẹ	sọ̀	kí	ó	dùn	ni
I	say	COMPL	it	hurts	us

Under English influence this complementizer was omitted in:

o	ma	Ø	mo	ṣe	ọmọ	yoroba
ó	mọ̀	kpé	mo	ṣe	ọmọ	yorùbá
he	knew	COMPL	I	be	descendant	Yoruba

2.0.24. The conjunction of reason, *lati,* was little used but occurred in:

mo	wa	lati	sọran	si	ọ
I	came	in order	to speak	to	you

2.0.25. The conjunction of consequence was also little attested except in Z's corpus:

nitoriti	anu	rẹ	li	awa	fẹ
because	mercy	your	FOC	we	want

2.0.26. Similarly, only Z used the clause conjoiner, pre-V *si*:

mo	si	ti	ni	ile	iwe	ekọ
I	CONJ	ANT	have	house	book	teaching

'and I had a school'

In other of Z's sentences, the nominal conjoiner, *ati,* was used as a clausal conjoiner, by analogy with the syntactic deployment of E 'and':

mo	le	ka	a	ati	emi	le	kọ	ọ
I	can	read	it	and	I	can	teach	it

2.0.27. The clause disjunctive, *ṣugbọn,* which occupies a parallel syntactic slot with English, occurred frequently in Z's texts.

3.0.0. **The Imperative Sentence**

3.0.1. The V stem, full and serial, suffices for singularity of address:

wa
come

wa	ba	mi
come	meet	me

3.0.2. Negative commands require pre-V *ma* ~ *mọ* (EY). The verb in this case may be elaborated into a serial structure involving use of *ṣe* 'do, perform, behave' in V_1 position.

ma ~ mọ	bu	Ṣango
NEG	abuse	Shango

ma	ṣe	lọ
NEG	perform	go

'don't go'

mọ	ṣe	binu
NEG	behave	be annoyed

'don't be annoyed'

3.0.3. The continuative pre-V marker *maa* can introduce a verb of motion:

maa	bọ
CONT	approach

'come'

maa	lọ
CONT	go

'go'

3.0.4. A negative continuative marker, *i*,[15] may follow *ma*.

ma	i	lọ
NEG	CONT	go

'don't go'

3.0.5. The pre-V intensifier *ma* ~ *mọ* may follow negator *ma*. In Y the two are tonally distinguished.

mọ	mọ	je	ko	le	mi	sarun	buruku
NEG	EMPH	let	VOL it	enable	me	make sickness	bad

3.0.6. Plurality of address or respect for a singular addressee is signaled by preposing $Pr_{2\,pl}$ to the V:

ẹ	ki	Yemanja
(you)	greet	Yemanja

ẹ	wa	jade
(you all)	come	come out

4.0.0. The Interrogative Sentence

4.0.1. Query in general is signaled by sentence initial *ṣe.*

ṣe	ara	le
INTERR	body	firm

'how are you?'

4.0.2. Sentence-initial *ta,* topicalized by the focus V, indicates query of human identity:

ta	ni	onibode
INTERR$_{Id}$	FOC	gatekeeper

'who is the gateman?'

ta	ni	wọ
INTERR$_{Id}$	FOC	you$_{emph}$

'who are you?'

The last sentence may be further focused:

iwọ	ta	ni
you$_{emph}$	INTERR$_{Id}$	FOC

'who are you?'

4.0.3. Sentence-initial *ki,* topicalized by the focus V, announces query of nonhuman identity:

ki	ni	mo	ṣe
INTERR$_{Id}$	FOC	I	do

'what did I do?'

ki	ni	oloriṣa	le	ṣe
INTERR$_{Id}$	FOC	*orisha* devotee	can	do

'what can the *orisha* believer do?'

4.0.4. Sentence-initial *nibo ~ ibo,* topicalized by the focus V, queries location:

nibo	ni	wa	ti	n	re
at place	FOC	we	ANT	CONT	travel

'where is it we have been traveling to?'

ibo	lo		n	lọ
ibo	ni	o	ń	lọ
place	FOC	you	PROG	go

'where are you going?'

Locative query may utilize *da* as focus V postposed to a NP:

iya rẹ da
mother your INTERR$_{loc}$
'where is your mother?'

4.0.5. Sentence final *bi* ~ *nkọ* ~ *sikọ* (EY) ~ *ra* ~ *re,* all of which are postposed to a focused NP, are semantically restricted to state or condition. *ra* ~ *re* may also be preposed to a V or verbal adjective. Thus:

ara ra le
body INTERR$_{cond}$ firm
'are you well?'

olukọ rẹ re
name your INTERR$_{cond}$
'what is your name?'

ara nle bi
ará nílé bí
members at home INTERR$_{cond}$
'how are the home folks?'

baba rẹ nkọ
father your INTERR$_{cond}$
'how is your father?'

iya rẹ sikọ
mother your INTERR$_{cond}$
'how is your mother?'

7

Lexicon

Analytical Procedures

For the sake of manageability, and also in order to identify the most relevant and functional areas of vocabulary retention, this examination of the TY lexical repertoire will be confined to the items that carried conscious semantic content for users. Among such items are word-list responses, words glossed from song lyrics, those occurring in songs composed by informants, and data from Z's taped interviews only, since the full range of his lexicon existed in written form and had been expanded from written sources.

In the initial stages of research, I used a word list of my own design. Reasons for its abandonment have already been explained.[1] Despite the failure of this methodology, fifty percent of the Swadesh (1955) two-hundred-word list was elicited, even without excepting Swadesh's ecology-specific terms like 'snow', 'fog', 'freeze', 'lake', culture-bound discriminations between 'foot' and 'leg', 'belly' and 'guts', 'wood' and 'stick', 'meat' and 'animal', 'brother' and 'sister', not to mention color categories and occupational lexicon. Sixty-four percent of the hundred-word list citation was elicited.

The lexicon generated was in part a response to specific data requested and was largely limited to concrete phenomena. Furthermore, through oversight and social proprieties of gender and age I never sought, for example, to establish the existence of a lexicon of sexual knowledge and behavior.

In part, lexical items were offered spontaneously, and thus they appear to represent readily remembered facets of Yoruba language culture. But the moribund condition of Yoruba language survival raises the issue of a possible distortion of the semantic field once covered by the TY lexicon since the aged informants were prone to memory lapses, the risk exists of a possible lack of representativeness in the semantic correspondence of unique citations, and conditions of data collection were artificial: in the main they excluded a sociocultural framework from which to assess the semantic range and symbolic expression of the citations. For example, the very ecological, not to mention social, environment in which the lexicon once functioned has changed significantly.[2] Nearly a century has elapsed since the most intensive period of Yoruba language functionality. In the intervening years Trinidad continued to receive its population from India and from other Eastern Caribbean islands; the Boer War and two World Wars colored the life, pace, and values of the little colonial outpost; and perhaps most significantly, oil discoveries at the turn of the century caused extensive repercussions on the economic, demographic, and agricultural contours of island life. In addition, because of the nonreciprocal use of TY at the time of collection, the lexicon presented here lacks the contextual resonances of interactive language. As a result, the semantic field and sociolinguistic context of these lexical items can hardly be gauged except where a contextual framework was provided or where a descriptive commentary on an item was advanced.

The referential range of the vocabulary therefore is limited largely to concrete objects of a domestic nature, to religious iconography, and to stative and kinetic verbs of routine activities and primary emotions. The conceptual framework is balanced by an awareness of good as well as adversity. The lexicon's contexts of use can be delimited as work, religion, entertainment, and camaraderie.

It is instructive, then, to observe that this TY lexicon differs from Oyelaran's Sierra Leone Yoruba word list in the absence from the present collection of words relating to guilds and masquerades, and in an impoverished list of clothes items and perjorative behaviors.[3] This difference may be attributable to a combination of factors. One factor is that my limited cultural knowledge prevented me from asking questions regarding these domains and thus blocked the emergence of recessed knowledge of such vocabulary on the part of informants. In this connection, it has since become apparent through translation and cultural analysis of the song corpus that songs dedicated to the Egungun did exist, as well as chants derived from the Ogboni cult. In one instance, the Oro cult is understood by a major speaker as linked with fighters in nineteenth-century Ibadan.[4] The other factor in the discrepancy between the lexicons of Yoruba in Trinidad and Sierra Leone is that certain organizations, artifacts, and hostile interpersonal attitudes perhaps did not persist long enough in Trinidad to be recalled by third-generation speakers.

The examination of song metaphors together with explanations of certain song contexts indicates that abuse was indeed a lively speech form in TY society. The presence in this vocabulary of terms such as *ọlẹ* 'lazy person', *panṣaga* 'prostitute', and *pọrunka de bọ* 'gossip, slanderer' only hint at the more extended range of abusive terms and expressive mechanisms.

Dialect Variation

Dialectally differentiated lexical choice appeared in the spoken corpus. One of the few cases that surfaced apppeared in this assertion by T: "We wouldn't say *agidi* . . . the Ẹkba people say *agidi*; well, we say *akasan*."

A parallel comment by S makes a point that is partly about lexical choice but that fundamentally concerns phonological variation in the same lexeme: "*Ile* is 'house', but *ule* is 'house' in *our* language." In citation, she advanced both *ba* and *uba* for 'father' although she consistently employed *baba* in sentences. K remarked that both *ọsẹ* and *ẹsẹ* denoted 'foot'. In fact, the data show acceptance of and productive competence in phonological variants of a lexeme, a fact that indicates a fluid language system—one that tolerated a fair degree of variation. Morphophonological free variants were the focus of alternations (or were they corrections?) in the following sequenced sentences by S:

a. **o s*ọ*s*ẹ* rẹ# o s*ẹ*s*ẹ* rẹ#**
   (Ek) (Ọyọ)
   'he bruised foot his'

b. **mo fẹran *ujo*# mo n jo pwikpọ l*ujo* ajeni# mo jo pipọ l*ijo* ajeni**
   (Ek) (Ọyọ)
   'I loved dancing# I PROG dance a lot in dance African# I danced a lot in dance African'

c. **maa domi gbigbona l*ilẹ*# l*alẹ***
   (Ọyọ) (Ek.)
   'I'm about to throw water hot at earth'

Free alternants *mo* (Eg) ~ mọ (Ọyọ) 'I', *ariko* (Eg) ~ *areko* (Ek) 'right time', *sure* (Ek) ~ *sare* (Eg) 'run', also distinguished a call-and-response performance between N and her son, F, and reflect divergent dialect sources of the same item. Here are four lines of the song:

F	**Ye,**	**tide**[5]	**ti**	**mo**		**de**
N	**O,**	**dide**	**ti**	**mo**		**de**
SY	**Yé,**	**dídé**	**ti**	**mo**	**ń**	**dé**
	Listen,	arrival	that	I	PROG	arrive

F	**Mo**	**n**	**de**	**sariko**
N	**Mọ**	**Ø**	**de**	**sareko**
SY	**Mo**	**ń**	**dé**	**sárinko**
	I	PROG	arrive	to propitious time

F **Sure manja ~ Sure maja ~ surem baja**
N **Sarem baja ~ Sare baja**
SY **Sáré- m̀- bọ́ja**
Run I reach market

F	**Mo**	**Ø**	**de**	**sariko**
N	**Mọ**	**n**	**de**	**sareko**
SY	**Mo**	**ń**	**dé**	**sárinko**
	I	PROG	arrive	to propitious moment

Lexical Organization

This vocabulary is organized around syntactic categories. However, the syntactic function of certain lexemes is an area of some controversy and of ongoing structural analysis. This reexamination resulted from attempts to liberate Y from the impositions of English class-category definitions. Further problems result from what appears to be the transitional, and therefore ambivalent, grammatical function of certain homophonous particles.

An early area of controversy centered around the various categorizations of certain lexemes as "adjectives," "predicative adjectives," "adjectival verbs," and "verbs."[6] Another grey area is the formal classification of English "notionally defined adverbs" and conjunctives, some of which Awobuluyi (1971; 1973) and Ọkẹ (1974) assess as verbal elements in serial structures, while Awobuluyi (1974) argues that some other traditionally perceived adverbials function in deep-structure as nominals. The status of "prepositions" is also in doubt. Several particles previously categorized as prepositions have been reclassified as verbs or verbal adjuncts.[7] By an analysis of locative, possessive, and comitative function words, Lord (1973) has shown that some particles with still-extant verbal function have evolved into prepositions and further into conjunctives. Y *ní* serves both verbal and prepositional function, *kpẹ̀lú* combines these with conjunctive use. The grammatical categories assigned below reflect some of these analyses.

Nouns

Anatomical Terms

The following occurred in single form:

Entries	*Etyma*
akpa: arm; district	**akpá**: arm
eti: ear	**etí**: ear
imu: nose	**imú**: nose
inu: stomach	**inú**: stomach
oju: eye	**ojú**: eye
ori: head	**orí**: head
ọkan: heart	**ọkàn**: heart
ọwọ: hand	**ọwọ́**: hand

Variants were cited for:

ara ~ **ọra**: body	**ara** (SY) ~ **ọra** (Ij, Ek): body
bọ ~ **erin** ~ **esumare** ~ **sumari**: hair	**ìbò**: type of male cap; **erun** (Ẹg, Ij, Yag, Ijb) **irun** (SY); **èsúmórí** < **è**: thing; **sú**: sprout; **mó**: join; **orí**: head
ẹjẹ ~ **ijẹ**: blood	**ẹjẹ** (SY) ~ **ijẹ** (Ek): blood
ẹnu ~ **ẹrun**: mouth	**ẹnu** (SY) ~ **ẹrun** (Ij, Ek): mouth
ẹsẹ ~ **ọsẹ**: foot	**ẹsẹ** (SY) ~ **ọsẹ** (Igbomina): foot
ẹhin ~ **ẹyin**: tooth	**ẹhín** (Ọyọ) ~ **enyín** (SY, Ij, Ifẹ): tooth

Semantic transference between associated referents appears to have occurred in the case of *bọ,* attested by one informant as 'hair', but which appears derived from *ìbò,* a type of male cap. Similarly *esumare* ~ *sumari,* both attestations for 'hair' from one informant, and closely resembling the formative for 'rainbow' (*òsùmàrè*) may have defined a hair-style, rather than 'hair' itself. Semantic extension characterized the idiosyncratic use of *akpa* to refer to 'section of a town'. At the same time, phonological similarity between *akpa* and *ọgba,* the more appropriate sememe for 'town quarter', may have produced a malapropism.

An instance either of borrowing or phonological convergence seems to apply to the term *chambo* to designate 'facial scarification'. Interestingly, the informant who supplied the term sang the Yoruba designation *ilà* in one of her songs. However, *chambo* appears closely related to *gọ̀m̀bọ́,* the specific designation for Ọyọ facial marks. The term may derive from a language in the vicinity of northern Yorubaland.[8] *Chambo* also appears to have had wider Caribbean currency, seeing that it is listed in the *Dictionary of Jamaican English,* where it refers to the Chamba people of the Nigeria-Cameroon hinterland. Whether an association existed between them and salient tribal scarifications is as yet unclear.

Human Categories

These constituted a fairly extensive inventory. Single form entries were:

Entries	*Etyma*
agonile: house occupant	**àgò**, **onílé**: permission, homeowner (to enter)
alejo: visitor	**àlejò**: stranger, visitor
arugbo: old person	**arúgbó**: old person
awe ~ **ọrẹ**: friend	**àwé** (Ek) ~ **ọ̀rẹ́** (SY): friend
aya: aunt	**aya**: wife
ẹgbọn: elder brother, elder friend	**ẹ̀gbọ́n**: elder sib
ẹni: people	**ẹni**: person
ẹnikan: somebody	**ẹnìkan**: somebody
gbẹna-gbwẹna: carpenter	**gbẹ́nà-gbẹ́nà**: carpenter
ibeji: twin	**ibéjì**: twin
igesi: Briton	**gèésì**: Portuguese, European
ikọle: builder	**ìkọ́lé**: builder
iku: the dead	**ikú**: death
iyawo: wife, bride	**ìyàwó**: wife, bride
oburin: woman	**obìnrin**: woman
oge: star performer, sweetheart	**oge**: ostentation, a dandy
ole: lazy person	**ọ̀lẹ**: lazy person
ologun ~ **oloro**: warrior	**oní ogun** > **ológun**: carrier (of) war; **oní oro** > **olóro** carrier (of) fierceness/terror/provocation
ọlọran: spokesman	< **oní ọ̀ràn**: carrier (of) matters
oyinbo: European	**òyìnbó**: white person; European
pọrun-kan-de-bọ: news-carrier, gossip	**kpurọ́**: lie; **ká**: go about; **dé**: reach; **bọ̀**: come

Synonyms and subcategorizations appeared in:

abura okori: younger brother	**àbúrò okùnrin**: younger sib male
aburo ~ **agburo**: younger sib	**àbúrò**: younger sib
ara ~ **ira**: people	**ará** (SY) ~ **irá** (Ij, Ek): people
ara ile ~ **arale** ~ **idile**: coresidential family	**ará ilé**: folk (of) home; **ìdílé**: clan-group with common male ancestor
aralu: fellow countryman	**ará ilú**: folk (of) town
baba ~ **uba**: father	**baba** ~ **bàbá** (SY) ~ **uba** (Ek): father, old man

baba agba ~ **baba nla**: grandfather	**baba àgbà** ~ **baba ńlá**: grandfather
eniyan: people	**ènìyàn** ~ **ènìyọ̀n**: people
enyan didun: black people	**ènìyàn dúdú**: people black
enyọn fifun: white people	**ènìyàn fífún**: people white
ẹru ~ **eru**: slave	**ẹrú** (SY) ~ **erú** (Ij, Ek): slave
iya ~ **yeye** ~ **eye**: mother	**ìyá** (SY) ~ **yeye** (Ek): mother, old lady
iya agba ~ **iya nla**: grandmother	**ìyá àgbà** ~ **ìyá ńlá**: mother old ~ mother great; grandmother
okunrin ~ **ọkọrẹn** ~ **okorira**: man	**okùnrin** (SY) ~ **ọkọrẹn** (Ijb): man ~ **okùnrin ará**: male person
okunrin didun: black man	**okùnrin dídùn**: male black
okunrin fifun: white man	**okùnrin fífún**: male white
ọba: king	**ọba**: king
ọbabirin: queen	**ọba obìrin**: ruler female
ọkọ ~ **ọkan**: husband, man	**ọkọ**: husband
ọlọkpa ~ **ọlọpwa** ~ **ọlọbọ**: policeman	**ọlọ́kpà**: policeman < **oní ọ̀kpá**: owner (of) stick; **oní ọgbà**: guardian (of) compound, enclosure
ọmọ ~ **ọma** ~ **ọmọde**: child, descendant	**ọma** (Ọyọ) ~ **ọmọ** (Ẹgba) ~ **ọmọdé**: child, descendant
ọmọbọrẹn: girl	**ọmọ obìnrin**: child female
ọmọdan: lady	**ọmidan**: young woman
ọmọkọrin: boy	**ọmọ okùnrin**: child male
panṣaga ~ **paṣanga**: prostitute	**kpańṣágà**: sexually uninhibited person

Semantic transfer occurs in the case of *aya,* aunt, replacing the original meaning 'wife' and the abstract *iku,* death, for the specific or collective concrete noun *òkú,* corpse, the dead. These are perhaps due to errors of memory. *ọmọdan* is somewhat semantically extended from 'young woman, pubescent female' to 'lady'. Z's knowlege of the term *ìdílé* 'clan-group descended from common male ancestor' derived no doubt from reading, since the more accessible term for and denotation of 'immediate family, household' was covered by *arale.*

Morphotactic change in the form of metathesis affects *panṣaga* ~ *paṣanga.* The latter was to become the name of a dance in Cuba. *Pọrunkadebọ* may be idiosyncratic, but nominals formed from serial verbs are common to Yoruba poetry especially. The normative vowel-initial has been deleted in the citation.

An interesting usage was the polyvalent *oge* 'star dancer, sweetheart'. In one of its original semantic fields as the abstract 'ostentation; beauty', it occurs in songs with lines like:

ila (r)	**oge**	**ki**	**mọ**	**wọ**	**lẹrun**
facial marks	attractive	that	I	wear	on cheeks

and

ko	**ma**	**soge**	**nihin**	**lẹhin**	**ọtẹ**	**fa**
NEG	EMPH	exist beauty/pride	here	after	rebellion	TAG

emo	**gboge**	**lọ**
disaster	carries glamor	go

Fauna

Nine of the fauna entries were unique contributions by the same informant. The item known to the widest number of people was 'chicken'. It is instructive that the total list includes creatures not indigenous to the Caribbean. The fact that items such as 'elephant', 'tiger/leopard', and 'lion' were attested by more than one informant indicates that the Y designations for these exotic animals were retained because they occurred in proverbs, folktales, or songs that were familiar to the informants. In fact, the gloss 'king bird' for *orofo* stems from its metaphoric use in a Y song sung in Trinidad. *Orofo* in fact refers to a type of wild pigeon.

Single forms were elicited for:

Entries	*Etyma*
adaba: dove	**àdàbà**: dove
aja: dog	**ajá**: dog
awọn: tortoise, land turtle	**awọn**: tortoise
ayan: cockroach	**aáyán**: cockroach
ejo: snake	**ejò**: snake
ekute: rat	**èkúte**: rat
elede: hog	**ẹlẹ́dẹ̀**: pig
eleti: rabbit	**elétí < oní etí**: bearer (of) ears
erin: elephant	**erin**: elephant
ẹfan: bull	**ẹfọ̀n**: bushcow, buffalo
ẹja: fish	**ẹja**: fish
ẹkun: leopard, tiger	**ẹkùn**: leopard
ẹyẹ: bird	**ẹyẹ**: bird
ẹyẹle: pigeon	**ẹyẹlé**: pigeon
idi: eagle	**ìdì**: eagle
kẹtẹkẹtẹ: donkey	**kẹ́tẹ́kẹ́tẹ́**: donkey
kiniun: lion	**kìnìún**: lion
kolokolo: fox	**kọ̀lọ̀kọ̀lọ̀**: fox
maluu: cow	**màlúù**: cow, ox
orofo: kingbird	**orófó**: type of wild pigeon
ọkẹn: peacock	**ọ̀kẹ́n** (Ijb) ~ **òkín** (SY): peacock
pẹkpẹyẹ: pigeon	**kpẹ́kpẹ́yẹ**: duck, goose
raṣmi: camel	**ràkunmí**: camel

Variants and subcategorizations occurred with:

adiẹ ~ **abo** ~ **abo adiẹ**: chicken	**adìẹ**: chicken ~ **abo adìẹ**: female fowl, chicken
ago pwẹnyẹn: guinea bird	**awó**: guinea fowl; **kpẹ̀kpẹ́yẹ́**: duck
agurukan: land turtle, (TE *morocoy*)	**awun òkun**: turtle
agutan ~ **agotan**: sheep	**àgùtọ̀n**: sheep
akukọ ~ **akikọ** ~ **akiko** ~ **atikọ** ~ **atiko** ~ **atikọ ganga**: cock	**àkùkọ̀** (SY) ~ **àkìkọ̀** ~ **àtìkọ̀** (Ij, Ek): cock; **àkùkọ̀ gàǹganràngan**: cock very large
ẹṣin ~ **eṣin**: horse, donkey	**ẹṣin** (SY) ~ **eṣin** (Ij, Ek)
ogungu ~ **ugungu**: ostrich	**ògòǹgò**: ostrich

Erroneous designations were *pẹkpẹyẹ* 'duck', for 'pigeon', *eṣin* 'horse', for 'donkey', and *ẹkun* 'leopard', for 'tiger'. *Ẹfan* 'bushcow' as a designation for 'bull' is a semantic extension, since *ẹfọn,* the etymon, refers to the buffalo or wild bull or cow, but was used by an informant as a non-specific designatum.

Eleti appears to be a coinage or a dialect variant. The Y lexeme is *ehoro.*

The fossilized form *atikọ ganga* 'cock' seems a variant of a term cited in Crowther (1852: 93): *àkùkọ̀ gàǹganràngan* 'very large cock'. In the Trinidad elicitation, the adjective has been abbreviated.

Gender specification was prefaced to a generic term in *abo adiẹ,* literally 'female fowl/hen', with the gender indicator serving as the unique designation for 'hen' in one idiolect, perhaps due to memory lapse.

Ago pwẹnyẹn 'guinea bird', presented a novel hybrid of two bird types: *awo* 'guinea bird' and *kpẹkpẹyẹ* 'duck'. If this unique attestation was indeed in general use, then it might have signaled that a comparison had been established between the duck and the guinea bird's disinclination to fly. However, the TY form shows a reversal of the sequential order of Y nouns in apposition; in Yoruba the generic reference normally precedes the specific. For example: SY *ẹyẹ* 'bird' + *awo* 'guinea fowl'.

Flora and Foods

To varying degrees, semantic shift has affected the designation of residual food types. Indeed, the main surviving context of Yoruba culinary function is that of religious ceremonial—as food for the *orisha* and celebrants, ancestors, and living relatives.

The best known foods were *agidi, akasan, akara, ọyọyọ,* corn, ochro (okra), yam, pounded yam, eddoe, plantain, sugarcane, and rum. Terms for generic 'food' were well known. The generic terms *igi* 'tree' and *ewe* 'leaf' were also frequently attested. A number of leaves were cited by a priestess in the context of sacral-medicinal function rather than in connection with food preparation: the *adọndọn, efirin aja, igbwese, ijogun,* and *ọlọrun.*

Single-form entries were:

Entries	*Etyma*
adọndọn: kalanchoe, TE 'wonder of the world'	**ọ̀dundún**: kalanchoe, an erect succulent shrub
agbo: long-necked calabash; 'goat calabash'	**agbò**: ram
agbọn: coconut	**àgbọn**: coconut
akara: fritter of beans, or of wheat flour and flaked fish; bread	**àkàrà**: fritter of ground beans; bread
alubasa: onion	**àlùbósa**: onion
ata: pepper	**ata**: pepper
ewe: leaf	**ewé**: leaf
ẹgusi: type of melon, seeds of which are ground and made into sauce of same name	**ẹgúsí**: type of melon
ẹkọ: corn porridge	**ẹ̀kọ**: corn porridge
ẹran: meat	**ẹran**: meat
igi: tree	**igi**: tree
igun: thorn	**ẹ̀gún**: thorn
ijogun: type of medicinal plant	**ìjòkùn**: type of trailing plant
ila: okra; okra stew	**ilá**: okra, *Hibiscus esculentus*; stew of chopped okra
iroko: African oak	**iroko**: African oak
iṣu: yam	**iṣu**: yam
obi: kolanut; cacao	**obì**: kola tree and fruit
okurọ: palmnut	**òkùrọ́** (Ek) ~ **èkùrọ́** (SY): palmnut with pericarp removed
olubọ: cassava flour	**èlùbọ́**: yam, plantain, or cassava flour
oro: mango	**òro**: wild mango
oyin: honey	**onyin**: honey
ọlọrun: plant with medicinal properties	**olóòrún**: leaf used as food flavoring
ọrẹyẹlẹdẹ: lard	**ọ̀rá ẹ́lẹdẹ̀**: fat (of) pig; lard
ọti: rum	**ọtí**: alcohol
ọyọyọ: shrub, leaves of which are used as *kalalu*	**ọ̀yọ́yọ́**: *Corchorus olitorius*
pokpondo: white beans	**kpòkpòndó**: *Canavalia papilonaccae*
wara: milk	**wàrà**: milk

Variant entries and subcategorization were offered in the case of:

abẹkẹ ~ ẹbẹkẹ: chopped or partly pounded plantain or yam cooked with onion and pepper	**ẹbẹtẹ** (Ek): crushed yam mixed with oil and seasonings
agbado ~ agbado: corn, maize	**àgbàdo**: maize
agidi ~ akasan: steamed cornbread	**àgìdí ~ àkàṣù ~ akasa** (Fon): loaf of *ẹ̀kọ,* steamed maize pap
amala ~ ẹba: cassava *kuku,* i.e., cassava flour stirred and steamed in water. To this mixture is optionally added dried pigeon peas (*gungu*), already stewed	**àmàlà**: stirred, steamed starchy flour; **ẹ̀bà**: cassava flour steamed and stirred
efirin: a type of mint	**efirin**: wild mint
efirin aja: a medicinal shrub	**efirin aja**: *Hyptis suaveolens*
egbwesẹ ~ egbwẹsẹ ~ igbwese: medicinal shrub	**ẹ̀gbẹ̀sì**: plant cure for measles and pimpled skin
elekadẹ ~ alẹkadẹ ~ eregede: pumpkin	**elégédé**: pumpkin
fufu ~ inyan ~ gunyan ~ wangu: pounded yam or cassava	**fùfú**: pounded starchy foods; **inyán**: pounded yam; **gún inyán**: pound pounded yam (V); **bángún**: pound with (V); **iyón**: pounded yam, i.e., pound yam with other starch
gbaguda ~ baguda: cassava	**gbágudá**: cassava
ijijẹ ~ jijẹ ~ ounjẹ ~ unjẹ: food	**jijẹ**: meant for food ~ **ounjẹ**: food
ikoko ~ koko: eddo, cocoyam, tannia	**kókò**: cocoyam, taro
ireke ~ ereke: sugarcane	**ìrèké**: sugarcane
iṣakpa ~ ṣakpa: white sorrel	**ìṣápá**: white sorrel, *Hibiscus sabdariffa*
iwa: peas; black-eyed peas	**ẹ̀wà**: cow pea
iwa ere: unspecified type of beans	**ẹ̀wà erèé**: beans cooked
iyefun ~ ifu: flour	**ìyẹfun**: flour
iyọ: salt	**iyọ̀**: salt, savor, sweetness
iyọ ~ iyọ didu ~ ibu: sugar	**iyọ̀ dídùn**; savor sweet; **òbú**: salt-bearing rock
iyọ fifun ~ iyọ fufu: white sugar	**iyọ̀ fífún ~ fúnfún**: savor white
ọbẹ: sauce, gravy	**ọbẹ̀**: sauce, gravy
ọbẹ ata: peppery soup or sauce	**ọbẹ̀ ata**: sauce (of) pepper
ọduku ~ oduku: potato	**òdùkún**: sweet potato
ọgẹdẹ ~ ẹgẹdẹ: plantain	**ọ̀gẹ̀dẹ̀**: plantain
ọka ~ ọkan: *kuku;* cornmeal steamed and stirred in water or coconut milk; pounded cassava and plantain	**ọkà**: cornmeal steamed in water
warakasi ~ walakasi: cheese	**wàràkàsi**: cheese

A meal described but undesignated may have been *èkuru àgbàdo,* a composite of corn well boiled with peas. The whole is flavored with black pepper, chives, garlic, onion, butter and "sweet oil," that is, olive oil. *Ekuru* appears to be a generic term. Abraham (1958) describes it as "a food made from *erèé,* the beans being ground and boiled in leaves," apparently synonymous with contemporary *mọ́ín mọ́ín.* But Clarke (1843: 36) describes it as being "prepared from the white beans of a creeping plant; the beans are divested of their husk, pounded and mixed with palm oil, shallots, Cayenne pepper" and then eaten with *àgìdì.*

The unitary terms *akasan* and *agidi* are more readily recalled than the mass designation *ẹ̀kọ.* Of the three terms, *akasan* was the most common. *Akasan* and *agidi* designate a loaf of *ẹ̀kọ.* The congealed gluttinous *ẹ̀kọ* passes through an earlier stage as porridge, *ògì,* a term not advanced in the corpus, though it was described. O, for instance, gave a partial account of the preparation of *akasan*: corn is grated, strained, and boiled into a porridge. T was more detailed. She first indicated a subethnic distinction between the use of the two lexemes. She described the preparation as involving corn soaked overnight in water, shelled, pounded, washed out "to get the cream of the corn," boiled, apportioned, and wrapped in leaves. Both T and Z attested to the fact that *akasan* was eaten with honey.

A degree of polyvalency appears to affect *ọkà* and *àmàlà.* Both denote a flour that is stirred in boiling water over low heat until the mass congeals. In Trinidad this food is called *kuku. Ọkà* seems largely to have referred to the product of cornmeal. The one attestation of *àmàlà* equates it with modern Y *ẹ̀bà* 'steamed, stirred cassava flour'. But Bascom (1951b: 126) indicates that in some areas *ẹ̀bà* is also called *ọkà.* However, the fact that modern Y preserves a designation like *àmàlà-láfún* (*àmàlà* prepared from *láfún,* a very fine cassava flour) indicates that *àmàlà* has generic connotations in spite of its present-day restriction in general to steamed and stirred yam flour. However, there appeared some confusion in T's mind as to the necessary difference between *ọkà* and *fúfú.* The latter is pounded, the former stirred, into a mass. *Bángún* is in fact the most appropriate term for pounded combinations like yam and cassava or cassava and plantain. Two other terms for pounded foods were presented: *gunyan* and *wangu. Gunyan* is a nominal derivation from the verb *gunyan* 'to pound yam' while *wangu* derives in contracted form from *báańgúnyán,* a type of pounded yam. Some uses of the TY *gunyan* may exhibit semantic extension from specific to nonspecific, in that *iyan* in some idiolects translates as 'pounded food' rather than Y 'pounded yam'. This TY usage signals nondifferentiation between *fufu* and *inyan*. In Y, *fúfú* can be a generic term for pounded starchy foods, but *inyan* specifically designates pounded yam.

Semantic extension also affected *ẹba*. It originally may have designated 'cassava flour steamed and stirred', but in Trinidad this basic recipe seems to have been elaborated by the addition to the mixture of stewed dried pigeon peas (*gungo*).

Another instance of semantic extension relates to *ewe* 'leaf', which one informant additionally glossed as 'bush'—a TE expression that signifies 'shrub', 'leafy bunch'.

Ẹwa seems a generic term in Y for 'peas' and is applied to the most common type of the subset in a locality. This specific and nonspecific use is reflected in the TY designations 'peas, black-eyed peas'.

Koko seems to have been extended from reference to cocoyam to include the larger but related root crop 'tannia'.

The voluntary attestation of *obi* as 'cocoa' unfortunately occurred only once and was not cross-checked with other informants. If, however, this semantic application did have currency and was not an incorrect correspondence, it provides another example of meaning extension. *Obi* occurs in *orisha* ritual contexts as 'kolanut', but its further reference to 'cacao'—in the pre-twentieth century an exotic tree and fruit to African eyes—may have stemmed from the similarity between the stacked appearance of cocoa beans in the pod and the clustered kola valves.

Akara has undergone semantic extension, both in Y itself and in TE. Perhaps because it is a breakfast meal, *àkàrà* was co-opted in the nineteenth century to designate 'wheat bread'. This usage is manifest in TY, probably brought about by folk-derived analogic processes and reinforced by the Y Bible translation.

Iyọ̀ signifies both salt and sugar. In modern Y *iyọ̀* exclusively connotes salt on a literal level, though metaphorically it retains its meaning 'savor'. *Iyọ̀ òyìnbó,* literally 'European salt', is the modern Y referent for 'sugar' when the English loan *ṣùgá* is not used. Interestingly, Crowther (1852) defines *iyọ̀* as 'savor', neutrally and inclusively salty and sweet. Confronted by a new factor in the environment, both Y and TY introduced differentiation by appending a qualifier; the two varieties differ, however, as to the choice of attributive. TY chose *iyọ̀ dídún,* literally 'sweet salt ~ savor', and further distinguished granulated sugar by its color as *iyọ̀ fífún ~ fúnfún* 'white salt'. The implication of the latter phrase is that *white* was a redundant qualifier for salt, while it was not with respect to sugar, since both white and brown varieties were available. As regards the cues that may have distinguished *salt* from *sugar,* we may speculate that context was one; another may have been a relative clause or reprise subject extension as articulated by N: *iyọ ọ se ounjẹ* 'salt—it cooks food'. The designation *ibu* < *òbú* 'sugar', was yet another instance of the adaptation of existing lexical resources to new environmental factors. Semantic change affected the pristine quality of taste association with *òbú* but its function as a food-flavoring was retained.

Omi bona ~ *omi bonẹ* 'tea, chocolate, coffee' < *omi gbígbóná* ~ *omi gbóna* 'hot water' is either a forerunner or a reinterpretation of TE *tea.* It demonstrates the Creole tendency to reduce all hot drinks to a common denominator. In TY they are analogically reduced, but more accurately to their common component—hot water.

I am still unsure as to the etymology of *kaṣibu,* but if it is in fact Yoruba, a probable morphosemantic composition has been attempted:

ewe kaṣibu ~ **kaṣibu**: leaf wrap for steamed pap; leaf plate on on which cooked food is placed	**ewé**: leaf; **ka**: fold; **ṣù**: knead; **bu**: bake

Physical Objects and Activities

Single-form entries were:

Entries	*Etyma*
ada: cutlass	**àdá**: cutlass
aga: chair	**aga**: chair
agba: calabash	**agbà**: receptacle; **igbá**: gourd; **agbè**: type of gourd
ahere: kitchen	**ahére**: farm-shack
akpa: area, locality	**akpá**: side, district
akpata: rock	**àkpáta**: rock
apekpe: ladder	**kpekpe**: altar, platform, shelf
asa: tobacco	**àásaà**: tobacco
aṣọ: clothes	**aṣọ**: cloth, clothes
ayo: seed used in now extinct draughts-like game	**ayò**: seed of tree; game played with seeds of the tree by same name
bata: shoe	**bàtà**: shoe
eni: bed	**ẹní**: mat, sleeping mat
eyiya: hair comb made of animal or fish bone	**òòyà**: comb

ẹnubode: TE *door mouth*; house entrance	**ẹnubodè < ẹnu ibodè**: mouth (of) house; house entrance
ẹyin: egg	**ẹnyin**: egg
fitila: drinking glass; long brass drinking utensil	**fìtílà**: lamp
gele: headtie	**gèlè**: headtie
idẹ: gold	**idẹ**: brass, money
ijoko: bench, chair	**ìjókó**: stool
ikakare: spoon	**kakara**: shell
ina: fire	**iná**: fire
irawọ: star	**ìràwọ̀**: star
iṣana: matches	**iṣaná**: match
itana: lamp	**ìtaná**: lamp
iyare: room	**ìyàrá**: room
kedegbe: gourd out of which food can be eaten	**akèrègbè**: long-necked gourd calabash for carrying water
kẹkẹ: carriage	**kẹ̀kẹ́**: carriage, bicycle
kini ~ nkan ~ ohun: thing, something	**kiní ~ nkan ~ ohun**: thing, something
lori ibudo: headquarters	**olórí ìbudo**: encampment, headquarters
odo: food mortar	**odó**: food mortar
ojo: rain	**òjò**: rain
oko: farm	**oko**: farm
okun: rope	**òkun**: rope
olori odo: pestle	**ọmọrí odó**: pestle
olu: hammer	**oòlù**: mallet
omi: water	**omi**: water
orun: cooking fire	**ooru**: heat, cooking fire
oṣukpa: sun	**òṣùkpá**: moon
otitan: chair	**otita** (Ij, Ọta): bench, chair
owo: money	**owó**: money
owu: lampwick, thread	**òwú**: cotton, thread, lampwick
ọdẹdẹ: drawing-room, hall	**ọ̀dẹ̀dẹ̀**: central corridor of house; verandah
ọgba: field	**ọgbà**: yard, cultivated field, enclosure
paṣan: whip	**kpàṣán**: whip of hippopotamus hide
ṣibi: spoon	**ṣíbí**: metal spoon
ṣokoto: trousers	**sòkòtò**: trousers
wura: gold	**wúrà**: gold

Variants and subcategorization applied with:

awo ~ awo ama: ware plate	**àwo**: plate; **ọmọ àwo**: ware container
ibi: place	**ibi**: place

ibuṣẹ: workplace	**ibi úṣẹ́** (Ek): place (of) work
ijo ~ **ujo**: dance	**ijó** (SY) ~ **ujó** (Ek): dance
ikoko ~ **koko**: pot; pipe	**ìkòko**: wide-mouthed pot; pipe
ile ~ **ule**: house	**ilé** (SY) ~ **ulé** (Ek): house
ule ẹja: fish market	**ulé ẹja**: house (for) fish
ule ọja: roofed market	**ulé ọja**: house (for) market
ule oriṣa: church	**ulé òrìṣà**: house (for) deities; temple
uluṣẹ: place of work	**ile iṣẹ́**: house (for) work
ilẹ ~ **alẹ**: earth	**ilẹ̀** (SY) ~ **alẹ̀** (Ek): earth, soil
ilẹkun ~ **ilẹko**: door	**ìlẹ̀kùn**: door
koko asa ~ **koko taba** ~ **koko itaba**: tobacco pipe	**ìkòko àásaà** ~ **ìkòko tábà**: tobacco pipe
ilu ~ **ulu**: town, city, natal land	**ìlú**: town, natal land
ilu ọja ~ **ulu ọja**: city, market town, San Fernando	**ìlú ọja**: town (of) market
ododo ~ **adodo**: red headtie, red cloth	**òdòdó**: flower, redness
okuta ~ **ọkuta**: stone, rock	**okúta** (SY) ~ **ọkúta** (Ifẹ, Yagba): rock, stone
ọmaleko: window	**ọmọ ìlẹ̀kùn**: small door; window
ọna ~ **ọnọ**: road, journey	**ọ̀nà**: road, journey
ọrun ~ **oorun**: sky	**ọ̀run** ~ **ọọ̀run**: sky
ọsẹ ~ **ọṣa**: soap	**ọsẹ**: soap
ṣaṣare ~ **ṣẹṣẹrẹ** ~ **ṣẹṣbẹ**: broom	**ṣaṣara**: worn-out palm-broom, broom; **ṣẹṣẹrẹ**: broom; **ṣaṣa ẹ̀bẹ**: broom for shavings

Musical Instruments and Rhythms

The single-form entries were:

Entries	*Etyma*
adan: a lively drum and dance rhythm	**adan**: that which excites
agbe: calabash surrounded by a net with buttons and made to clatter rhythmically	**agbè**: gourd, calabash
igbandu: type of large drum	**gbàndú**: huge; **ìgbèdu**: large drum beaten to call a meeting of community leaders
kankan: type of dance	**gangan**: type of large drum
kẹrẹ: type of drum rhythm	**kẹrẹ-kere-ẹ̀tu** ~ **kẹrẹ-kẹ́rẹ-ẹ̀tu**: powder horn, calabash or flask of gun powder

kongo:[9] a small drum played together with the *dùndún* drum	**kòngó ~ kòǹọngó**: type of drum
kọkọrọ: hooked drumstick	**kọ́kọ̀rọ́**: key, hooked drumstick
ṣẹkẹrẹ: ideophone suggestive of the timbre of the calabash drum	**ṣẹ̀kẹ̀rẹ̀**: calabash drum netted with cowries

Variants occurred with:

bẹmbẹm ~ ibẹmbẹ ~ bẹbẹ rigidi: largest drum used during *orisha* ceremonies; also called mother drum	**bẹ̀m̀bẹ́**: type of round drum; **bẹ̀m̀bẹ́ bìrìkìtì**: stout *bẹ̀m̀bẹ́* drum
umele ~ omele: the medium-sized drum among the three used in *orisha* ceremonies	**umélé ~ emélé ~ omélé**: type of small drum

Temporal Divisions

Single-form entries:

Entries	*Etyma*
ana: yesterday	**àná**: yesterday
eto: time, occasion	**ọ́tẹ̀**: time, occasion
igba: time	**ìgbà**: time, period
ojuma: daylight	**ojúmọ́**: daybreak
oni: today	**òní**: today
oru: night	**òru**: night
ọdun: year	**ọdún**: year, anniversary
ọdun to kọja: last year	**ọdún ti ó kọjá**: year which it passed; last year
ọla: tomorrow	**ọ̀la**: tomorrow
ọsan: midday, afternoon	**ọ̀sán**: daylight
ọsẹ: week	**ọ̀sẹ̀**: week
ọṣu to kọja: last month	**ọṣù ti ó kọjá**: month which it passed; last month
ọtunla: day after tomorrow	**ọ̀túnla**: day after tomorrow
titi: long duration	**tītí**: long duration

Variant forms occurred with:

alẹ ~ asalẹ: evening, night	**alẹ́**: evening; **àsálẹ́**: evening
aurọ ~ owurọ ~ owurọn ~ ọwurọn: morning	**àwúrọ̀ ~ òwúrọ̀**: morning

Days of the Week

Entries	*Etyma*
ijọ osi: Sunday	**ijọ́ ìsin**: day of worship
iju kan lọsẹ: Monday	**ijọ́ kan lọ́sẹ̀**: one day in the week
ijọ meji lọsẹ: Tuesday	**ijọ́ méji lọ́sẹ̀**: two days in the week
ijọ meta lọsẹ: Wednesday	**ijọ́ mẹta lọ́sẹ̀**: three days in the week
iju marun[10] **lọsẹ**: Thursday	**ijọ́ maarun lọ́sẹ̀**: five days in the week
ijọ merun[10] **lọsẹ**: Friday	**ijọ́ mẹẹrin lọ́sẹ̀**: four days in the week
iju mefa lọsẹ: Saturday	**ijọ́ mẹfa lọ́sẹ̀**: six days in the week

This catalog of the days of the week was read by T from a notebook. Its sequence was computed numerically rather than ordinally as would be acceptable in Yoruba. In any case, under the influence of evangelization and trade, modern Yoruba has borrowed English weekday names rather than retain its own four-day week related to indigenous trade and religious festival routines. The person or persons from whom T had learned these terms followed Christian tradition in referring to Sunday as "the day of worship," but contrary to that tradition treated Monday, rather than Sunday, as the first day of the week.

Numeration[11]

Entries *Etyma*

Single-form entries were:

eje: seven	**eje**: seven
ejọ: eight	**ẹjo**: eight
arindilogun: fourteen	**erìnlàá**: fourteen
arundilogun: fifteen	**arùúndínlógún ~ èédógún**: fifteen
erindilogun: sixteen	**erindilogun**: sixteen
mẹtadilogun: ?	**ẹ̀tàdínlógún**: seventeen (num); **mẹ́tàdínlógún**: seventeen (adj)
mejidilogun: ?	**éjìdínlógún**: eighteen (num); **méjìndínlógún**: eighteen (adj)
aadọọrun: ninety	**àádọ́ọ̀rún**: ninety

Multiple forms were rendered for the lower digits, in the case of 1 on account of lexical variation, but sometimes because of vowel length variation or denasalization, and sometimes because of a confusion of numeral and adjectival forms:

ọkọn ~ **eni** ~ **ini**: one	**ọkọn** ~ **ení**: one
eji ~ **meji**: two	**ejì**: two; **mejì**: two (adj)
ẹta ~ **ẹẹta** ~ **mẹta** ~ **mẹẹta**: three	**ẹta**: three; **mẹta**: three (adj)
ẹrin ~ **ẹẹrin**: four	**erin**: four
arun ~ **aru**: five	**arùún**: five
ẹfa ~ **mẹfa**: six	**ẹfà**: six; **mefà**: six (adj)

Abstract Concepts

Single-entry forms:

Entries	*Etyma*
anu: mercy	**àánú**: pity, mercy
ara: self	**ara**: self
are: amusement, entertainment	**aré** ~ **iré**: amusement, a play
are: misery, wretchedness	**àre**: misery, distress
aye: world	**ayé**: world, life
ede: language	**èdè**: language
eleyi: this one	**eléyìí**: this one
eyo: that matter	**ènyùn**: that thing/matter
ẹgan: mockery	**ẹ̀gàn**: contempt
idi: opinion	**ìdí**: opinion, reason
iku: death	**ikú**: death
ilọ: journey	**ilọ**: the going, journey
imọle: light	**ìmọ́lé**: light, deity
inu: mind, psyche	**inú**: mind
ire: goodness	**ire**: goodness
iyin: praise	**ìnyìn**: praise
ogun: war	**ogun**: war
ohun: voice; pitch, lexical tone	**ohùn**: voice; **ohùn oro**: pitch (of) words/syllables
oro: bitterness, trouble	**oró**: poison, difficulty, terror
ọgbọn: wisdom	**ọgbọ́n**: wisdom
ọkpọlọkpọ: abundance	**ọ̀kpọ̀lọ́kpọ̀**: abundance
ọran: matter	**ọ̀rọ̀n**: affair, trouble
ọrọ: word	**ọ̀rọ̀**: word
ọru: heat	**oru**: heat

Multiple entries:

ajo ~ **ajọ**: journey	**àjò**: journey
alafia ~ **alalfia**: peace	**àláfíà**: health, well-being
ayọ ~ **ayo**: joy	**àyọ̀**: joy
ebi ~ **abi**: hunger	**ebi**: hunger
iṣẹ ~ **uṣẹ**: work	**iṣẹ́** (SY) ~ **uṣẹ́** (Ek): work
orukọ ~ **ọrukọ** ~ **oruko** ~ **oluko**: name	**orúkọ**: name
otitọ ~ **ọọtọ**: truth	**òtítọ́** ~ **òótọ́** (SY) ~ **ọ̀títọ́** (Ek): truth
ọna ~ **ọnọ**: journey	**ọ̀nà**: road, journey
orin ~ **ẹrin**: song	**orin** (SY) ~ **erin** (Ek): song

Places and Nationalities

Single-entries:

Entries	*Etyma*
Abomi: a Dahomey town	**Abòmè** ~ **Agbòmè**: capital of old Dahomey
Agido: district in Lagos	**Agìdó**: district in Lagos
Aja: a people	**Àjà**: a region and people of old Dahomey
Ajasẹ: Yoruba-speaking people; people of Porto Novo	**Àjàṣẹ́**: Porto Novo and its Yoruba speakers
Arigidi: Yoruba town in eastern Ekiti	**Arìgìdì**: Yoruba town in eastern Ekiti
Asanti: Ashanti people	**Àṣàǹti**: Ashanti nation
Awari: southern Yoruba subgroup near Dahomey	**Àwórì**: Yoruba subgroup, also called (A)Nago
Ekiti: a region of Yorubaland	**Èkìtì**: region of northeast Yoruba-land
Eko: a Yoruba town	**Èkó**: Lagos
Ẹgbaragidi Ẹgbado: a Yoruba people	**Ẹ̀gbádárígí Ẹ̀gbádò**: Ẹgbado people from Badagry
Fulani: a people	**Fúlàní**: Fula people
Hausa: a people	**Aúsa**: a people
Ibadan: a Yoruba town	**Ìbàdàn**: A Yoruba town
Ijẹbu: a Yoruba place	**Ìjẹ̀bu**: a region and people in south-east Yorubaland
Ikọle: "a place where builders live"; builder	**Ìkọ̀lé**: name of towns in Ijẹsha and Ekiti districts
ile Afrika: Africa the homeland	**Ilé Afrika**: home(land) Africa

Ilu Oyinbo: England	**Ìlú Òyìnbó**: town/land (of) Europeans
Iluwaye: Africa	**Ìlú ayé**: land (of) the world
Kramanti: a people	**Kòròmantì**: a town and people on the Gold Coast
Kumasi: a town in Ashanti	**Kúmasí**: capital of Ashanti
(O)luwu: a people	**Olúwu < oní Òwu**: chief/lord (of) Owu, a Yoruba town
Okiti: a place	**Òkìtì**: hilly district in eastern Yorubaland
Ọta: a Yoruba town	**Ọ̀tà**: a southern Yoruba town
Ọyẹ: a Yoruba town	**Ọ̀ye**: a town in Ekiti
Undo: a Yoruba town	**Oǹdó**: an eastern Yoruba town

Multiple entries were given for:

Abẹkuta ~ **Abọọkuta** ~ **Ọdọọkuta**: a Yoruba town	**Abẹ́òkúta**: southern Yoruba town, meaning 'under (the) rock'; **ọ̀dọ̀ ọkútà**: site (of the) rock
Egosi ~ **Igosi**: a Yoruba town	**Ègòsì**: an Ekiti town
Ẹgba ~ **Ẹkba**: a Yoruba people	**Ẹ̀gbá**: a southern Yoruba people
Ẹgbado ~ **Ẹkbado**: a Yoruba people	**Ẹ̀gbádò < Ẹ̀gbá odò**: Ẹgba (of the) coast
Ibadan ~ **ule Ibadan**: a Yoruba town	**Ìbàdàn** ~ **Ilé Ìbàdàn**: Ibadan; the hometown Ibadan
Ifẹ ~ **Ufẹ** ~ **ule Ufẹ**: a Yoruba holy city	**Ifẹ̀** (SY) ~ **Ufẹ̀** (Ek, Ij) ~ **Ulé Ufẹ̀**: Ifẹ; Ifẹ, the home; Yoruba town credited as site of human origin
Ọyọ ~ **Ọyọle**: a Yoruba town	**Ọ̀yọ́**: capital city of Yoruba Empire, and name of its people; **Ọ̀yọ́ Ilé**: Ọyọ homeland
Sa Liọnn ~ **Sa Lionn**: a place, a king	**Sàró**: Sierra Leone
Yoruba ~ **Yọruba** ~ **Yoroba** ~ **Yooba** ~ **Yuroba** ~ **Yeraba** ~ **Yaraba**: Ọyọ people; Yoruba speakers	**Yorùbá**: Ọyọ people; Yoruba language speakers

Verbs

Single-entries:

Entries	*Etyma*
ba: receive	**gbà**: receive
bajẹ: spoil	**bàjẹ́**: spoil

bere: ask
bẹ: be (location)
bi: give birth to
binu: be angry
bọ: cover
bukun: bless
buru: be bad
darugbo: grow old
de: happen
di: tie
dide: stand up
dubulẹ: lie down
dun: hurt
fadara: endure
fẹ: wish, want to
fẹran: love, want to, like to
fo: jump
fọ: burst
fun: give
ga: be high
gbagbe: believe
gbe: support, succour
gbe: take, carry away
gbede: understand a language
gbọ: hear
gbwe: live
gọ: be stupid
ja: fight
jale: steal
jẹrẹ: have good luck
ji: wake
jina: be far, distant
jo: dance
jo: burn
joko: sit
jọba: bring a court case against somebody
ju: verb intensifier
ka: read
kago: ask permission to enter
ke kpe fun: call out to
kere: be small
ki: greet
kọja: pass, pass by
kọ: teach
kọrin: sing

bèèrè: ask
bẹ: exist, be (position)
bí: give birth to
bínú: be angry
bo: cover
bùkún: bless
búrú: be bad
dárùgbò: grow old
dé: happen
di: tie
dídé: stand up
dubulẹ̀: lie down
dùn: hurt
faradà: endure
fẹ: wish
fẹ́ràn: love
fò: jump
fọ́: burst
fún: give
ga: be high
gbàgbé: believe
gbè: support
gbé: carry
gbédè: understand a language
gbọ́: hear
gbé: live
gọ̀: be stupid
jà: fight
jalè: steal
jẹre: have luck; **jère**: profit
jí: wake
jìnà: be far, distant
jó: dance
jò: burn
jókòó: sit
jọba: govern, be king over
jù: exceed, be excessive; more than, very[12]
kà: read, count
káàgò: ask permission to pass/enter
ké kpé fún: call say give/call out to
kéré: be small
kí: greet
kọjá: pass, pass by
kọ́: teach, learn
kọrin: sing

kpa: kill
kpamọ: hide
kpe: call
ku: die
ku: remain
kun: be full
le: well (of body)
le: be able
lo: grind
lu: hit
mọwọ: marry
mu: drink
ni: equative verb
ni: have
pa: wash (of clothes)
pinu: agree
ra: buy
ran: send
ranti: remember
reti: hope, wait for
rẹ: be weary
ri: see
rin: walk
rọ: rain
rọra: be careful
se: cook
si: exist—used after negative particle
sin: follow, guide
sun: sleep
ṣagbe: shake calabash rattle
ṣan: chew
ṣe: offend, grieve
ṣire: play and dance, be merry
ṣomele: beat the *omele* drum
ṣọ: guard, preserve
tẹ: crush, step on
ti: not be (of fact)
tọ: urinate
tun + NP + **ṣe**: renew, help
wẹ: bathe
wo: look at
wọle: enter
wu: attract, appeal to liking of
wuwo: be heavy
yọ + NP + **lẹnu**: disturb, annoy

kpa: kill
kpamọ́: hide
kpè: call
kú: die
kù: remain
kún: be full
le: be strong
lè: be able
lọ̀: grind
lù: hit
mú ọwọ́: take hand
mu: drink
ni: equative verb
ní: have
kpa: rub, bring into contact
kpínú: agree
rà: buy
rán: send
rántí: remember
retí: await
rẹ̀: be weary
rí: see
rìn: walk
rọ̀: rain
rọra: be careful
sè: cook
sí: exist, be (location)—used after negative particle
sìn: follow, accompany
sùn: sleep
jí ṣẹ̀kẹ̀rẹ̀: shake calabash rattle
ṣan: chew
ṣè: offend
ṣiré: play, enjoy oneself
lù omele: beat the *omele* drum
ṣọ́: watch, guard
tẹ̀: step on, bend, crush, press
tì: not be (of fact)
tọ̀: urinate
tún + NP + **ṣé**: repair
wẹ: bathe
wò: look at
wọlé: enter
wù: catch fancy of, appeal to senses
wúwo: be heavy
yọ + NP + **lẹ́nu**: annoy, disturb

Multiple entries and synonyms:

ba ~ **kpade**: meet	**bá**: meet, be with; **kpàdé**: meet
beru ~ **gberu**: fear	**bèrù**: fear
bọ ~ **ṣubu**: fall	**bó**: fall (inanimate); **ṣubú**: fall (animate)
bọ ~ **bọ wa** ~ **wá**: come	**bọ̀** ~ **bọ̀ wá** (Ẹg): come ~ **wá**: come
da ~ **dara**: be well	**dá** ~ **dára**: be well/good
dun ~ **nyun-nyun**: be sweet, delicious	**dùn** (SY) ~ **nyun-nyun** (Ek): be sweet, tasty
gbẹ ~ **bwa**: make thirsty	**gbẹ**: dry, make thirsty
jade ~ **kúrò**: leave, originate	**jáde**: come out, leave; **kúrò**: leave, originate
jẹ ~ **je**: allow	**jẹ́** (SY) ~ **jé** (EY): allow
jẹ ~ **jẹun**: eat	**jẹ** ~ **jẹun**: eat
jiba ~ **juba**: pay homage, give thanks, bow	**jíbà** (Ek) ~ **júbà** (Ọyọ): give homage
lọ ~ **la** ~ **re**: go (to)	**lọ** (SY) ~ **la** (Ọyọ): go, go to; **rè**: go to
mọ ~ **ma**: know	**mọ̀** (SY) ~ **ma** (Ọyọ): know
ni ~ **sọrọ** ~ **sọran** ~ **wikpe**: speak, discuss, say	**ní**: say ~ **sọ̀rọ̀** < **sọ̀ ọ̀rọ̀**: speak words; **sọ̀ràn** < **sọ̀ ọran**: speak matters; **wíkpé**: say COMPL
sare ~ **sure**: run	**sáré** (SY) ~ **súré** (Ek): run
ṣe ~ **se**: do, make, be; play an instrument	**ṣé** (SY) ~ **sé** (Ọyọ): do, be; play an instrument
ṣi ~ **pa** + NP + **mọ**: shut	**ṣi**: shut; **kpa** + NP + **mọ́**: join + NP + join
ṣiṣẹ ~ **ṣuṣẹ**: work	**ṣiṣẹ́** (SY) ~ **ṣuṣẹ́** (Ek): work

Jọba presents a telling instance of semantic shift occasioned by the absence of royal and chieftaincy institutions in a colonial and overseas political framework. However, the TY meaning, 'to bring a court case against', invokes one of the Yoruba king's functions, that of hearing cases and appeals, but that power became vested in the British judicial system as agent of the British Crown. The idiom suggests that the Verb's Subject aligns him/herself with the colonial authority against another citizen and derives a sense of status from so doing.

Mọwọ is a TY calque of the E idiom 'take hand in marriage'. The Y idiom, on the other hand, is *gbé ìyawó* 'take/carry wife'.

Semantic extension seems to have affected *ṣe* which, in addition to the Y meaning 'do', also means in TY 'play a musical instrument', thus supplying an invariant verb for a variety of verbs which in Y are deployed in connection with various instruments.

Adjectives

Single entries:

Entries	*Etyma*
buruku: bad	**burúkú**: bad
didun: happy	**dídùn**: sweet, happy
didun: black	**dídún** (Ij) ~ **dídú** ~ **dúdú** (SY): black
dudan: young	**dúdán** (Ek): young, glossy
gbigbona: hot	**gbígbóná**: hot
giga: high	**gíga**: high
kan: one	**kan**: one
kekere: small	**kékeré**: small
mejeji: both	**méjèjì**: both
meji: two	**mejì**: two
mẹta: three	**mẹ́ta**: three
mimọ: holy	**mímọ́**: clean, holy
rere: good, well	**rere**: good
wẹwẹ: small	**wẹ́wẹ́**: minute

Variants were found in:

fifun ~ **funfun**: white	**fífun** (SY) ~ **funfun** (Ẹg): white
nikọn ~ **nukan**: alone	**nikọn** (SY): alone

Adverbials

Single entries:

Entries	*Etyma*
bẹẹni: truly, indeed	**bẹ́ẹ̀ni**: thus, in fact
bi: how?	**bí**: how?
diẹ: a little	**díẹ̀**: a little
tete: soon, just (of time)	**tètè**: soon, just (of time)

Variants occurred with:

boya ~ **bọya**: perhaps	**bóyá**: perhaps
dara ~ **daada**: well	**dára** ~ **dáadáa**: well
kpukpọ ~ **kpikpọ**: very much	**kpúkpọ̀** (SY) ~ **kpíkpọ̀** (Ek): very much

A number of semantic adverbials are prepositional phrases headed by *ní* 'in/at' and *sí* 'to':

lana: yesterday	**láàná**: yesterday
lọla: tomorrow	**lọ́la**: tomorrow
nigba: at the time, when	**nígbà**: in/at the time
ninu: inside	**nínú**: inside
niwaju: in front	**níwájú**: at the front
sibe yi: to this place	**sí ibè yìí** (Ek): to this place
sohun: to over there	**sóhùn**: to that place
soke: upward	**sókè**: upward
titi: a long time, until	**tító**: a long time

Variants occurred in:

lọjọjumọ ~ **lojojuma**: daily	**lọ́jọ́jumọ́**: daily
nibẹ ~ **nubẹ**: there	**níbẹ̀**: there
nibi ~ **nihin** ~ **nihi**: here, in the place where	**níbi**: here, in the place where; **nihin**: here
nisisiyi ~ **nisisiyin** ~ **nisinsin** ~ **nisiyin**: now, at present	**nísinsin yìí** ~ **nísin yìí**: now, at this time

Prepositions

Single entries:

Entries	*Etyma*
laarin: among	**láàrìn**: in the center, among
lat': from	**láti**: from
lẹhin: after	**lẹ́hìn**: after
nibọju: in the presence of, before	**níbojú**: in front of
pẹlu: with	**kpẹ̀lú**: with
si: to, into, toward	**sí**: to, into

Variants:

ni ~ **li**: in, at	**ní** (SY) ~ **lí** (Ẹg): in, at

Connectives

Single forms:

Entries	*Etyma*
ati: and	**àti**: and
oun: and	**òun**: and

si: pre-verbal clause conjoiner	**sì**: pre-verbal clause conjoiner
ṣugbọn: but	**ṣùgbọ́n**: but
tabi: or	**tàbí**: or
ti: of	**ti**: of

Variants:

pẹlu ~ **kpelu**: and	**kpẹ̀lú**: with
ti ~ **ki**: which, who	**tí** (SY) ~ **kí** (Ek, Ij): which, who

---

Complementizers

Entries	*Etyma*
bi: if, as, since	**bí**: if, as, since
ki: that	**kí**: that
lati: in order that	**láti**: in order that
nitoriti: because	**nítorítí**: because

Salutations; Exclamations

Phrases	*Cognates*
ago: give way, please	**àgò**: permission
ai lọ run ~ **ayu lọ run**: a goodwill greeting	**ẹ ńlé run** (Ek) < **ẹ kpẹ̀lẹ́ rọ̀**: you gently support
ara ba ti le: 'asking if you feeling good' ~ **ara ra le**: how are you?	**bí ara ba ti le** < **bí**: if; **ara**: body; **bá**: HYP; **ti**: EMPH; **lé**: firm; how is your body, how are you? ~ **ara rà le** (Ek): body INTERR firm
ara le diẹ ~ **o le díẹ̀**: 'I'm fair'——response to 'how are you?'	**ara le díẹ̀**: body firm a little ~ **ó le díẹ̀**: it firm fairly, lit. I am fairly well
ara mle bi: how is everyone at home?	**ará nílé bí**: people at home how?
dukpẹ ~ **mo dupẹ** ~ **mo dupwẹ** ~ **mo dupẹn**: thanks	**dúkpẹ́**: thank (V); **mo dúkpẹ́**: I thank
ẹ rọra: be careful	**ẹ rọra**: you sustain body, lit. be careful
ka ti ri: how are things	**kí lo ti rí** < **kí**: what; **lo**: be you; **ti**: have; **rí**: be
mo jiba: thank you	**mo jíbà** (Ek): I render respect

o ba ti ṣe: how are you?	**o ti ṣe**: you have been?, lit. how are you?
o dijọ meeri: goodbye	**ó di ijọ́ mérin**: it passed days four, lit. until we see (soon)
o jare: good morning (in reply)	**o jàre**: acknowledgement of a casual greeting
o ji ire ~ o jire ~ wo o ji ire o: good morning	**o ~ ìwo ò jí ire**: you not woke healthy?
o ku abọ: welcome	**o kú àbọ̀**: you are greeted (on) approach
o ku alẹ: good evening	**o kú alẹ́**: you are greeted (in) evening
o ku aurọ ~ o ku owurọn: good morning	**o kú àwúrọ̀ ~ òwúrọ̀**: you are greeted (in) morning
o ku jare: good morning	**o kú, jàre**: you are greeted, I heard your greeting
o kuluwu, ọmọ are Afrika: a greeting	**o kú Olóòwu, ọmọ àrè Afrika**: you are greeted, King of Owu, child exiled (of) Africa
o kuluwu, ọmọ ọdọ Abẹokuta: a greeting for Ẹgba people	**o kú Olóòwu, ọmọ ọ̀dọ̀ Abẹ́ọ̀kúta**: you are hailed, King of Owu, citizen (of) place Abẹokuta
okun ~ okun o: "keep heart"; good morning	**okun**: strength; greetings (Ek)
o ku ọsan ~ o ku asan: good afternoon	**o kú ọ̀sán**: you are greeted (in) afternoon
siọ: exclamation from spectators during stickfights	**síọ̀**: expression of contempt, defiance
sun daada ~ sun ire: sleep well	**sùn dáada**: sleep well; **sun ire**: sleep healthily

Sentence Tags

Entries	*Etyma*
nọ: indicates encouragement or decision to choose an option	**nọ́**: sentence-final index of persuasion or decision to accept one of a number of options
o ~ u: yes, I'm hearing	**o**: reply of approval; an intervention registering attention to statement by interlocutor

Lexical Loans

Entries	*Etyma*
Afrika: Africa	**Africa** (E)
Ajini ~ **Ajeni**: Africa, African	**Guinée** (Fr): Africa, Guinea, African
aroye: rice	**arroz** (Port., Span.): rice
ayo: goodbye	**à Dieu** (Fr): goodbye
banga: bunch of oilpalm nuts	**banga** (Wolof): small gourd; palm kernel
bẹnẹ: sesame, sesame seeds, *žižiwi* (Fr Cr)	**beni** (Wolof); **nyàmọ̀ti** (SY): *Sesamum indicum*
but	**but** (E)
chambo: facial scarification	**?gọ̀m̀bọ**: Ọyọ facial marks; **?chaba** (Hausa): to slash
di: say	**dire** (Fr): say
epi: with, also	**et puis** (Fr): and then
even	**even** (E)
ijakato: small bitterish fruit used in *kalalu*	a fruit (Wolof)
la: DEF	**la** (Fr): DEF$_{fem}$
mwè: I	**moi** (Fr): I$_{emph}$
o ~ **or**	**or** (E)
so	**so** (E)
ṣinikafa: rice; *kuku*	**shinkafa** (Hausa): flour

Among several possibilities, Hancock (1978: 60) notes the Wolof term *banga* as carrying meanings close to that conveyed by the Trinidad Yoruba denotation. The word, however, is not listed in either Abraham (1958) nor in *A Dictionary of the Yoruba Language* (1959). It is probably in restricted dialect usage, and appears to have been borrowed from one or more West African savanna-based languages. Interestingly, Bascom (1969: 14) quotes Bowen (1858: xvi) as declaring that Ifa, the Yoruba deity of divination, "is called Banga, the god of palm-nuts." The Yoruba divination system involves the casting of a rosary of palm nuts on to a sanded board. Bascom defines *bángá* as "'a head' or bunch of fruit of the oil palm," but notes that by the twentieth century Dalziel (1937: 499) found that "the word does not seem to be so used at the present." The lexeme is, however, indicated as synonymous with a Yoruba term in Bascom's explanation (1969: 26) that "The oil palm (*ọpẹ*) or *Elaeis guineensis* bears fruit (*ẹyin*) in large bunches (*idi ẹyin, banga*); each fruit consists of a palm nut covered with a reddish-orange pericarp from which palm oil (*epo*) is extracted for cooking and for export.

The nuts (*ekurọ*) themselves are about an inch long, ovoid or egg-shaped, with hard black shells marked with lengthwise grooves. Both palm nuts and palm kernels are ordinarily known as *ekurọ*."

Hancock (1987: 274) lists Krio *jakato* ~ Cameroonian *njakatu* as derived from Wolof, but does not give the Wolof form. Its meaning is given as 'garden egg', but that in the Caribbean is understood as *Solanum melongene,* in TE both *melongene* and Hindi *baigan.* But this does not accord with the fruit description given by informants. Rather, that description fits the *Solanum americanum,* called *aguma ~ aguma bhaji* in Trinidad, and clearly related to or identical with *susumba* in Jamaica. These the *Dictionary of Jamaican English* (1967: 430) names as *Solanum torvum* and *Solanum mammosum.* However, the *DJE* (1967: 248) also lists *jocato* and adduces Twi and Ewe cognates referring to plants "of Solanum type." The botanical identification for *jocato* is however given there as "[t]he plants *Phytolacca rivinoides* and *P. icosandra,* used as a soup-green and in folk remedies. Also called 'mountain calalu'."

Present-day Yoruba uses the English loan-word *irési* for 'rice'. It is interesting that Koelle's 1843 lexicon shows that his Sierra Leone-based informants had difficulty glossing this dietary innovation. Some did attest *ṣinkafa,* also acknowledged in Crowther (1852: 11, 50), but in Koelle the most frequent designation was *iṣu* 'yam', the more familiar meal-base. *Ṣinkafa* also occurs in Olmsted (1953). The identification between *shinkafa* and *kuku* expands the Hausa generic term for 'flour' to encompass a food item prepared from a type of flour, in this case cornmeal steamed in boiling water and stirred until it becomes a gelatinous mass.

Another new concept that necessitated a loan word was 'Africa', a term that embraced all peoples from the continent without respect to their national identities. French Creole speaking people had already borrowed the European designation *Guinea,* and Trinidad Yoruba rephonologized Fr. Cr. /žine/ to /ajini ~ ajeni/.

Part Three

The Dialectics of Obsolescence and Creolization

8

Language Recession within a Creolized Context

In terms of speaker competence, TY displays the wide proficiency range typical of moribund languages receding in speaker affiliation, functional domain, and stylistic register. This language recession has come about partly as a result of language contact in an asymmetrical socioeconomic context and has been exacerbated by TY's physical severance from its linguistic and cultural matrix. As a result, many Y descendants have either rejected or neglected Y language and culture, but there are those who have been imperfect or careless learners. Yet again, others, like the eight individuals whose raw data has enabled this analysis, have cultivated, cherished, practiced, and even actively promoted their Y linguistic skills.

That this range of language competency and loyalty has typified second- and third-generation TY over at least three decades is apparent from the ethnographic recordings made in Trinidad in 1939 by Melville and Frances Herskovits. Their corpus contains several renditions, both individual and communal, of phonologically varying *orisha* chants, evidence of TY dialect variation as well as of interference from languages in contact. Similarly, the Herskovitses also recorded renditions of secular and religious songs by Margaret Buckley of Toco, a second-generation Yoruba descendant, whose TY linguistic skill in song is similar to that displayed by the major informants for this study. Her songs reveal convergence of dialect forms and tonal accuracy in melodic line, but her glosses indicate either a generalized or partially accurate comprehension of the pieces she renders.[1]

Factors Favoring Language Conservation

Ancestral language retention is prompted by a complex of factors operating within the cultural conservationist: individual personality traits, social conditioning, mental capacity, and linguistic flair.

Personal and Social Factors

Z was a man of great determination, independence of character, and a fierce sense of loyalty to his ethnic past. He was also inclined to scholarship and brought an unrelenting dedication to learning and to the dissemination of his knowledge.[2] But underlying all of these qualities was an equation of cultural loyalty with personal love for family members who embodied that culture. This personal devotion was more strongly articulated by T and L. In T, a strong sense of ethnic loyalty combined with family pride and a self-sacrificing religious dedication. In contrast with Z, none of the women gave evidence of scholarly inclination. Indeed, O, N, S, and L expressed their love of "pleasure," and Yoruba was one of the avenues through which gaiety had come into their lives. In addition, B, N, and S had good memories. S combined a good memory with a quick mental grasp, a natural ability to discern objective data, and a general shrewdness. She herself claimed that her "head was light," by which she meant that her powers of mental assimilation were quick and her retentive abilities good.[3]

Age

As demonstrated by the synchronous proficiency continuum and revealed by the diachronic profile between 1939 and the 1960s, it is misleading to automatically attribute greater linguistic accuracy to older speakers rather than younger ones. The very frequency of variation in the utterances of both old and young warns against such an assumption. A fine example of phonetic inconsistency as well as the sometimes greater reliability of a younger speaker's text was afforded by the consecutive rendition of the same song by N and her son, F:

N	**Ijọ m ba ku kwaiwo ~ Ijọ m ba ku kwariro**				
F	**Ijọ m ba ku kwariwo**				
SY	**Ijọ́**	**m̀**	**bá**	**kú,**	**kpariwo**
E	Day	I	HYP	die,	make noise
	'The day I die, make noise [beat drums]'				

N	**Oku o mei ya ige ~ Oku o meyin aye gwe ~ Oku o ge haye ma**
F	**Oku o me haye ma**

SY	**Okú**	**ò**	**mẹ̀hìn**	**ayé**	**mọ́**
E	Corpse	NEG	know behind	world	still

'The dead no longer know the world they have left behind'

TY Speaker Competence

Fluency

In a situation of language decline, fluency may not be an exclusive index of language competence.[4] In this study, we may compare O's halting sentences during her first interview with the evenly paced authoritative texts of Z. Repetition, hesitancy, and substitution characterize O's search for the normative syntax in which to couch her ideas:

Mo ...	**kpukpọ ...**	**mo**	**kọrin**	**kpukpọ ...**	**mo**	**ma**	**kọrin ...**
I	a lot	I	sang	a lot	I	know	sing

Mo	**fẹ**	**kọrin ...**	**mo**	**ma**	**kọrin ...**	*but*	**mo**	**gbagbe**	**edee**
I	wish	sing	I	know	sing	but	I	forgot	language

mi ...	**edee**	**mi**	**mo**	**gbagbe ...**
my	language	my	I	forgot

Her equally distracted apology for her disjointed expression, perforce, had to be rendered in English:

> "I don't want to speak it out of the way [badly]. . . . You see, in the twang of the changing of the words sometime, I forgot that . . . so long . . . haven't nobody to speak to. All my people [friends] is English [speaking] people. . . . But the real, *my* language, I cannot unfold it as I should."[5]

In fluency, Z's performance was diametrically opposed to O's. However, his Yoruba idioms were sometimes misapplied, and his syntactic ordering betrayed a transliteration from English and Trinidad English idioms. Inappropriate lexical and idiomatic choice is underlined.

<u>Nisisiyi</u>,[6]	**ede**	**naa**	**mo**	**mọ**	**ọ**	**rere.**	**Mo**	**le**	**sọrọn**
Now,	language	DEF	I	know	it	well.	I	can	speak

rẹ. Mo le ka a, ka a, ati emi le kọ Ø
it. I can read it, read it, and I can write [it]

nitoriti mo si ti ni ile iwe ekọ ni akpa
because I also ANT have house book teaching in side

naa ti a n kpe ni Diego Martin. Nisisiyi,
DEF which we HAB call say Diego Martin. Now,

ede ya[7] mo fẹ ki o run soke ...
language this I wish VOL it achieve prominence ...

Code-switching

Within the TY corpus, code-switching occurs between two and at times three languages. Of particular significance is the co-option into TY of French Creole and English Creole, languages in which informants had the greatest productive competence. Phrase-length code-switching is not as noticeable a feature as might have been expected in the corpus of an obsolescent language, but this crutch was obviated by the brevity of most of the TY productive discourse. The bilingual crutch was more evident in longer prose discourse. The unsolicited folktale collected from N was narrated in English Creole, although the song refrain was in Yoruba. And in Z's long expository statements, English grammatical structures lie below the surface of his formulations in Yoruba while English pronouns and greetings, Creole phatic expressions like *é é!* and introductory narrative leads like *he say* increase in frequency as he proceeds, leading to the eventual translation into English of an already formulated Yoruba sentence:

Li ọjọ kan nigbati mo te mi ṣiṣe ni Waterloo,
In day one when I ANT CONT work in Waterloo

mo kpade ọkọren kan ti mo ma ti a n kpe
I met man one who I know that we HAB call

ni Robote, Roboto. *E e!* **Awa ti ma ọkan**
say Robert. [Surprise] We_{emph} ANT know one_{num}

ati ikeji ni *Sandi Gran.* **Nigbati mo wọ ninu**
and two_{ord} in Sangre Grande. When I entered inside

ile ọja kan mo pade rẹ. O ke kpe si
house market INDEF I met him. He called said to

mi. O wi kpe *'Helo!* **Ki ni iwọ n ṣe**
me. He said called 'Hello. What FOC you_{emph} PROG do

niyin?" **Mo** **wi** **fun** **Ø** **"Awa** **m ...** **emi** **m**
in here?" I said give [him] "We$_{emph}$ PROG I$_{emph}$ PROG

ṣiṣẹ **nile** **olo** **naa ...** **ọlọ** **ireke** **naa."** *He say*
work in house grinding DEF ... mill sugar DEF" He said

"Ki **ni** **wọ** **ṣe** **nibẹ?"** *A* **wi ...** **mo** **wi** **fun** **Ø**
"What FOC you$_{emph}$ do in there?" I said I said give [him]

"Emi **n** **ṣiṣẹ** **gbẹna-gbwẹna** **bi** **wọ** **ti** **ma."** *A*
"I$_{emph}$ PROG work carpenter as you$_{emph}$ ANT know." I
said, "Well, I'm working as a carpenter, as you know."

In songs, code-switching tended to occur during line-tags. Such tags were variants of *mo ní* 'I say'. *Mo di* or *Mwè di* occurred, utilizing French Creole *mwè* 'I' and *di* 'say'. In this case, lexical transfer was facilitated by the alliterative harmony between Y and Fr. Cr. first person pronouns—*mo* and *mwè* respectively, and then by the vowel rhyme and shared alveolar locus of the consonants in Y *ní* and Fr. Cr. *di*. At the end of a song, O sang *ayo,* Fr. Cr. meaning 'goodbye', the more apt meaning in context, though it could also have been Y *ayọ̀* 'joy' or *àyò* 'beloved'.

The substitution of *mwè* for *mo* also occurred in a limited way outside of tag phrases. There were also code-switched song lines. Such songs are likely indications of second-generation transition from ancestral to primary language, in this case French Creole. O, for instance, replaced the stanza-ending *Ó dẹ̀ mí lọ* 'I must leave' with *dudu, mwè kale* 'sweetheart, I am leaving'. A secondary informant sang verses from a Christmas serenade that featured tag- and intersentential switching:

Fwè *Žinai!*
Brothers (of) Africa

Mo **forí** **bálẹ̀** **fágbàgbà**
I put head meet ground give elders
'I pay respect to the elders'

Mwè *di,* **fágbàgbà**
I say, give elders

Žan *Domnik*
Jean Dominique

Mwè **jago** **lọna** **o** **< mo kágò lọ́nà o**
I ask permission to go on roadway EMPH

Ago **m** **rele** **< Àyò ń relé**
Beloved one PROG go home

The following song by a secondary informant incorporated Yoruba, English Creole, and French Creole variants of the same line:

O ẹ̀gbọ́n
Oh elder brother/friend

Yuh doh know mi now
You don't know me now, i.e., you're ignoring me now

O ò mọ̀ kúrá e
You NEG know rascal EMPH

Ha ha ha!
[Laughter]

O ẹ̀gbọ́n
Oh elder kinsman

U te pa kònèt mwè
You PERF NEG know me

There was one instance of code-switching between Yoruba and Hausa in song. In addition, some informants showed familiarity with songs and phrases in African languages other than Yoruba—KiKongo, Hausa, Arabic, and Fon.

TY Linguistic Structures

Diachronic Considerations

The degree to which first-generation TY can be reconstructed from third-generation TY texts is, to say the least, problematic. The only nineteenth-century Trinidad Yoruba text of which I am aware so far is the war cry of the 1837 West India Regiment mutineers at the St. Joseph barracks. It was led by Daaga, the Popo prince-turned-soldier. But the contiguity of Ewe-speaking Popo ~ Gun and Yoruba-speaking Ajasẹ in multiethnic coastal Dahomey, and the fact that some of Daaga's followers, including one of his chief aides, were Yoruba raised for me the possibility that the war song might be in the Yoruba language. The song text—partially written in French-based orthography—was recalled as:

Dangkaree	*Dangkarée*
Au fey	*Au fey*
Olu weree	*Oluu werrei*
Au ley[8]	*Au lay*[9]

Its meaning was glossed and framed in doggerel as:

> Come to plunder, come to stay
> We are ready to obey.

On attempting a Yoruba reconstruction, a coherent text emerged:

Idà ~ àdá	**ń**	**kárí ~ Idà**	**ńkà**[10]	**ré**
Sword/cutlass	PROG	suffice ~ Sword	cruel	behold!

Ó	**fé**
It	slices

Ó	**lù**	**wéré**
It	strikes	without mercy/madly

Ó	**lé**
It	be hard/strong/firm

This text exhibits no significant difference in grammatical form or lexical choice from the TY corpora available in this century. The type of crux presented by *ida n kare ~ kari* is similar to other conundrums in the present corpus. In this case, the phrase must have been a military term whose currency has passed, along with its meaning. The phrase occurs as well in one of the 1939 Herskovits song texts by Margaret Buckley.

Dialect Convergence

Clearly, the Yoruba civil wars precipitated intensive dialect contact both in Yorubaland and its overseas diaspora. This leveling process would have been further accelerated once individuals entered a settled existence in tightly knit communities in Trinidad. No doubt the process was accompanied by some amount of friction and misunderstanding. Present-day differences over idiomatic and contextual choices, and probably over phonological variants,[11] had their nineteenth-century precedents. B recalls her grandmother's dismissal of Yoruba phrases learned by her children from other Yoruba people. Her blunt comment that the utterance was wrong could have been a negative judgment either on her children's tonal rendering or lexical choice (or both) or it could have implied disagreement with the grammatical structure used.

Certainly, the direction of linguistic consensus would have been dictated at various points in time by factors inherent in the perceived social hierarchy of the Yoruba community on the island as a whole, or of each isolated grouping, or of both. But we lack information as to the identity of those who became role models within the group, whether this was based on civic role, occupational skill, oratorical command, wealth, resistance to colonial laws and standards, or mediation of them.[12]

But to the extent that the TY synchronic data afford a partial reflection of nineteenth-century linguistic processes, we see indications in the twentieth-century corpus of Ọyọ-Ekiti dialect interaction in particular. The prominence of these two dialects is evidenced in both the spoken and sung corpus. Analysis demonstrates Ọyọ dialect input into the syntactic, idiomatic, and lexical usage of informants with Ekiti heritage, and into songs that by reference are of Ekiti provenance. Similarly, Ekiti influence is present in lexical choices, idioms, and idiolectal intonation contours, particularly those of S and N, both of whom had Ekiti family connections. This interdialect code-switching is similarly a feature in the phonology. Examples of this polydialectal language are evidenced in the rendition of the following songs and analyzed in the chart below:

a.

Báyì	**náà**	**ni,**	**'mọ**	**Ekiti**
Thus	that	FOC,	children	(of) Ekiti

Kíni	**a**	**lè**	**ṣé,**	**ayé?**
What FOC	we	can	do,	world?

b.

Ogé,	**gbé**	**mi**	**délé**	**o**
Plover bird,	carry	me	reach home	EMPH

Iọ[13]	**mọ̀**	**í**	**ràjò**
Person	NEG_{emph}	PROG	go journey

Kó	**bàa**	**nyúlé**	**o**
REL he	HYP_{neg}	reach home	EMPH

Ogé,	**gbé**	**mi**	**dé**
Plover bird,	carry	me	arrive

Ọyọ/Ekiti Dialect Comparison

	Ọyọ form	*Ekiti form*
Lexical choice	dé	nyú
Morphophonology	bẹ̀ẹ̀	báyì/báà
	kíni	kayi
	ìwọn	iọ
	ama	ọmọ
	se	ṣe
	mà	mọ̀
Syntax	kì í mà í	mọ̀ í

It is not clear whether some Yoruba dialects remained mutually unintelligible in the Trinidad locale. But the extent of phonological alternation in twentieth-century TY indicates that a koine was in the process of evolution. However, TY was neither sufficiently isolated nor a primary language long enough for this process to become consolidated, as occurred in the case of Trinidad Bhojpuri, a now-receding language spoken by Trinidad Indians.[14]

Syntax

There was, generally speaking, a loss of formal/informal, emphatic/nonemphatic differentials between the two personal pronoun paradigms of Yoruba. In any case, the artificial conditions of data collection together with a likely restricted interlocutor context of language use in the later days of its communal function precipitated overuse of the first person pronoun and to a lesser degree the second. It also led to nonattestation, in self-generated discourse, of the plural pronoun imperative, used in Y for plurality of address as well as to convey respect toward a singular addressee. Tonal leveling, on the other hand, accounted for frequent deletion of the post-verbal vowel signaling the third person singular pronoun, which in Y replicates the vowel-final of the verb but with tonal differentiation.

Perhaps because of the contraction of reference inward toward speaker perceptions, feelings, and immediate environment, the normally marked proximate demonstrative deictics have survived to the virtual exclusion of the distal.

Single-component and contiguous serial verbs occurred in original discourse more frequently and with greater accuracy of usage than serial verbs of the disjunct variety. It may be of some significance that TE lacks disjunct serial verbs so that the creole would not have acted as a reinforcing agent in this matter. Another likely area of creole impact may be seen in the fact that while TY has largely retained the continuous/habitual marker, differentiation between punctual and nonpunctual aspects of the anterior tense has been suppressed in favor of the punctual, structurally expressed in the unmarked verb. In creoles, the punctual, expressed by the unmarked verb stem, enjoys high frequency. The future tense was rarely attested in TY productive discourse, while the hypothetical occurred only in mnemonic data. However, the hypothetical clause was liable to lose its clause initiator *bí,* although its disjunct preverb marker *bá* remained tied within the verb phrase.

Deletion of the Y equative verb *jẹ́* was noted in specific semantic contexts.[15] Topicalized sentences occurred mostly in recollected texts but were also creatively used. On the other hand, sentences with reduplicated Subject occurred more frequently in the productive corpus than they do in SY. This grammatical feature has been shown to give transparence to an underlying pronoun functioning as a reduplicated Subject in SY and other Y dialects.[16] The pronoun is, however, overt in non-SY dialects, at least in specific constructions. Similar Subject reduplication also characterizes KiKongo.[17]

A variety of orthodox interrogative sentences was attested. Declarative sentences were overwhelmingly of the simple type, and the main productive embedded clause was the relative, largely coreferential, though both S and Z constructed relative clauses with noncoreferential subject. Clause-conjoined sentences were noticeably avoided by most speakers, and, where attested, rule violation betrayed weakness at coordinate junctures. Verb negators were productively used but nonverb negation only minimally so. The embedded volitive clause was used, headed by its initiator *kí.*

The predominance of simple syntactic structures in self-generated discourse is typical of informal speech style, and indicates the familiar and casual contexts in which the language largely operated. Furthermore, the extent of the speakers' reliance on parataxis went beyond the norms of oral discourse in English Creole. In TY, parataxis functioned to bypass lexical items such as complementizers and, by extension, to avoid clause connecting and embedding. By contrast, such parataxis would not have characterized contemporary Creole English formulations of the following TY statements:

S	**Mo**	**n**	**lọ**	**soko**	**mi,**	**lọọ**[18]	**ṣuṣẹ**	**diẹ.**
	I	PROG	go	to garden	my +	will go	do work	a little#

'I am going to my garden to work a little.'

N	**Mọ**	**lọ**	**sulu**	**ẹja.**[19]	**Mo**	**ra**	**bogbo**	**nkan.**	**Iyọ,**
	I	went	to town	fish#	I	bought	all	thing#	Salt +

'I went to the fish town. I bought everything. Salt,

mo	**gbagbe.**
I	forgot#

I forgot.'

Z	**Akoko**	**ti**	**m**	**bọ**	**iwọ**	**a**	**rin**	**kẹkẹ**	**n**
	Time	REL	PROG	come +	you	FUT	see	carriage	PROG

'In time to come, you will see a carriage

rin. **Ko** **si** **ẹṣin** **ninu** **rẹ.**
walk# NEG exist horse inside it$_{compl}$#
moving. There will not be any horse inside it.'

Phonology

TY shows less deflection towards non-Yoruba languages than an unfinished process of Y dialect intermingling.[20] As shown by the high incidence, at idiolectal level and in general, of vowel and consonantal variation, of cognation between full and syncopated, nasalized and denasalized forms, the main dialects in contact in TY emerge as Ọyọ and Ekiti/Ijẹsha in particular, with other features derived from Ẹgba, Ondo, Ijẹbu and Yagba. We therefore witness in TY a series of incomplete sound changes, a situation of high fluctuation in which variants enjoy optionality.[21] This condition confirms the accuracy of Labov's observation concerning the dissolution in living language of "the assumed association between structure and homogeneity" since "heterogeneity is not only common, it is the natural result of basic linguistic factors" (Labov 1972: 166).

The main divergences from the majority of mainland Yoruba dialects lie in rounding segmentation of coarticulated stops; suppression of the syllabicity of the Y syllabic nasal and its assimilation as syllable-final to the preceding vowel; irregular application of vowel harmony rules; virtual loss of the alveo-palatal nasal glide [ɲ]; nasalization across word boundaries, most likely under the influence of French Creole; French-influenced word-final pitch raising; and, in speakers most influenced by English, detonalization and modified stress substitution. Tone deletion also effected loss of tonal markers of syntactic juncture—in the Noun + Poss genitival phrase, and to signal postverbal third person pronoun Complement.

Contact with Ewe/Fon, English, and French accounts for sporadic labial substitution of [v] for [f] and [b]. Both English and French must have accounted for the substitution of aspirated [p'] for the Y implosive labiovelar [kp]. On the other hand, Yoruba and other African languages with nondifferentiation between [s] and [š] in certain dialects would account for similar nondistinctiveness in the English articulated by such native speakers.[22]

The contest between [ɔ] and [a] for phonemic status in TY would have contributed to the salience of [a] and its high functional load in conservative TE dialects. French Creole and English Creole use of peripheral vowels was compatible with the TY phonemic inventory, and perhaps—though the sociohistorical data are insufficient—may have helped to consolidate the vowel phonemes of the creoles themselves. Whatever the case, it is of some significance that high lax vowels, such as [ɪ] and [ʊ], so prominent in EY phonology, and a distinctive aspect of S's and N's TY, do not appear to have impacted on the phonological systems of either Trinidad's French Creole or conservative English Creole.[23] On the other hand, the occurrence in cognates of lax vowels on the part of Barbadian and Jamaican Creoles as against tense ones in Trinidad English Creole raises the possibility of the greater impact of languages like Igbò, among others, in Barbados and Jamaica.

Idiosyncratic tone and tonal decay in TY permit some qualification to the apparently reasonable generalization regarding language contact situations supported in Campbell and Muntzel (1989: 186): "Distinctions with a functional load which is high (in terms of phonology and/or morphology) will survive longer in the speaker's use of his or her weaker language than distinctions which have a low functional load." On the basis of functional load TY would have been expected to retain tonal distinctions as a general rule, but this has not proven so. Two of the speakers for whom tonal contours were an index of language competence were third-generation descendants (S, O), the other was a second-generation speaker (L). Generational proximity to first-generation native speakers, therefore, is not the substantive difference. Instead, tonal retention by subsequent generations appears concomitant with a wide lexical and stylistic range, and indicates a level of language competence which such speakers once commanded. On the other hand, tone lost salience when frequency of use, lexical inventory, stylistic range, and functional domain contracted to the point that the phonemic distinctiveness of tone ceased to be a barrier to communicative ability.[24]

Lexicon

The form-meaning relationship between the Yoruba and Trinidad Yoruba lexica indicates that the majority of items are cognates. Tonal differences excepted, most lexemes share identity of form and meaning. The following comparative comments must, all the same, be understood as being made in the light of the dialect- and register-restricted entries available in the more accessible Yoruba dictionaries. Such lexical information has been supplemented by entries listed in articles on Yoruba linguistics.

Instances of differentiation between Y and TY words with related form and identical meaning are due to:

a. changes in segmental phonology, for example *baguda* < *gbágudá* 'cassava', *erin* < *erun* 'hair'.
b. prefixation of related SY lexemes, for example *ibẹmbẹ* 'type of large drum', *igesi* 'European', *akpekpe* 'ladder'. These are possibly, however, examples of prefix retention by TY in cases no longer observed within dialects contributing to SY, though such forms may exist in other Y dialects.
c. loss and probable loss of prefixation, for example *daromi* < *idaarò mi* 'my lament'; *gunyan* 'pounded starchy food' < *gún* + *inyán,* analyzable as Ø N_{prefix} + 'pound' (V) + 'pounded yam' (COMPL).
d. appositive, attributive, and genitival compound NPs internalized as bound forms, for example *ago pwẹnyẹn* 'guinea bird' < *awo* 'guinea fowl' + *kpẹkpẹyẹ* 'duck'; *atikọ ganga* 'cock' < *àtìkọ̀ gànganràngan* 'large cock'; *ọpware* 'tray' < *ọkpọn ọrẹ* 'tray (containing) sacred offering'.
e. frozen phrases internalized as lexemes, and the extension of such context-bound phrases to designate an act, event, or person, for example *agonile* 'householder' < *àgò, onílé* 'permission (to enter), householder'; *daromi* 'solemn chant' < *idaarò mi* 'my lament'.
f. the application of an abstract sememe to a concrete phenomenon, for example *iku* < *ikú* 'death' > 'dead person'. This example could also qualify as inappropriate prefix choice, i.e. *ikú* 'death', rather than *òkú* 'corpse'.

New environmental factors and needs account for semantic reinterpretations and lexical innovations. In this category are:

a. formally distinct lexemes with analogic semantic content, for example *akpekpe* 'ladder' < *kpekpe* 'altar, shelf'; *mamalawo* 'female diviner-priestess' < *babalawo* 'male diviner-priest'.
b. apparent coinage formed by word compounding, for example *kaṣibu* 'leaf-wrap for steamed food' < ? *ká* 'fold' + *ṣù* 'make into balls' + *bú* 'bake', or *ewe kaṣibu* < ? *ewé kí a ṣù bú* 'leaf that we make into balls bake';[25] *ọlọran* 'government leader' < *oní* 'governor (of)' + *ọ̀ràn* 'words, affairs'.
c. semantic extensions of Yoruba sememes, for example *ikakare* 'spoon' < *kakara* 'shell'; *juba* 'perform rituals honoring *orisha* Eshu, in order to dismiss evil from sacred precincts' < *jùbà* 'pay respects to'; *kẹrẹ* 'type of drum rhythm' < *kère-kẹ́rẹ-ẹ̀tu* 'gunpowder calabash/container (probably used as a drum)'; *obi* 'kolanut, cacao' < *obì* 'kolanut'; *ododo* 'red cloth, red headtie' < *òdòdó* 'redness, flower'.
d. rephonologized loan words, for example *aroye* < *arroz* (Span., Port.) 'rice'; *ṣinikafa* 'rice' < *shinkafa* (Hausa) 'flour'.

It is difficult to hypothesize the stage at which each of the lexical changes noted above entered TY. Some are likely to have been Y dialect forms introduced with the first generation immigrants, particularly those that show, in form, either prefix retention or loss: *akpekpe, ibẹmbẹ, idaaro, igesi*. The loan of Hausa *shinkafa* 'flour' for 'rice' appears to have originated in Sierra Leone and the shipboard contact environment, as it appears in the 1937 Oxford *Dictionary of the Yoruba Language* and also in Olmsted (1953). *Aroye* 'rice', on the other hand, appears to be unique to Trinidad and as such was most likely assimilated from Portuguese shopkeepers or from Spanish neighbors of TY speakers. Indeed, one realization of the TY term by T carried a Spanish laryngeal coloring to the back mid vowel [aro^{h}ye].

Words that were introduced in the second and third generations would more likely be frozen-phrase lexemes, as at e. above, and analogic neologisms for new cultural designations, such as *mamalawo* 'female diviner', based on *babalawo* 'male diviner'.

Whatever the generational differentiation, however, it may be deduced from the lexical inventory presented that the number of lexical innovations recalled is small. This may indicate, cross-generationally, a limited productive response to the new physical and social ecology, no doubt because the new environment already supplied lexemes to denote its peculiar features.

All the same, one must bear in mind the fact that the ideological and economic environment of the mid twentieth century has been, in emphasis and sometimes in essence, quite removed from that obtaining in the mid to late nineteenth century. It is therefore quite possible that TY either innovated or semantically changed or extended Y lexemes to denote concepts and persons related to plantation culture: master, overseer, driver, housekeeper, concubine, boilerman; estate tools and manufacturing processes, slave rebellion, work strike; religious and ethnic types and hybrids like Indian, Hindu, Moslem, Spanish, Chinese, Portuguese, mulatto, sambo, and that plethora of distinctions that have been spawned by a color-conscious society. Since this cultural construct had lost currency, the research defaulted by failing to take account of its past valency. As such, deductions about lack of innovation must necessarily be cautious.

This said, it is however noteworthy that the innovations and readaptations apparent in the data arise in the domains of food preparation, botany, and religious observance. This pattern highlights the fact that the major conceptual parameter of at least the second- and third-generation lexicon is concrete rather than kinship-oriented, administrative, or abstract. This lexical contraction may have originated from the severe limitations placed on the politico-economic self-determination of the immigrant Yoruba group. In addition, the youthfulness of its members would mean that their full lexical range would not yet have blossomed. Hypothetically, lexical impoverishment among the first generation could also be ascribed to inventory decay on the part of dialectally marginalized groups and the apparently brief life span of the language as an exclusive communicative medium. The resultant lexical narrowing and decline in polyvalency are also facets of the restricted stylistic code in TY and the artificial conditions under which the data were collected.[26] Furthermore, loss of tonal distinctions must have contributed to the discarding of homonyms, a significant factor in general lexical fading.[27]

9

Creolization Processes in Broader Perspective

Although this study in the main addresses an instance of language obsolescence, there is an existential sense in which death resists finality. This ontological perspective finds corroboration not only in the interdependence of life and death in nature but can also be observed in the fact that obsolescent languages endure for several generations in conditions of decline. Even more instructively, I note in the Introduction above the semantic and functional limitations on the notion of language death, in that *languages have conventionally been spoken of as 'dead' because they have ceased reciprocal function,* but that this ascription denies their survival in nonreciprocal contexts, or in the lexica of interactive languages, or by retention of a surrogate life through their phonological, syntactic, or idiomatic penetration of other languages.

We now turn to an examination of the subtle and therefore unrecognized ways in which Yoruba, through TY, may be seen to have impacted on other languages in contact—languages that still enjoy vibrant life, and through whose forms Y and TY live a limited and surrogate existence.

African Language Persistence During Slavery

As a by-product, this study throws light on the process of language shift across three generations. This shift has meant the increasing dominance of European lexifier Creoles over African mother tongues. Unfortunately, the period of language shift treated in this study—the nineteenth and twentieth centuries—falls well outside the time frames most significant for the genesis of the Atlantic creoles: the sixteenth and seventeenth centuries. Additionally, the socioeconomic context of African languages in the Caribbean was changed by the emancipation of Africans in 1838 from the restrictions of plantation culture. This act liberated Africans to live their culture more fully than was previously possible, albeit still under the shadow of powerful colonial constraints. But the sociocultural context of post-Emancipation life would have become more favorable for self-expression and would have bonded members of particular ethnic groups, both pre-Emancipation slaves and post-Emancipation indentured workers. One cannot therefore imply that the three-generational profile afforded by this study replicates the factors of language shift under the conditions of plantation enslavement. But the mental and phatic processes are likely to have been similar and therefore to prove illuminating.

For one, the study does serve to insert *the role of the individual personality, of personal relationships, communal will, and identity into the model of cultural change.* This is an antidote to mechanistic and deterministic interpretations of language use and language change. We need to remember that while, on one level, laws are inherent in nature, in society, and in behavior, at another level humankind is in dialectical relationship with these laws and with the physical and social environment, modifying them and negotiating its own trajectories. The factors of individual personality and talent at work in language retention and propagation, the evidence of linguistic alternation and dialect convergence in the TY corpus attest to the elements of choice, aesthetic attraction, and idiosyncrasy in human activity.

The evidence of this study, for instance, exposes the overemphasis in the interpretation of Caribbean social history on the notion that Africans were deprived of their languages by the harshness of slave laws and the plantation regime. This one-sided interpretation ignores the gaps that have always existed and that persist between laws, their implementation, and their observance. Indeed, the periodic reintroduction of the same slave laws indicates constant breakdowns in reconciling theory and practice. Another assumption is that on any one plantation—particularly on large ones—there were no two slaves who spoke the same language. This assumption flies in the face of the laws of probability, and ignores evidence that large national groups arrived on each shipment. This clustering greatly increased the probability that a buyer purchasing more than one slave might well have come away from the auction with at least two compatriots. In any case, there is evidence that, on the one hand, buyers had ethnic preferences and, on the other, that slaves of the same linguistic group formed themselves into social and pressure groups.[1]

As such, this study shows that transatlantic slavery precipitated experiences and responses generally classified as typical of *exile,* and that Africans functioned under these conditions as does any other immigrant group. Concrete factors revealed here allow us to extrapolate that even during slavery there *was* continued use of African languages, given factors such as ethnic clustering and language loyalty that encouraged affective and symbolic roles for mother tongues as well as conscious language transmission to subsequent generations. African languages functioned actively in domestic domains, in ritual activity, and in work arenas involving ethnically homogeneous individuals and groups. In such environments, an African language could become the mother tongue of second-generation descendants and could entrench itself in the children's formative years in situations in which the ethnic group was demographically well represented.

Conversely, aptitude in and the functionality of African languages declined in environments where and at periods when the removal of children in particular (and even adults) from African-speaking locations was endemic. Furthermore, perhaps only in circumstances of maroonage, that is, physical, sociopolitical and economic estrangement of African language groups from non-African linguistic environments, could African languages flourish independently, in conditions closely akin to those in Africa. Even so, Maroon settlements were likely to be multidialectal as well as multiethnic, which meant that processes of linguistic convergence also operated there.

Generational Processes of Language Loss

The evolution of monolingual persons to bi- or tri-lingual under high-pressure slavery and immediate postslavery conditions is a process still subject to much conjecture. But happily Cruickshank (1916, 1917) has documented the initial stages of that process in British Guiana and recent studies on bilingualism assist a reconstruction.

Accordingly, the incorporation of the target language into the incipient bilingual's language repertoire began with isolated words, set phrases, and idioms, as these least disturbed the mother-tongue syntactic frame. Increasingly, mother-tongue syntactic structures would have provided a skeletal frame on which to map newly acquired target referents. But expansion beyond these fixed forms in order to improve comprehensibility would gradually put a brake on the extent to which African syntactic structures could be variously copied and reinterpreted. Reinterpretation would be guided by the underlying conceptual dictates inherent in the mother tongue. Linguists who deny or undervalue mother-tongue transfer erroneously assume an equivalence between child and adult language acquisition.[2] The adult is far less innately programmed than the child, for with the adult the determinism of nature and genetics has been modified by enculturation and environmental factors. And if elements of mother-tongue phonology remain to mark second language production, why should one suppose that mother-tongue influence would completely erase itself from other facets of second language competence?

Slightly later in the process of second language acquisition, universal tendencies of imperfect language manipulation come into play, among them parataxis, pro-drop, preposition deletion, the multifunctional use of the unmarked verb and a preverbal negative particle, invariant declarative and interrogative word order. These standard interlanguage shorthand devices also provide a recourse for the second language learner.[3]

Thus the new speaker's comprehensibility in the target language depended on realignments over time in the relative weighting of factors such as: mother-tongue transference of syntax, grammatical and conceptual categorization, reproduction of target language structural models and concepts, the formal economy precipitated by language contact trauma, and command of paralinguistic features.

This research project unfortunately overlooked elicitation of data on the linguistic behavior of nineteenth-century second-generation African descendants. Speaking of British Guiana in the early twentieth century, Cruickshank (1917: 79) commented that "most of the Yoruba Creoles 'hear' Yoruba—that is, understand it—readily. Many of them speak it well, a few fluently." But fluency may not have equated totally with the grammatical and stylistic performance of their parents. On the other hand, African Creoles whose mother tongue was African had had to undergo processes similar to those undergone by their parents in the acquisition of both French and English creoles or of either one of them. Yet there were differences.

Some adult Africans must have functioned essentially as coordinate bilinguals, proceeding to a subordinate bilingualism in which their mother tongue preserved principal subjective value. On the other hand, their offspring proceeded from compound to subordinate bilingualism. Coordinate bilingualism "arises when the two languages are learned in different learning environments, which are experienced as being completely separate." It "ordinarily implies biculturism." However it is unimaginable, with respect to exiles in the ad hoc learning conditions and the disadvantageous circumstances of slavery and indenture, that coordinate bilingualism involved suppression of the need for translation.[4] The evidence of calquing and grammatical transfers belies this conclusion.

In infancy, second-generation Yoruba would have performed as compound bilinguals, living as they did "within a fused learning environment . . . [one] not clearly differentiated." The words they learned in Yoruba and in Creole would have been "conceived of as being nearly identical." Increased exposure to European languages and European-lexifier Creoles eventually would have induced Yoruba-subordinate bilingualism where "one name is understood to be a substitute for the other." This approach to language learning would also typify a situation in which "a language or dialect with a low cultural or social standing still exists beside a language with a higher standing in a bilingual setting" (Dahlstedt 1972: 346). Second-generation Africans came into contact with European languages at an earlier age than parents who had entered slavery as teenagers and adults, in addition to which their linguistic environment once outside their immediate neighborhood was creole. They were therefore likely to be more fluent in the creoles than their parents and would make an earlier transition to European lexical dominance in their bilingual repertoire than had their parents. Their bilingual language style and competence was probably matched by those of first-generation African children who must have shown the linguistic flexibility so characteristic of minors. A few examples of adult second-generation conversation indicate a French Creole matrix with embedded Yoruba lexemes:

Oburin,	i	fashé	epi	mwè
woman	$Pr_{3\ sg\ Subj}$	be annoyed	with	me

'She, my girlfriend, is angry with me.'

Greetings such as *Okun o* (Ek.) 'Keep well', and *O jire* (Ọyọ) '[May you] Wake in health', littered their speech, along with *O jare o,* a reply to these greetings.

Another difference between the first-generation adult Africans and their children lay in the European language models available to a minority of the latter. It must be realized that British English or metropolitan French was not the target language of the majority of first-generation Africans.[5] Perhaps with the exception of the few who were domestic slaves or servants, the target language was the creole or creoles they heard from their workmates and those with whom they shared their living quarters. There was no need for them to speak other than a creole since everyone in their environment, including Europeans, had passive (and often active) competence in it.

While Creole served as linguistic goal of the second generation African, the few who attended school and excelled did so in part because they came to master Standard English or Standard French, or both, or even Latin. Such students modeled their language skills on those displayed by Barbadian and British teachers, clergy, and magistrates.

The majority, however, were largely illiterate or semiliterate, and with educational and occupational opportunities minimal, creole was their linguistic ambit. Thus the attestation that several second-generation Africans spoke English well probably had more to do with fluency in English Creole and with deployment of polysyllabic words (such as typified West Indian tea-meetings and some earlier calypsos) than with the ability to articulate Standard English.[6]

It is no doubt at this generational layer that macaronic African and Creole language songs appeared. These were songs that intercalated lines in an African language with lines in a European-lexifier creole, the latter glossing the meaning of the preceding African phrase. Sometimes this translation device proceeded by stanzas rather than lines. Further analysis of such texts from Trinidad, Jamaica, and Colombia promises to be instructive in identifying the reciprocal transfer of lexical, phonological, syntactic and idiomatic features between African and Creole languages.[7]

The extent of second-generation multilingualism would have been a major factor in destabilizing the African languages that were still used in home situations. Destabilization would have increased at the turn of the twentieth century when the first-generation African community declined in numbers and public activity. But destabilization would also have been caused by the multidialectal variations of the African languages to which speakers and young learners were exposed. Uncertainties and conflicting opinions over competing forms, combined with a decrease in the monitoring of language orthodoxies by senior speakers, must have become a disincentive to use.

Thus, one is left to hazard a guess as to the generational layer that began the process of syntactic restructuring of ancestral languages in the phonological and syntactic mold of creoles and European metropolitan languages in contact. It is indeed likely to have been both less competent second-generation African language speakers as well as many third-generation ones. This brings us to the point that language changes did not proceed in the sequential manner suggested by a surface appraisal of a generational schema: not only could the same individual be both second- and third-generation at the same time depending on which ancestral line one reckoned by, but it should be realized that *persons of varying generational layers coexisted synchronously.* This point needs to be borne in mind in order to appreciate the living dynamic of language-internal variability and the process of simultaneous retention and rejection involved in internal and cross-systemic language changes.[8]

Structural Characteristics of First-Generation English

Evidence from third-generation Africans provides a helpful indication of the English Creole competence of their African-born grandparents. Examples of their speech as imitated by their descendants give syntactic evidence less of the 'foreigner-talk' stage of their second language acquisition than of developed creole formulations and mother-tongue transfers.

Example a. appears to exhibit a basilang theme-rheme structure. But since this occurs in the expression of identity, it invites comparison with Y and TY structures utilized in the same semantic context. Thus,

a. *me* *yoroba*
I Yoruba [statement of ethnic affiliation]

invites comparison with TY:

emi *yoroba*
I Yoruba [statment of ethnic identity][9]

Furthermore, the use of E $Pr_{1\,sg\,Obj}$ in the Eng. Cr. Subj slot suggests the concatenation of TY $Pr_{1\,sg\,Subj}$ variant *emi,* in apocopated form, with the E Obj form *me,* itself phonetically analogous to the Y and TY $Pr_{1\ sg\ Obj}$ form *mi.* Additionally, the weight of the bilabial nasal in other Y and TY forms, such as *mo ~ mọ,* and in Fr. Cr. *mwè,* itself borrowed into TY, suggests that a bilabial nasal expression of the $Pr_{1\ sg\ Subj}$ would gain ascendancy over the marked E /ai/, *I.*

Example b. also invites categorization as basilang because of its theme-rheme structure. But it may also be structurally analyzed as Creole and as Y. Yet in totality, it is neither of the two.

b. *suwa swit* (Be) soup sweet?

It is ascriptive, with the ascription *sweet* functioning verbally in accordance with Y, TY, and TE grammars. However, unlike TE and creoles, no definer qualifies the noun, though Ø definite article conforms to this context in Y and TY grammars. Yet unlike T and TY the sentence bears no overt segmental marker of interrogation. Such a marker would have preceded the theme or subject. Apart from these syntactic issues, both sememes in b. exemplify the multifunctionality of L_2 lexical items in the early stages of second language learning. The E words are calques of Yoruba lexes. (The original speaker was first-generation Yoruba.) *Soup* designated E 'soup', 'broth', and 'gravy'. The latter is the semantic application here, just as it is in conservative Jamaican Creole as well as in contemporary West African "pidgins."[10] *Sweet* functions here, not as a property of sugar as it may also have meant, but as 'pleasant ~ appropriate to taste', a Y semantic application.

The following examples differ syntactically from a. and b. in that they contain, from an E perspective, overt Verb Phrases; but their formal distinctiveness from E lies in the following usages: *-am* transitive invariant object pronoun (examples c, d, e, h, and i below); *fo* as complementizer (example h); the topicalizing verb particle *a* (examples h, i); invariant *nɔ ~ na* as preverb negator (examples e, h); invariant SVO sequence for questions (example g); and *mi* as first person singular possessive (example f).

c. sutam
shoot you ~ him

d. kalam jaka
call him Jack

e. nɔ mainam
don't mind him
'don't pay him any attention'

f. yu šapi mi dag
you chopped my dog
'you cut my dog with a cutlass'

g. aveli,[11] yu kyan cedi nini
Evelyn, you can thread the needle?

h. a nɔ so fo seam
FOC not so to say it
'that's not the way to say it'

i. a nɔ doam so
FOC nut(s) do it so
'It is nuts that have done [flavored] it like that'

Further examples generally reinforce the phonological patterns observed above:

j. has — horse
k. baks — box
l. bwai — boy
m. gan pikini — grand-children
n. salfis ana poka — saltfish and pork

Of note are the occurrence of epenthetic vowels and avoidance of consonant clusters (though it is likely that the third-generation English Creole speaking informants did not reproduce all the possible cases, cf. /baks/). Both processes bring the phonological structure of words into line with the open-syllable structure of the Yoruba and KiKongo mother tongues in these instances.[12] In addition, there is glide insertion in *bwai*;[13] s ~ š and š ~ c variation, the former typical of dialect differences within both Yoruba[14] and KiKongo; and the high functional load of the /a/ phoneme (already noted as a dialect alternative to /ɔ/ in Y),[15] and of cardinal vowels in general.

Trinidad Yoruba to Trinidad Creole Transfer

Some of the second and third generation began as African mother tongue speakers, but soon proceeded to become in their lifetime both French Creole and English Creole primary speakers with English Creole assuming predominance in the second half of their lives. Such a progression in primary language use must necessarily have involved the dialectical process whereby (a) some language traits were transferred from one language to another, and (b) the restructuring tendencies produced by language trauma affected the recessive languages.

(a) With regard to Yoruba to English Creole transfer, the following categories of influence are apparent in Trinidad English Creole as a legacy of the contact between these two languages on the island:

Lexical Loans

ago	permission requested of Earth to throw water upon it in libation; permission requested of persons to clear area for pouring of libations < *àgò,* request for permission to pass or pour water
akra	fried paté of wheat flour and flaked cooked fish < *akara,* fried paté of bean paste, sometimes containing fried shrimp
dada head	'matted hair' < *Dàdá,* god with matted hair
futi	be likely to (emph.), implying an understood reluctance < *futẹ* 'be inclined to', cf. TE *you futi go* 'you had better go'
nə	final tag in instruction or request supporting one action (expressed in preceding V) of an implied alternative < *nọ,* S-final tag following V that suggests one action rather than an implied other, e.g. *jóòkò nọ* 'sit (rather than stand)'. This *nọ* differs from that in *it hot, nuh,* where the tag implies 'is it not?' with the semantic content of Fr. S-final *non.*
(w)oya!	Start! Said by dance orchestra leader to start band or by calypso singer to signal the accompanying orchestra to begin[16] < *ó yá* 'it be alive/ready to begin'; 'Ready!'
shango	deity of thunder and lightning; religion venerating Yoruba deities or *òrìṣà* < *Ṣàngó,* deity of thunder and lightning
susu	'system of pooled savings' < *èsúsú* 'system of pooled savings'

Discourse Analogies

rọra	**o**	> TE *take it easy!* Advice of caution
support body	EMPH	against hotheadedness
fig. be careful!/Go slowly.		

(ṣé)	**kpẹ̀lẹ́**	> TE *cool it.* Expression of comfort,
(do/perform)	gently	reassurance, kindly caution

Calqued Idioms and Syntax

Y **domi** **sí** + NP
throw/pour water to + NP
TE throw water to + NP, i.e., pour water on

Y **èmí** **níkan**
$I_{emph.}$ $one_{adj.}$/alone
TE me one. (Both words are emphatic)

Y **ènìyà** **ni**
person/human FOC
TE *X is people,* i.e., X is worthy of regard ~ of being treated as a human being rather than an animal

Y **ẹṣin** **òrìṣà**
horse deity, i.e., chameleon, praying mantis that acted as horse of the deity who first came from heaven to earth
TE *god horse,* i.e., 'praying mantis'

Y **jókò** **síbẹ̀**
sit to there
TE *sit there!* i.e., 'you'd be foolish not to take any action; you'd be foolish to be so complacent'

Y **kí** **ló** **ṣé** **ẹ?**
what be it does thing to you?
TE *what do you?* i.e., 'what's the matter?'

Y **ọ̀kọn-ọ̀kọn ~ kọ̀ọ̀kọn**
one-one, i.e., distributive, meaning 'one by one; scattered'; 'in small number'
TE *one-one,* i.e., few and scattered

Y **kúrò** **níbẹ̀**
leave in there
TE *come out in there,* i.e., 'come out of there'

Y **mo ń lọ (sí ~ ní)**[17] **ilú**
I PROG go (to ~ in) town
TE *I going (in) town,* i.e., 'I plan to go to town'

Y **mura kpa**
be ready ~ dressed kill
TE *dress to kill,* i.e., 'to dress ~ be dressed in such a way as to create an impression'

Y **nígbà gbogbo**
in time all
TE *all time,* i.e., 'always'

Y **otútù mú** + NP_{obj}
coldness seizes/holds + NP_{obj}
TE *the cold (flu) have* + NP_{obj}, i.e., 'NP_{subj} has the flu'

Y **sọ̀rọ̀ burúkú**
say words bad
TE *to bad talk,* i.e., 'speak ill of'

Y **ẹnu dídùn**
mouth sweet i.e., flattering speech
TE *sweet mouth,* i.e., flattery, flattering language

Y **ọmọ ilé**
child ~ slave house, i.e., off-white house-dwelling lizard
TE *wood slave*

Interaction of Y and E Syntax

An area of some interest for understanding the composite elements within TE involves a unique TY Ø occurrence of locative verb in O's

nibo wọ?
in place you_{emph}

This formulation appears to calque TE *where you?,* itself a structure in which TE differs from several creoles which overtly express a verbal locative in the cognate sentence:

we yu de?
where you be_{loc}?

Y itself expresses location in an interrogative sentence by the verb *dà,* a corollary to *wà* in declarative sentences. Thus:

ìwọ	**dà**
you_{emph}	be $located_{interr}$

One may therefore wish to argue that TE *where* in *where you?* functions analogously to Y as verb, with its sentence-initial position deriving from sentence-initial positions of English WH- words.

Further evidence of the interweaving of Y, TY, E, and TE semantico-syntactic formulations is offered by L's TY sentence:

ọkan	**de**	**nibẹ**
one	there	in there

In Y this would be:

ọkan	**wà**	**níbẹ̀**
one	be_{loc}	in there

In basilectal TE and other Creoles this surfaces as:

one	de	de
one	there	there

with *there*$_1$ functioning as locative verb, and *there*$_2$ as adverbial. L's TY sentence is a lexical and syntactic intercalation of Yoruba and English. A comparable substitution of *there* for Y *wà* occurs in the TE noncommittal response to greetings such as *how you?*[18] or *how you do?*

A	de	~ A diə
I	there	

The Y equivalent is:

mo	**wà**
I	be_{loc} ~ exist

TY, however, supplied a variant of this expression in

mo	**mbẹ**
I	there

which S articulated within the evening prayer she recited (see chapter 4, "Yoruba in Ritual Language"). This grammatical form may represent an archaism or regionalism. In fact, Rowlands (1969: 154) regards *wà* and *mbẹ* as "basically dialectal variants." SY, for its part, utilizes the segmental shape *mbẹ*

i. as an adverbial contraction of *ní ibẹ̀* 'in there', occurring uniquely with the verb *wà*. Thus:

ó	**wà**	**ḿbẹ̀**
he	be_{loc}	there

ii. as a verb phrase with the meaning 'exist'. *bẹ* now carries mid rather than low tone, and is used solely in the progressive/continuative/habitual aspect. Thus:

ó	**ḿ**	**bẹ**
he	PROG	exist

Ọlọ́run	**ḿ**	**bẹ**
God	PROG	exist

Apart from near homophony, there does appear to be some overlap in both the semantic content and restrictive occurrence of *ḿbẹ̀* and *ḿ bẹ,* conditions that may relate to the generally unstable relationship between some verbs and adverbs in Y.[19]

The issues surrounding the possible verbal status of TE *where* and *there* prompt, on the converse, consideration of TY sentences with zero verb. Such sentences were produced by various primary informants.

olukọ babaa mi Oguntusi
orukọ iyaa mi Asato
orukọ iya mi Ọṣuntoki ~ iya mi ni Ọṣuntoki

This structure echoes an example of nineteenth-century English as produced by an African-born Yoruba:

me yoroba

TE now uses E lexical forms of the verb *be* as equative. But with regard to the nineteenth-century antecedent (or at least, one of the available options), what is significant here is that the zero verbal exponent of equation occurs in the semantic expression of personal or ethnic identity. This TY syntactic pattern is typical of colloquial Y, although Y does possess equative verbs. But *jẹ́,* the Y equative expressive of permanent characteristics relative to natural identity, status, and occupation, is marginal to the Y verb system. "The meaning of *jẹ́* is such that forms other than the simple stem do not often occur" (Rowlands 1969: 153). Bamgboṣe (1966: 41–42) further supplies instances in which *jẹ́* is deleted in favor of a structure using the focus verb *ni.*

àjé	**ni**	**dọndọn**
witch	FOC	certainly

tíṣà	**ni**	**mí**
teacher	FOC	me

which he derives from the respective underlying sentences:

< **àjé**	**ni**	**ó**	**jẹ́**	**dọndọn**
witch	FOC	he/she	EQU	certainly

< **tíṣà**	**ni**	**mo**	**jẹ́**
teacher	FOC	I	EQU

Another area of syntax that invites consideration is the TE treatment and interpretation of serial verbs. Although in contemporary TE serial verb constructions are rare, nineteenth-century TE displayed structures with *gie* ~ *gib* as V_2: *he begin fou read gib naga* 'he began to read to the Blacks'; *he no sell rattin beef gie awee* 'he did/ would not sell rotten beef to us'.[20] Fr. Cr. correspondingly featured structures with *bai* as V_2—*pale bau* 'speak to you'; *mete limie bai Congo Bara* 'put light (candle) for Congo Bara'. However, the expressive formulation of some of the serial verb units hints at another area of amalgamated English and Yoruba semantics, syntax and lexicon. Note S's

TY	**lọ**	**mumi**		**fun**	**mi**	**wa**
SY	**lọ**	**mú**	**omi**	**fún**	**mi**	**wá**
	go	take	water	give	me	come
Fr Cr	*ale*	*pòte*	*glo*	*ba*	*mwè*	
	go	carry	water	give	me	
TE	go bring the water for me ~ go and bring the water for me					

TY	**ta**	**jí**	**wá**
	which we	open eyes to the world (re waking, birth)	find

TE expression by same informant:

me open me eyes see them do it so, i.e., it was done that way before I was born

and L's

TY	**kú**	**lọ**
	die	go

Informant's gloss:

dead and gone, i.e., died a long time ago

Differentiation appears to have taken place in Trinidad creoles with regard to the expressive formulation of the serial verb. *ji wa* has been rendered as a split verb: 'open my eyes see'; while *lọ mu* + NP

+ *fun* + NP + *wa* treats its two semantic constituents differently. In *go take water come, bring* conceptually accounts for *take . . . come,* thus obviating the need for V_2, which would now redundantly convey direction. However, the initial directional verb is retained. Purpose —*give*—in *bring water give me* is expressed prepositionally, thus *bring water for me.*

Apart from that, *go bring* and *die go* can both be rendered by a conjoining structure: *go and bring* in the instance where motion is literal and precedes the action conveyed by V_2. On the other hand, in *dead and gone* the motion verb is partly literal since the ghosts of the dead can move, but *gone* also figuratively suggests distance. This is why *gone* is an elaboration of the event of death and occupies V_2 slot here.

Further consideration can be given to the conjoining option. This may have its source in the optional expression of the serial verb string in Y and Twi, for example.[21] Although only V_1 in the string usually takes preverbal markers in the documented varieties of these languages, there *are* semantic environments and specific verbs with which V_1 or V_2 (or both) are marked for aspect and tense. Comparable examples in TY exhibit V_2 marking to the exclusion of V_1.

Ọya	**gbe**	**n**	**sa**
Ọya	continue	CONT	run

Ọlọpa	**wa**	**m**	**bọ**
Police	come	PROG	approach

Such options imply the possibility, within African languages, of disaggregating the concepts conveyed in the compound structures of serial verb strings, and it would appear that the conjoint verb structure is an exploitation of this underlying semantico-syntactic reality. Further evidence of this reality is presented in the example quoted by Stahlke (1970: 62):

Mo	**fi**	**ọgbọn**	**fi**	**àdá**	**gé**	**igi**
I	took	cleverness	took	machete	cut	tree

where concepts of manner, instrumentality, and conclusive action are not only quasi-independently expressed, but where the sentence also makes reduplicated use of the verb lexeme *fi.*

The conjoint verb structure thus represents an analytical reformatting of the synthetic serial verb string. Trinidad creoles have therefore exploited, not one, but a range of options in reformulating the grammatical options offered by African languages in the context of the grammar and lexicon of European languages.

The analyses presented above also serve to highlight two points. One is the *significance of dialects in the study of African languages. What is or is not permissible in an African language cannot be adjudged on the basis of documented or standard language forms only.* The other point is *the pivotal role played by semantics in the determination of lexical and grammatical choice.*

Issues Posed by Culture Contact

The preceding instances of language transfer are not meant to make an exclusive claim for substrate theory relative to Trinidad's creoles, nor even to register an exclusive role for Yoruba in what might be perceived as the substratal blueprint of those creoles. With regard to the latter, we recognize that other African languages predated Yoruba in the Trinidad environment and, even more importantly, that other African mother tongues arrived with slaves brought into the colony from French territories—New Orleans, Saint Domingue, Guadeloupe, Martinique, and Grenada among them—from the closing years of the eighteenth century and into the nineteenth. But lateness of arrival need in no way debar a culture from making its impact on the preexisting cultural amalgam once other factors allow it some advantage. In Trinidad, moreover, the notion of lateness is noticeably relative, given that the slave population became significant only in the late eighteenth century. By the time slavery was abolished in 1838, that institution had only reached its apogee during the preceding fifty years! The French and English creoles spoken on the island must then in large measure have reproduced creoles native to other environments.

The Y and TY transfers into Trinidad creoles, rather, provide concrete instances in which a language present in Trinidad's sociohistorical evolution has influenced the lexicon and expressive discourse of a succeeding language. For this reason, Yoruba influence on Trinidad Creole would better be described as adstratal, that is, part of the ongoing process of language evolution. And dynamic change is my emphasis, which is why, regardless of time of introduction or of maximal influence, I prefer to dispense with the notions of substrate and superstrate that, in the first place, suggest static entities and static interrelationships. Such concepts lead to the notion that lects are fixed and homogeneous and, in particular, that the opaque presence of African languages in creoles is restricted to a seminal phase of these new languages.

Some of the transfers may originate uniquely in Yoruba, but only further work will indicate the extent and nature of reinforcement from convergent features in other contact languages, whether typologically similar or diverse, whether African or European. We will need to consider inter-African contact features, borrowings from African into European speech cultures, and vice versa. Insights into language universals provide a useful key to contact phenomena, but address to a more abstract level of language processing ought not to be exclusive. Cultural and historical specifics, rather than being bypassed, anchor the processes of change in concrete data and thus merit insertion into the paradigm of genetic relationship.

The Chronology Factor

The relationship of TY to Trinidad's creoles raises at least two conceptual and procedural issues. One concerns the interrelation between earlier and later inputs into a new linguistic entity: Does it involve the dominance of Input_1 over later inputs, or the displacement of Input_1 by later elements? Clearly, both processes can come into play. While a founder language is well placed to stamp its imprint on new language formation, the possibility of late-arriving communities inputting idioms, calques, and grammatical particles must be admitted.[22] Indeed, the very lateness of the input may account for its salience and may even lead to the displacement of earlier lexical, grammatical, and phonological characteristics.

Comparative Cultural Deductions

Using comparative data from other disciplines, one may arrive at the following observations with regard to the variety of processes at work in the culture contact situation. These processes are discussed here with specific reference to the African contribution to Caribbean culture. Such research indicates, first of all, the need for sensitivity to factors of *heterogeneity and chronological change within cultural experience*. African retentions in the Caribbean may thus be categorized as:

1. the result of historically recent cultural inputs, which because of their recency have not been supplanted by other African, creole, or European modalities, but are nevertheless affected by them; or
2. may be based on a structural or conceptual framework established by another or an earlier group, whether aboriginal, African, or European.

A. Both 1. and 2. are syncretic forms since they assimilate elements from other cultures. Syncretism may produce:

i. additional morphologies—elements not present in the original structure. These elements may be absorbed by a group through culture contact with another; even so, the donor group in one instance may also be the receptor in another. Consider, for example, consultation of *orisha* priests or priestesses by non-*orisha* worshippers, on the one hand, and the use of the shepherd's crook and lighted candles from Christian iconography in *orisha* ceremonies; the "pretty mas" aspect of Trinidad carnival grafted onto the "ole [old] mas" component—the former a decorative and colorful extension of European masked ball costumery, the latter African in origin, raggedy in appearance, satiric in emphasis, and using African religious color symbolisms.

ii. parallel morphologies, for example, the Catholic saint and Rada *vodũ* identities of *orisha,* in addition to their Yoruba nomenclatures (see chapter 4, "Religious Terminology")

iii. synthesized morphologies, for example, *bubulups* 'fat' < KiKongo *bubulu* 'fat, ungainly' + E word ending *-ps,* ?by analogy with *oops*

iv. within a given typology, the replacement of morphological elements, their redistribution, and reconstitution into novel combinations. For example, steamed starchy flours are common as a carbohydrate meal base in West Africa. Also, boiled starches are pounded together to constitute a meal base. These two types of foods are retained to varying extents in the Caribbean. But extensions to the morphology and changes of methodology have taken place. In the Eastern Caribbean, cassava flour is mixed with grated coconut and optionally with grated pumpkin. To this spices, sugar, and fat are added and the pappy mixture baked to make "pone." In Jamaica, grated sweet potato, grated coconut, and wheat flour constitute the pap to which sugar and flavorings are added and the mixture baked. The identity of the carbohydrate base of such foods and their consistency are such that Africans can recognize a cognate food. However, in the Caribbean, "pones," being sweet, are eaten as cake or dessert. Such changes may be analyzed as due to (a) the use of high-profile agricultural products in the environment, such as sugar, coconut, and pumpkin (a low prestige food in parts of West Africa), and (b) contact with non-African cultures, in this case European. Europe has contributed the concept of dessert and the salience of sweet foods.

B. Contact phenomena also include fragmentation of various kinds:

v. polyvalency of a cultural label. For example, *candomblé* in Brazil applies to a religious ceremony and religion, while in Uruguay *candombe* applies to a musical type; *kandongo* in Puerto Rico pertains to a type of secular dance,[23] but in Jamaica it is a name for a religious ceremony.

vi. multiple labels for the same cultural item within a given geographical area. For example, *kumina* is also called *kandungo*;[24] *marijuana*—an aboriginal term—is called in Jamaica *ganja* (Hindi), *dyamba, chianga, makoni* (KiKongo).[25]

vii. reallocation of function. Yoruba *akara* is composed of the flour of ground beans, which is seasoned, made into a paste, and fried. In the Caribbean wheat flour is the base of *akra,* to which is added seasoning and pieces of cooked or salted fish. The paste is fried. Process iv. is involved here. With regard to function, in both locales the food is primarily a breakfast meal, but can be bought in restaurants as a snack. In recent years in the Caribbean, it has come to serve as a cocktail hors d'oeuvre also.

C. Contact situations also give rise to new cultural items and behaviors. These may be:

viii. inspired by or patterned after features peculiar to artifacts, habits, or concepts within one or more cultures in the environment. Trinidad steelband is a case in point. It was developed out of the percussive emphasis in African music and instrumentation. In addition, the concept of an orchestral morphology based on the same instrument sectionalized into pieces at differing pitch levels has many African precedents, and the orchestra incorporates a cognate of the African gong-gong as a metronome. But the instrument itself is neither African nor European. In recent years European traps have been added to the orchestra.

ix. entirely new and outside the previous experience of the community. The satellite dish and the computer are cases in point with respect to Caribbean communities.

Some of the instances of syncretism and bifurcation as well as the factors of chronology and simultaneity may be elaborated by reference to Jamaican *kumina* and Trinidad *orisha,* calypso, and *bɛlɛ. Kumina* is an ancestrally focused religious ceremony and belief system practiced, apparently since the latter part of the nineteenth century, by the Congo and their descendants. It appears, therefore, to be a recent cultural input and utilizes a Congo cosmology and sung liturgy. But its name (< *akom* 'possession' + *ana* 'ancestors'), its drum rhythms, and oral traditions of Maroon-Congo fraternal relations, suggest a previous identity with Akan Maroon religious ritual. The latter is still practiced but carries the English-lexifier label 'business dance', 'play ~ Kramanti play'.[26]

For its part, the Eastern Caribbean dance form and social event called *bɛlɛ* by the turn of this century became synonymous in certain contexts with the Yoruba and Hausa religious ancestral ceremony, *saraka*. On such occasions, it retained *saraka* religious elements such as animal sacrifice and offerings of food to the ancestors, but it now became an African transnational event, known in Carriacou, Tobago, and Trinidad as 'nation dance'. Such a *bɛlɛ* event was an outgrowth of originally ethnic-based socioreligious ritual. It later gave way in some situations to a fully creole dance form and secular occasion. However, all form and function layers could coexist simultaneously in a geographical locale.

In the case of Trinidad's calypso (originally *kaiso,* a word of Efik/ Kalabari provenience), it would appear that in the melodic line and rhythm of some early nineteenth-century performers, it manifested Senegambian influence. But later African adstrates have been the Congo-Kimbundu *kalinda,* Yoruba *orisha* chants, and Efik/Ibibio/ Igbo 2/2 staccato rhythms, not to mention the input of Portuguese chording, Latin American rhythms and tempo, and of African-American popular melody. A calypsonian may use either of these adstrates as a dominant form or elect to blend them. But can we find evidence any longer of its earliest layer? Was that earliest form itself monolithic? Or may it not have evinced different styles according to the ethnic provenience of its singers and in keeping with various song types even within the same ethnic culture? Has not the form itself changed radically and periodically, with certain news, satiric, and entertainment functions remaining constant? All the same, if an earlier function such as lament now seems incongruous, functional change has certainly affected this artistic act as well.[27]

What we are dealing with is the dialectical relationship between dynamism and homeostasis—in nature, human society, and culture. Dynamism suggests the capacity of an entity to generate new ideas, new institutions, new speech forms; on the other hand, homeostasis allows a community to absorb new features while retaining enough of its conventions to allow the community to recognize itself as the same as, or similar to, what it was before it admitted innovation. This is why innovation tends to carry the germ of some precedent. So the form-meaning-function correspondence between the old and the new cannot match exactly, and thus would be an inadmissible requirement for genetic relationship to be acknowledged.

Language Genesis: The Centripetal Model

The other conceptual issue raised by the relationship of TY to Trinidad creoles concerns the appropriateness of a hierarchical model of language genesis. This model has arisen from the historical recency (and therefore relatively detailed documentation) of European maritime trade and African slavery, together with the unequal power relations thus engendered. These particular circumstances have, for better and for worse, laid their stamp on analyses of the process of creole language formation and acquisition, and of language creation and learning in general. The debate over creole language genesis has been dominated by reference to the relationship of the creole to its *substrate* and *superstrate*—hierarchical terms which seem to me misleading and unhelpful in the understanding of linguistic and cultural synthetic (creolization) processes.

The most consensual definitions of *substrate* and *superstrate* concern inferiority and superiority in sociopolitical and economic power relationships.[28] While these relationships accord with the historical realities under which creoles were formed, the term *superstrate* carries the implication that it is more important than the *substrate* as regards attention merited, more powerful in terms of influence, and structurally better—notions that once openly bedeviled the literature on creolization, but that still inform the subtext of the debate.

In addition, the concept of *a* substrate and *a* superstrate with reference to any one creole or group of creoles suggests monolithic uniformity within each stratum, a concept that belies the linguistic reality of synchronic variability.[29] Furthermore, the notion of a target language—the superstrate, of course!—implies that the language community in question shares a consensus as to what homogeneous language they aim to approach and command. The reality, on the other hand, is far more varied: differing sectors of the language community resist or, on the other hand, desire achievement of such a goal. Yet the ideological assumption within creolistics has tended toward an exclusively unidirectional ("upward") flow of cultural attraction.

But if even one were to go along with the notion of a "substrate" language, one would also need to take cognizance of the fact that any one speech community contains within it not one substrate, but several. In the context of Caribbean social history, any one locality would have hosted speakers of more than one African language (not to mention class and occupational and other jargons, which are capable of making tremendous inroads into mainstream art and speech forms). This is not to deny the usefulness of identifying the preponderant African ethnicities in specific locales at particular periods with a view to gauging more concretely the impact of a particular African mother tongue on the creole that evolved there. But there are at least four factors that undercut, or at least qualify, the appearance of certainty about this suggested precondition for positing African linguistic influence.

The first and most obvious factor is that such information may not be available in every instance, because of paucity of records, their deliberate eradication, loss by fire or natural disasters, the extensive contraband trade in slaves, and the geographical movement of masters, slaves, and runaways during the long slavery era.

Second, considerable controversy surrounds quantitative historiography with regard to the slave trade. While Curtin, a pioneer in this field, is often quoted in linguistic treatises, other historians have challenged or modified his estimates.[30]

Third, African language artifacts are themselves of considerable importance in the reconstruction of Caribbean social history and the determination of cultural (if not also numerical) weight. They provide verbal archaeological evidence of the presence of particular ethnic groups in a particular locale, and indicate by their semantic content the areas of human activity emphasized by that people. Indeed, the retention of a single African word within a particular domain may indicate the salience of the involvement of an ethnic group in relation to a particular activity. For example, *kalinda* in Trinidad, a martial art/game/dance/song, was dominated by Central Africans. On the other hand, the retention of several words of Ewe/Fon provenience on the island of Curaçao with respect to folk festivals and religious belief reveals Curaçao as an area of not insignificant Ewe/Fon ethnocultural influence. This finding is further supported by the tonality and melodic line of certain archaic "Guene" songs known by elderly people on the island. But similar findings also establish the cultural prominence of Congo song and musical instrumentation in the cultural amalgam of Curaçao. So that proof of ethnic presence and impact may proceed from linguistic evidence rather than from historical documentation.

Fourth, as advanced in the previous paragraph, transdisciplinary research into the dynamic impact of Africa on cultural forms in the Americas has demonstrated that one particular ethno-linguistic group did not necessarily dominate cultural domains across the board. Rather, it is evident that synchronically (and also, but not necessarily, diachronically) one linguistic group may have put its stamp on religion, another on a musical form, yet another on masquerade, and so forth. Analogically, then, may the influence of one ethnolinguistic group not be more significant with regard to lexis, another in relation to syntax, another with respect to segmental phonology, another with respect to suprasegmentals?

The same argument holds with respect to European languages. There was no one superstrate but an adhesion of differing regional and class varieties, with some dominating at one historical period and being diachronically superceded by others.

I wish to propose then that *adstrate or donor language is a more useful and less negative, less exclusive concept than are substrate and superstrate.* "Adstrate" and "donor" emphasize a concern with convergent features of languages and dialects, a focus that nullifies the assumption of homogeneous language systems as conveyed in the terminology "substrate" and "superstrate." Abandonment of "sub" and "super" terminology would also modify the emphasis on dominance of one language over another, given that elements of two or more donor languages are likely to be very closely interwoven at all linguistic levels of the new synthesis.

Indeed it is, more precisely, *features of adstrate or donor languages* that need to be identified, since languages in contact would tend not to borrow entire systems, but would borrow selectively, a process that would be even more apropos in the context of the evolution of a new language synthesis. Furthermore, as dialect-based variability within TY and Y shows, and as demonstrated in the analysis of Y syntactic options in relation to TE above, more than one lexical token, more than one grammatical form is available within a given African language.

Deductions Regarding Creole Genesis

We may now consider the theories of creole language genesis from the standpoints of (a) the centripetal model of creative activity and of (b) synchronic and diachronic systemic heterogeneity in language. We need to ask then whether there has ever been just one phase in the very varied, historically protracted, and geographically wide contact areas and situations of the West (including Central) African slave trade, when stability of trade and social relations could have allowed a unique African language or dialect to fuse with another unique European language or dialect? Practically speaking, there must have been numerous local "pidgins" and interlanguages, both coastal and hinterland, only some of which would have impacted on the development of the eventual Atlantic creoles.[31] In turn, the interlanguages developed at the most vigorous trade sites would have moved away very quickly from their most rudimentary forms in order to cope with increasing trade volume. And even this acceleration would have been outstripped by the daily work and social routines on the slave plantations themselves. Such a "pidgin" predecessor or predecessors must have had extremely short life spans.

Is one then not chasing a chimera in seeking *the* original pidgin progenitor of the transatlantic creoles? Might one not more profitably address oneself to the ongoing absorption of African and European adstrates in the evolution of present-day creoles? And, as we notice in the instances of *kumina, bɛlɛ,* and *kaiso,* could structural optionality in creoles be seen not only as due to target language approximations and autonomous formations, but also to variable adstrate alternatives?

Conclusion

The retrieval and analysis of Trinidad Yoruba has profited from some of the available analyses in Yoruba dialectology, a field, however, that is still in its infancy. Certainly, it is hoped that this study will add to the overall body of knowledge that eventually will be compiled on this topic, and thus assist in comparative analysis both within the Americas as well as between African-based and transatlantic Yoruba dialects.

Furthermore, this research has helped in elaborating the presently underdifferentiated mapping of the African-Caribbean and African-American social, historical, and linguistic past and the way in which Africans of varying ethnocultural origins have shaped patterns of thought, life, and behavior in this hemisphere. It also involves a recognition that conditions *did* exist for the survival of African languages and culture patterns on this side of the Middle Passage. The assumption that African languages died out once a slave was "seasoned" derives ultimately from racist premises that dissociate Africans from culture, cultural loyalty, an affective being, and intellect. With minds unclouded by such racist notions, linguists and other academicians should realize how preposterous it is to conceive of any body of immigrants not carrying in their memories and somatic behavior certain parameters of knowledge and conditioned motor skills. From this angle, the attempts to shunt aside African influence in creoles is ideologically suspect, in addition to which it runs counter to observations of African retentive or inspirational influence in other cultural areas such as dance, vocal style, and musical rhythm and composition, not to mention oral literary traditions and religion. Certainly, descriptive analysis of the phonology, syntax, and lexicon of a language used by Africans and their descendants in a transatlantic diaspora setting furnishes us with much-needed data as to the conceptual categorizations and linguistic structures in which they were traditionally programmed.

Both the sociocultural and formal linguistic data also point to the need to approach human phenomena—including language convergence and linguistic change—with an appreciation of multidimensionality and dialectics as fundamental to nature, human experience, and behavior rather than by way of exclusive, unilinear, and deterministic interpretations. Here, we have seen in a microcosm the multiplicity of subjective and objective factors at work in the process of individual, generational, and communal language loss (or recession) and second language acquisition, and this among the very ethnic groups and in the very locations—though in a later time-frame—where the Atlantic creoles had been developed, if not necessarily engendered.

Appendix: Trinidad Yoruba Lexicon in Alphabetical Order

■ *Trinidad Yoruba*	■ *Cognates*
ababo ~ lababo: yodel made to welcome advent of *orisha*; used also as verb	**awóbóbó** (Fon): ululation to welcome or express joy
Abalofa: Eternal Father, King of Kings	**Ọbalufọn**: god who invented weaving; Lord of Speech
aadọọrun: ninety	**àádọ́ọ̀rún**: ninety
abẹkẹ ~ ẹbẹkẹ: chopped or partly pounded plantain or yam cooked with onion and pepper	**ẹbẹtẹ** (Ek): crushed yam mixed with oil and seasonings
Abẹkuta ~ Abọọkuta ~ Ọdọọkuta: a Yoruba town	**Abẹ́òkúta**: southern Yoruba town, meaning 'under (the) rock'; **ọ̀dọ̀ ọkútà**: site (of the) rock
abo ~ abo adię: female fowl, chicken	**abo adìẹ**: female fowl, chicken
Abomi: a Dahomey town	**Abome ~ Agbome**: capital of old Dahomey
abuke ~ abukẹ: dwarfed hunchbacks who live on the far side of the sun	**abuké**: hunchback
abura ọkọri: younger brother	**àbúrò okùnrin**: younger sib male
aburo ~ agburo: younger sib	**àbúrò**: younger sib
ada: cutlass	**àdá**: cutlass
adaba: dove	**àdàbà**: dove
adan: a lively drum and dance rhythm	**a-dan**: that which excites
Adangbe ~ Adangwe: serpent god	**Dangbwe** (Fon): serpent god, associated with the source of energy, movement, life. Christian counterpart: God Almighty
adię: chicken	**adìẹ**: chicken
adọndọn: kalanchoe, TE 'wonder of the world'	**ọ̀dundún**: kalanchoe, an erect succulent shrub
Adosoji: Banyan, St. Anthony	**Da Zoji** (Fon): god of smallpox. Trinidad Catholic counterpart: St. Anthony

adura: prayer	**àdúrà**: prayer
Aflɛgɛdɛ ~ **Aflegede**: Ọya	**Avlekete** (Fon): goddess of wind and lightning. Catholic counterpart: St. Catherine
Afrika: Africa	**Africa** (E)
aga: chair	**aga**: chair
agba: calabash	**agbà**: receptacle; **igbá**: gourd; **agbè**: type of gourd
agbado ~ **agbado**: corn, maize	**àgbàdo**: maize
agbe: calabash surrounded by a net with buttons made to clatter rhythmically	**agbè**: gourd, calabash
Agbemiji ~ **Agbemeje** ~ **Agbwemiji**: honorific of Ósain	**Agbe meji**: two touraco birds, emblem of Ọsanyin's mystical knowledge ~ **a-gbé-ìmí-jí**: supporter of the breath of life
agbo: long-necked calabash; "goat calabash"	**agbò**: ram
agbọn: coconut	**àgbọn**: coconut
agidi: steamed cornbread	**àgìdí**: steamed maize pap
Agido: district in Lagos	**Agìdó**: district in Lagos
Aginju: St. George	**Aganjù**: Shango's knife, one of Shango's insignia
ago: make way, stand clear; water is about to be thrown	**àgò**: make way, clear the way; permission
agonile: house occupant	**àgò, onílé**: permission (to enter), homeowner
ago pwẹnyẹn: guinea bird	**awó**: guinea fowl; **kpẹ́kpẹ́yẹ́**: duck
agurukan: land turtle. TE *morocoy*	**awun òkun**: turtle
agutan ~ **agotan**: sheep	**àgùtọ̀n**: sheep
ahere: kitchen	**ahére**: farm-shack
ai lọ run ~ **ayu lọ run**: a goodwill greeting	**ẹ nlẹ́ run** (Ek) < **ẹ kpẹ̀lẹ́ rọ̀**: you gently support
Aja: a people	**Àjà**: a region and people of old Dahomey
aja: dog	**ajá**: dog
Ajasẹ: Yoruba-speaking people of Porto Novo	**Ajàṣẹ́**: Porto Novo, its Yoruba speakers, the latter also called (E)Gun
Ajini ~ **Ajeni**: Africa, African	**Guinée** (Fr): Guinea, Africa; African
ajo ~ **ajọ**: journey	**àjò**: journey
akakũ: Guinea pepper	**àtákṹ** (Fon): Guinea pepper (*Afromomum melegueta*)
akara: fritter of beans, or of wheat flour and flaked fish; bread	**àkàrà**: fritter of ground beans; bread

akasan: steamed cornbread	**àkàṣù** ~ **akasa** (Fon): loaf of *ẹ̀kọ*, steamed maize pap
akpa: area, locality	**akpá**: side, district; arm
akpata: rock	**àkpáta**: rock
akukọ ~ **akikọ** ~ **akiko** ~ **atikọ** ~ **atiko** ~ **atikọ ganga**: cock	**àkùkọ̀** (SY) ~ **àkìkọ̀** ~ **àtìkọ̀** (Ij, Ek): cock; **àkùkọ̀ gànganràngan**: cock very large
alejo: visitor	**àlejò**: stranger, visitor
alafia ~ **alalfia**: peace	**àláfíà**: health, well-being
alẹ: evening, night	**alẹ́**: evening
alubasa: onion	**àlùbọ́sa**: onion
amala : cassava *kuku,* i.e., cassava flour steamed and stirred in water. Optionally, dried pigeon (*gungu*) peas are stewed and added to the starchy mass.	**àmàlà**: stirred, steamed starchy flour, whether of yam or cassava
ana: yesterday	**àná**: yesterday
anu: mercy	**àánú**: pity, mercy
apekpe: ladder	**kpekpe**: altar, platform, shelf
ara: self	**ara**: self
ara ~ **ọra**: body	**ara** (SY) ~ **ọra** (Ij, Ek): body
ara ~ **ira**: people	**ará** (SY) ~ **irá** (Ij, Ek): people
ara ba ti le: 'asking if you feeling good'	**bí ara bá ti lé** < **bí**: if; **ara**: body; **bá**: HYP; **ti**:EMPH; **lé**: firm; i.e., how is your body, how are you?
~ **ara ra le**: how are you?	**ara**: body; **rà**: INTERR; **le** (Ek): firm, i.e., are you well?
ara ile ~ **arale**: coresidential family	**ará ilé**: folk (of) home
ara le diẹ ~ **o le diẹ**: I'm fair (response to "How are you?")	**ara le díẹ̀**: body firm a little; **ó le díẹ̀**: it firm fairly
ara mle bi: how is everyone at home?	**ará nílé bí**: people at home how? i.e., how are the home-folks?
aralu: fellow countryman	**ará ìlú**: folk (of) town
are: amusement, entertainment	**aré** ~ **iré**: amusement, a play
are: misery, wretchedness	**àre**: misery, distress
Arigidi: Yoruba town in eastern Ekiti	**Arìgìdì**: Yoruba town in eastern Ekiti
arindilogun: fourteen	**ẹrìnlàá**: fourteen
aroye: rice	**arroz** (Port, Span): rice
arugbo: old person	**arúgbó**: old person
arun ~ **aru**: five	**arùún**: five
arundilogun: fifteen	**arùúndínlógún** ~ **èédógún**: fifteen
asa: tobacco	**àásaà**: tobacco
asalẹ: evening, night	**àsálẹ́**: evening, night
Aṣanti: Ashanti people	**Àṣàǹtí**: Ashanti people

aṣọ: clothes	**aṣọ**: cloth, clothes
ata: pepper	**ata**: pepper
atare ~ **ata ire**: guinea pepper	**ataare** ~ **ata ire** (Ketu): Guinea pepper (*Afromomum melegueta*)
ati: and	**àti**: and
aurọ ~ **owurọ** ~ **owurọn** ~ **ọwurọn**: morning	**àwúrọ̀** ~ **òwúrọ̀**: morning
Awari: southern Yoruba subgroup near Dahomey	**Awórì**: Yoruba subgroup, also called Anago or Nago
awe ~ **ọrẹ**: friend	**àwé** (Ek) ~ **ọ̀rẹ́** (SY): friend
awo ~ **awo ama**: ware plate	**àwo**: plate; **ọmọ àwo**: ware container
awọn: tortoise, land turtle, TE *morocoy*	**awọn**: tortoise
Awoyo: honorific for Yemanja	**Awoyo** (Fon): honorific of the sea
aya: aunt	**aya**: wife
ayan: cockroach	**aáyán**: cockroach
aye: world	**ayé**: world, life
Ayira: honorific of Shango	**Àrìrà**: thunderbolt; honorific of Shango
ayo: seed used in now-extinct draughts-like game	**ayò**: seed of Heloptelea tree; game played with seeds of the tree by same name
ayo: goodbye	**a dieu** (Fr): goodbye
ayọ ~ **ayo**: joy	**àyọ̀**: joy
ba: meet	**bá**: meet, be with
ba: receive	**gbà**: receive
baba ~ **uba**: father	**baba** ~ **bàbá** (SY) ~ **uba** (Ek): father, old man
Baba: God	**Bàbá**: father
baba agba ~ **baba nla**: grandfather	**baba àgbà** ~ **baba ńlá**: grandfather
babalawo: *orisha* priest	**babaláwo**: diviner priest, i.e., priest of Ifa
bajẹ: spoil	**bàjẹ́**: spoil
banga: oil palm nut	**banga** (Wolof): small gourd, oil palm kernel
Banyan: St. Anthony, 'barrister of the heavenly court'	**Banyani**: Shango's sister
bata: shoe	**bàtà**: shoe
bere: ask	**bèèrè**: ask
beru ~ **gberu**: fear	**bèrù**: fear
bẹ: be (location)	**bẹ**: exist, be (position)
bẹẹni: truly, indeed	**bẹ́ẹ̀ni**: thus, in fact
bẹmbẹm ~ **ibẹmbẹ** ~ **bẹbẹ rigidi**: largest drum used for *orisha*	**bẹ̀mbẹ́**: type of round drum; **bẹ̀mbẹ́ bìrìkìtì**: stout *bẹ̀mbẹ́* drum

ceremonies; also called *mother drum*	
bẹnẹ: sesame, sesame seeds	**beni** (Wolof); **nyàmọ̀tí** (SY): *Sesamum indicum*
bi: how?	**bí**: how?
bi: if, as, since	**bí**: if, as, since
bi: give birth to	**bí**: give birth to
binu: be angry	**bínú**: be angry
bọ: hair	**ìbò**: type of male cap
bọ: cover	**bo**: cover
bọ ~ **bo wa**: come	**bọ̀** ~ **bọ̀ wá** (Ẹg): come
bọ: fall	**bọ́**: fall (inanimate)
boya ~ **bọya**: perhaps	**bóyá**: perhaps
Bo Zewɔ̃ ~ **Bɔ̃ Zewa**: a healing deity, rarely manifesting in contemporary times; Shakpana, St. Jerome	**Bo Zuõ** (Fon): a deity with control over sickness and evil spirits
bukun: bless	**bùkún**: bless
buru: be bad	**búrú**: be bad
buruku: bad	**burúkú**: bad
but	**but** (E)
chambo: facial scarification	?**gọ̀m̀bọ́**: Ọyọ facial marks; ?**chaba** (Hausa): to notch, slash
da ~ **dara**: be well	**dá** ~ **dára**: be well, good
dabi cloth: red cloth on which kolanut valves are thrown for divination	**dà obì**: cast kolanut lobes for divination
Dada: patron of children	**Dàda**: Shango's brother, a lover of children and art
dara ~ **daada**: well	**dára** ~ **dáadáa**: well
daromi: solemn a capella hymn sung in preliminary stages of religious ceremony; also called 'litany'	**ìdáròò mi**: my lamentation
darugbo: grow old	**dárùgbò**: grow old
de: happen	**dé**: happen
desunu ~ **desuni** ~ **deshɔne**: sacred ceremony in which priest makes incisions on devotee's head and body, and anoints head with olive oil, and with leaves and celts steeped in water. Synonymous with *singbere*.	**désùnu** (Fon) < **désù**: atonement/purification ceremony; **-nu**, matters pertaining to
di: tie	**di**: tie
di: say	**dire** (Fr): say

dide: stand up	**dídé**: stand up
didun: happy	**dídùn**: sweet, happy
didun: black	**dídún** (Ij) ~ **dídú** ~ **dúdú** (SY): black
dię: a little	**díẹ̀**: a little
Dɔmbala: St. Dominic	**Dambala**: serpent god. Catholic counterpart: St. Dominic
drazɔ̃: vigil to start *orisha* ceremonies, during which prayers are said and a capella chants are sung	**dró zã** (Fon): keep [the] night; to to keep a vigil
dubulę: lie down	**dubulẹ̀**: lie down
dudan: young	**dúdán** (Ek): young, glossy
dukpę ~ **mo dupę** ~ **mo dupwę** ~ **mo dupęn**: thanks	**dúkpẹ́**: thank (V); **mo dúkpẹ́**: I thank
dun: hurt	**dùn**: hurt
dun: be sweet, delicious	**dùn** (SY): be sweet, tasty
ebi ~ **abi**: hunger	**ebi**: hunger
ede: language	**èdè**: language
edi: trouble, malignant magic	**èdì**: charm to cause irrational behavior
eyo: that matter	**ènyùn**: that thing/matter
efirin: a type of mint	**efirin**: wild mint
efirin aja: a medicinal shrub	**efirin aja**: *Hyptis suaveolens*
egbwesę ~ **egbwęsę** ~ **igbwese**: medicinal shrub	**ẹ̀gbẹ̀sì**: plant cure for measles and pimpled skin
Egosi ~ **Igosi**: a Yoruba town	**Ègòsì**: an Ekiti town
eje: seven	**eje**: seven
eji ~ **meji**: two	**ejì**: two; **mejì**: two (adj)
ejọ: eight	**ẹjo**: eight
ejo: snake	**ejò**: snake
Ekiti: a region of Yorubaland	**Èkìtì**: region of northeast Yorubaland
Eko: a Yoruba town	**Èkó**: Lagos
ekpo: olive oil	**ekpo**: oil; palm oil used in religious rites
ekute: rat	**èkúte**: rat
elede: hog	**ẹlẹ́dẹ̀**: pig
elekadę ~ **alękadę** ~ **eregede**: pumpkin	**elégédé**: pumpkin
eleti: rabbit	**elétí < oní etí**: bearer (of) ears
eleyi: this one	**eléyìí**: this one
eni: bed	**ẹní**: mat
eniyan: people	**ènìyàn** ~ **ènìyọ̀n**: people
enyan didun: black people	**ènìyàn dúdú**: people black
enyọn fifun: white people	**ènìyàn fífún**: people white

epi: with, also	**et puis** (Fr): and then
erin: elephant	**erin**: elephant
erin: hair	**erun** (Ẹg, Ij, Yag, Ijb) ~ **irun** (SY): hair
Erinlẹ ~ **Eilẹ**: water dẹity	**Erinlẹ̀** ~ **Eilẹ̀**: hunter who metamorphosed into a river deity
Eṣu: "a troublesome fellow," an agent of evil contained within God's Providence	**Eṣù**: god of chance, amoral trickster deity
esumare ~ **sumari**: hair	**esumare** < **è**: thing; **sú**: sprout; **mọ́**: join; **orí**: head; rainbow
eti: ear	**etí**: ear
eto: time, occasion	**ọ́tẹ̀**: time, occasion
even	**even** (E)
ewe: leaf	**ewé**: leaf
ewe kaṣibu ~ **kaṣibu**: leaf wrap for steamed pap; leaf plate on which cooked food is placed	**ewé**: leaf; + **?ka**: fold; **ṣù**: knead; **bu**: bake
eyiya: hair comb made of animal or fish bone	**òòyà**: comb
ẹba: steamed cassava flour	**ẹ̀bà**: cassava flour steamed and stirred
ẹbọ ~ **ẹgbọ**: sacrificial feast for *orisha*, small religious feast	**ẹbọ**: sacrifice, feast involving sacrificial offering
ẹdilogun ~ **mẹẹdologun**: thanksgiving feast a fortnight after the end of an *ẹbọ*	**ẹ́ẹ̀dínlógún**: sixteen (num); **mẹ́ẹ̀dínlógún**: sixteen (adj)
ẹfa ~ **mẹfa**: six	**ẹfà**: six; **mẹfà**: six (adj)
ẹfan: bull	**ẹfọ̀n**: bushcow, buffalo
ẹgan: mockery	**ẹ̀gàn**: contempt
Ẹgba ~ **Ẹkba**: a Yoruba people	**Ẹ̀gbá**: a southern Yoruba people
Ẹgbado ~ **Ẹkbado**: a Yoruba people	**Ẹ̀gbádò** < **Ẹgbá odò**: Egba (of the) coast
Ẹgbaragidi Ẹgbado: a Yoruba people	**Ẹ̀gbádárígí Ẹgbádò**: Egbado people from Badagry
ẹgbọn: elder brother, elder friend	**ẹ̀gbọ́n**: elder sib
ẹgusi: type of melon, seeds of which are ground and made into sauce of same name	**ẹgúsí**: type of melon; sauce made from seed paste
ẹhin ~ **ẹyin**: tooth	**ehín** (Ọyọ) ~ **enyín** (SY, Ij, Ifẹ): tooth
ẹja: fish	**ẹja**: fish
ẹjẹ ~ **ijẹ**: blood	**ẹjẹ** (SY) ~ **ijẹ** (Ek): blood
ẹkọ: corn porridge	**ẹ̀kọ**: corn porridge
ẹkun: leopard, tiger	**ẹkùn**: leopard
Ẹmilalẹ: Mother of the Earth	**Ẹmílálẹ̀**: Spirit in Earth; Earth Mother

Ẹlefọn ~ **Ẹlẹfan**: Eternal Father; Holy Ghost; appellation for the Supreme God	**Ẹlẹ́fọ̀n**: appellation for the Supreme God
ẹni: people	**ẹni**: person
ẹnikan: somebody	**ẹnìkan**: somebody
ẹnu ~ **ẹrun**: mouth	**ẹnu** (SY) ~ **ẹrun** (Ij, Ek): mouth
ẹnubode: *door mouth* (TE); house entrance	**ẹnubodè** < **ẹnu ibodè**: mouth (of) house; house entrance
ẹran: meat	**ẹran**: meat
ẹrin ~ **eerin**: four	**ẹrin**: four
ẹrindilogun: sixteen	**ẹrindilogun**: sixteen
ẹ rọra: be careful	**ẹ rọra**: you sustain body, lit. be careful
ẹru ~ **eru**: slave	**ẹrú** (SY) ~ **erú** (Ij, Ek): slave
ẹsẹ ~ **ọsẹ**: foot	**ẹsẹ** (SY) ~ **ọsẹ** (Igbomina): foot
ẹṣin ~ **eṣin**: horse, donkey	**ẹṣin** (SY) ~ **eṣin** (Ij, Ek): horse
ẹta ~ **ẹẹta** ~ **mẹta** ~ **mẹẹta**: three	**ẹta**: three; **mẹta**: three (adj)
ẹyẹ: bird	**ẹyẹ**: bird
ẹyẹle: pigeon	**ẹyẹlé**: pigeon
ẹyin: egg	**ẹnyin**: egg
fadara: endure	**faradà**: endure
fẹ: wish, want to	**fẹ**: wish
fẹran: love, want to, like to	**fẹ́ràn**: love
fifun ~ **funfun**: white	**fífun** (SY) ~ **funfun** (Eg): white
fitila: drinking glass; long brass drinking utensil	**fìtílà**: lamp
fo: jump	**fò**: jump
fọ: burst	**fọ́**: burst
fufu: pounded yam or cassava	**fùfú**: pounded starchy foods
Fulani: a people	**Fúlàní**: Fula people
fun: give	**fún**: give
ga: be high	**ga**: be high
gbagbe: believe	**gbàgbé**: believe
gbaguda ~ **baguda**: cassava	**gbágudá**: cassava
gbẹ ~ **bwa**: make thirsty	**gbẹ**: dry, make thirsty
gbe: support, succour	**gbè**: support
gbe: take, carry away	**gbé**: carry
gbede: understand a language	**gbédè**: understand a language
gbẹna-gbwẹna: carpenter	**gbẹ́nà-gbẹ́nà**: carpenter
gbigbona: hot	**gbígbóná**: hot
gbọ: hear	**gbọ́**: hear
gbwe: live	**gbé**: live
gele: headtie	**gèlè**: headtie
giga: high	**gíga**: high
gọ: be stupid	**gọ̀**: be stupid

gunyan: pounded yam or cassava	**gún inyán**: pound yam (V)
Hausa: a people	**Aúsá**: a people
hekpa: exclamation pronounced during divination	**heèkpa ~ éékpà**: exclamation of surprise uttered by *babalawo* on recognizing the cabalistic sign made by casting beads or kola lobes; an interjection denoting profound awe and reverence
hubunu: divinely appointed slayer of sacrificial animals	**hobonu** (Fon): sacred slayer of animal to be sacrificed
hũsi ~ ũsi ~ osi: devotee	**hũsi** (Fon): an initiate able to assist in priestly functions
huto: lead drummer in *ẹbọ* ceremony	**hũto** (Fon): lead drummer in *vodũ* ceremony
Ibadan: a Yoruba town	**Ìbàdàn**: a Yoruba town
ibeji: twin	**ibéjì**: twin
Ibeji: Sts. Peter and Paul	**Ibéjì**: patron deity of twins
ibi: place	**ibi**: place
ibu: sugar	**òbú**: salt-bearing rock
ibuṣẹ: workplace	**ibi uṣẹ́** (Ek): place (of) work
idẹ: gold	**idẹ**: brass, money
idi: eagle	**ìdì**: eagle
idi: opinion	**ìdí**: opinion, reason
idile: coresidential family	**ìdílé**: clan-group with common male ancestor
Ifẹ ~ Ufẹ: a Yoruba holy city	**Ifẹ̀** (SY) ~ **Ufẹ̀** (Ek, Ij): Yoruba town credited as site of human origin
igba: time	**ìgbà**: time, period
igbandu: type of large drum	**gbàndú**: huge; **ìgbèdu**: large drum beaten to call a meeting of community leaders
igesi: Briton	**gèésì**: Portuguese, European
igi: tree	**igi**: tree
igun: thorn	**ẹ̀gún**: thorn
ijakato: small bitterish fruit used in *kalalu*	a fruit (Wolof)
Ijẹbu: a Yoruba place	**Ijẹ̀bu**: a region and people in southeast Yorubaland
ijijẹ ~ jijẹ: food	**jijẹ**: meant for food, food
ijo ~ ujo: dance	**ijó** (SY) ~ **ujó** (Ek): dance
ijogun: type of medicinal plant	**ìjòkùn**: type of trailing plant
ijoko: bench, chair	**ìjókó**: stool
ijọ meji lọsẹ: Tuesday	**ijọ́ méji lọ́sẹ̀**: two days in the week
ijọ merun lọsẹ: Friday	**ijọ́ mẹẹrin lọ́sẹ̀**: four days in the week

ijọ mẹta lọsẹ: Wednesday	**ijọ́ mẹta lọ́sẹ̀**: three days in the week
ijọ osi: Sunday	**ijọ́ ìsin**: day of worship
iju kan lọsẹ: Monday	**ijọ́ kan lọ́sẹ̀**: one day in the week
iju marun lọsẹ: Thursday	**ijọ́ maarun lọ́sẹ̀**: five days in the week
iju mẹfa lọsẹ: Saturday	**ijọ́ mẹfa lọ́sẹ̀**: six days in the week
ikakare: spoon	**kakara**: shell
ikoko ~ koko: eddo ~ cocoyam, tannia	**kókò**: cocoyam, taro
ikoko ~ koko: pot; pipe	**ìkòko**: wide-mouthed pot; pipe
Ikọle: "a place where builders live"; builder	**Ìkọ̀lé**: name of towns in Ijẹsha and Ekiti districts
ikọle: builder	**ìkọ́lé**: builder
iku: death; the dead	**ikú**: death
ila: okra; okra stew	**ilá**: okra (*Hibiscus esculentus*); stew of chopped okra
ile ~ ule: house	**ilé** (SY) ~ **ulé** (Ek): house
ile Afrika: Africa the homeland	**Ilé Afrika**: home(land) Africa
ilẹ ~ alẹ: earth	**ilẹ̀** (SY) ~ **alẹ̀** (Ek): earth, soil
ilẹkun ~ ilẹko: door	**ìlẹ̀kùn**: door
ilọ: journey	**ilọ**: the going, journey
ilu ~ ulu: town, city, native land	**ìlú**: town, native land
Ilu Oyinbo: England	**Ìlú Òyìnbó**: town ~ land (of) Europeans
ilu ọja ~ ulu ọja: city, market town, San Fernando	**ìlú ọja**: town (of) market
Iluwaye: Africa	**Ìlú ayé**: land (of) the world
imọle: light	**ìmọ́lé**: light, deity
imu: nose	**imú**: nose
ina: fire	**iná**: fire
inu: mind, psyche; stomach	**inú**: mind; stomach
inyan: pounded starchy food	**inyán**: pounded yam
irawọ: star	**ìràwọ̀**: star
ire: goodness	**ire**: goodness
ireke ~ ereke: sugarcane	**ìrèké**: sugarcane
iroko: African oak	**iroko**: African oak
iṣakpa ~ ṣakpa: white sorrel	**ìṣápá**: white sorrel (*Hibiscus sabdariffa*)
iṣana: matches	**iṣaná**: match
iṣẹ ~ uṣẹ: work	**iṣẹ́** (SY) ~ **uṣẹ́** (Ek): work
iṣu: yam	**iṣu**: yam
itana: lamp	**ìtaná**: lamp
iwa: peas; black-eyed peas	**ẹ̀wà**: cow pea
iwa ere: unspecified type of beans	**ẹ̀wà erèé**: beans cooked
iya: mother	**iyá**: mother, old lady
iya agba ~ iya nla: grandmother	**ìyá àgbà ~ ìyá ńlá**: mother old ~ mother great; grandmother

iyare: room	**ìyàrá**: room
iyawo: wife, bride	**ìyàwó**: wife, bride
iyefun ~ **ifu**: flour	**ìyẹ̀fun**: flour
iyin: praise	**ìyìn**: praise
iyọ: salt	**iyọ̀**: salt, savor, sweetness
iyọ ~ **iyọ didu**: sugar	**iyọ̀ dídùn**: savor sweet
iyọ fifun ~ **iyọ fufu**: white sugar	**iyọ̀ fífún** ~ **fúnfún**: savor white
ja: fight	**jà**: fight
jale: steal	**jalè**: steal
jẹ ~ **je**: allow	**jẹ́**: allow
jẹ ~ **jẹun**: eat	**jẹ** ~ **jẹun**: eat
jẹrẹ: have good luck	**jẹre**: have luck; **jère**: profit
ji: wake	**jí**: wake
jiba ~ **juba**: pay homage, give thanks, bow	**jíbà** (Ek) ~ **júbà** (Ọyọ): give homage
jina: be far, distant	**jìnà**: be far, distant
jo: burn	**jò**: burn
jo: dance	**jó**: dance
joko: sit	**jókòó**: sit
jọba: bring a court case against somebody	**jọba**: govern, be king over
ju: verb intensifier	**jù**: exceed, be excessive; more than, very
juba ~ **mọjuba**: act of reverence; perform ritual to reverence Eshu at beginning of *ẹbọ* and at close of sequence of six days of *orisha* ceremonies	**júbà** (V): pay reverence; **ijúbà** (n): act of reverence
ka: read	**kà**: read, count
kabiyesi ~ **kabiyesilẹ**: expression of thanks during divination	**ka bì iyé sí ilẹ̀**: long live the Earth; we prostrate before Earth
kago: ask permission to enter	**káàgò**: ask permission to pass/enter
kan: one	**kan**: one
kankan: type of dance	**gangan**: type of large drum
ka ti ri: how are things	**kí lo ti rí** < **kí**: what; **lo**: be you; **ti**: have; **rí**: be
kedegbe: gourd out of which food can be eaten	**akèrègbè**: long-necked gourd calabash for carrying water
kekere: small	**kékeré**: small
ke kpe fun: call out to	**ké kpé fún**: call say give/call out to
kere: be small	**kéré**: be small
kẹkẹ: carriage	**kẹ̀kẹ́**: carriage, bicycle
kẹrẹ: type of drum rhythm	**kẹrẹ-kere-ẹ̀tu** ~ **kẹrẹ-kẹ́rẹ-ẹ̀tu**: powder horn, calabash or flask of gun powder
kẹtẹkẹtẹ: donkey	**kẹ́tẹ́kẹ́tẹ́**: donkey
ki: greet	**kí**: greet

ki: that	**kí**: that
kini ~ **nkan** ~ **ohun**: thing, something	**kiní** ~ **nkan** ~ **ohun**: thing, something
kiniun: lion	**kìnìún**: lion
kiriṣa: chants in honor of an *orisha*	**oríkì òrìṣà**: praise song to *orisha*
kobabo: ululate to welcome deity	**?kọ ababo**: sing *ababo*; **?kí ababo**: greet with ululation
koko asa ~ **koko taba** ~ **koko itaba**: tobacco pipe	**ìkòko àásaà** ~ **ìkòko tábà**: tobacco pipe
kolokolo: fox	**kọ̀lọ̀kọ̀lọ̀**: fox
kongo: a small drum	**kọ̀ǹgó** ~ **kònọngó**: type of drum played together with the *dùndún* drum
konkoto: tray with African foods from which children eat after the food has been offered as sacrifice to an *orisha*; also used as V.	**konkoto**: anything used by children at play to represent the worship of the *orisha*
kọ: teach	**kọ́**: teach, learn
kọja: pass, pass by	**kọjá**: pass, pass by
kọkọrọ: hooked drumstick	**kọ́kọ́rọ́**: key, hooked drumstick
kọrin: sing	**kọrin**: sing
kpa: kill	**kpa**: kill
kpamọ: hide, conceal	**kpamọ́**: hide, conceal
kpe: call	**kpè**: call
kpẹlu ~ **kpelu** ~ **pẹlu**: and, with	**kpẹ̀lú**: with
kpukpọ ~ **kpikpọ**: very much	**kpúkpọ̀** (SY) ~ **kpíkpọ̀** (Ek): very much
Kramanti: a people	**Kòròmantì**: a town and people on the Gold Coast
ku: die	**kú**: die
ku: remain	**kù**: remain
kun: be full	**kún**: be full
Kumasi: a town in Ashanti	**Kúmasí**: capital of Ashanti
kwe: earthen *orisha* altar	**kpè** (Fon): earthen *vodũ* altar
la: DEF	**la** (Fr): DEF$_{fem}$
laarin: among	**láàrìn**: in the center, among
lana: yesterday	**lááná**: yesterday
lat': from	**láti**: from
lati: in order that	**láti**: in order that
le: be able	**lè**: be able
le: well (of body)	**le**: be strong
lẹhin: after	**lẹ́hìn**: after
lo: grind	**lò**: grind

lori ibudo: headquarters	**olórí ìbudo**: encampment, headquarters
lọ ~ la ~ re: go (to)	**lọ** (SY) ~ **la** (Ọyọ): go, go to; **rè**: go to
lọjọjumọ ~ lojojuma: daily	**lọ́jọ́jumọ́**: daily
lọla: tomorrow	**lọ́la**: tomorrow
lu: hit	**lù**: hit
maluu: cow	**màlúù**: cow, ox
Mama Latè ~ Mama Late ~ Mama Leta: Earth; Oshala	**Maman La Terre** (Fr): Mother Earth
mamalawo: *orisha* priestess	*mama* 'mother' + **aláwo** 'possessor of divination secrets'
meji: two	**mejì**: two
mejeji: both	**méjèjì**: both
mejidilogun: ?	**éjìdínlógún**: eighteen (num); **méjìndínlógún**: eighteen (adj)
mẹta: three	**mẹ́ta**: three
mẹtadilogun: ?	**ẹ̀tàdínlógún**: seventeen (num); **mẹ́tàdínlógún**: seventeen (adj)
mimọ: holy	**mímọ́**: clean, holy
mo jiba: thank you	**mo jíbà** (Ek): I render respect
mọ ~ ma: know	**mọ̀** (SY) ~ **ma** (Ọyọ): know
mọngba ~ amọngba ~ ọmọgba ~ magba ~ mungwa ~ amungwa ~ omunga: *orisha* priest	**mọ́ngbà**: priest of Shango
mọwọ: marry	**mú ọwọ́**: take hand
mu: drink	**mu**: drink
mwè: I	**moi** (Fr): I_{emph}
Naite: Virgin Mary	**Naetɛ** (Fon): a water goddess; St. Philomen in Trinidad *vodũ*
ni ~ li: in, at	**ní** (SY) ~ **lí** (Ẹg): in, at
ni: equative verb	**ni**: equative verb
ni: have	**ní**: have
ni ~ sọrọ ~ sọran ~ wipe: speak, discuss, say	**ní**: say **sọ̀rọ̀** < **sọ̀ ọ̀rọ̀**: speak words; **sọ̀ràn** < **sọ̀ ọ̀ran**: speak matters; **wí kpé**: say COMPL
nibẹ ~ nubẹ: there	**níbẹ̀**: there
nibi ~ nihin ~ nihi: here, in the place where	**níbi**: here, in the place where; **nihin**: here
nibọju: in the presence of, before	**níbojú**: in front of
nigba: at the time, when	**nígbà**: in ~ at the time
nikọn ~ nukan: alone	**nikọn** (SY): alone
ninu: inside	**nínú**: inside
nisisiyi ~ nisisiyin ~ nisinsin ~ nisiyin: now, at present	**nísinsin yìí ~ nísin yìí**: now, at this time

nitoriti: because	**nítorítí**: because
niwaju: in front	**níwájú**: at the front
nọ: indicates encouragement or decision to choose an option	**nọ́**: sentence-final index of persuasion or decision to accept one of a number of options
nyun: be sweet, delicious	**nyun** (Ek): be sweet, tasty
o ~ or	**or** (E)
o ~ u: yes, I'm hearing	**o**: reply of approval; an intervention registering attention to statement by interlocutor
Obakuso ~ Ọbakuso ~ Abakoso ~ Abakuso: honorific of Shango	**Ọbakòsó**: king did not hang; an honorific of Shango
o ba ti ṣe: how are you?	**o ti se**: you have been?, i.e., how are you?
ọbẹ: sauce, gravy	**ọbẹ̀**: sauce, gravy
ọbẹ ata: peppery soup or sauce	**ọbẹ̀ ata**: sauce (of) pepper
obi: kolanut; cacao	**obì**: kola tree and fruit
oburin: woman	**obìnrin**: woman
o dijọ mẹẹri: goodbye	**ó di ijọ́ mẹ́rin**: it passed days four, i.e., until we see (soon)
oduku ~ ọduku: potato	**òdùkún**: sweet potato
odo: food mortar	**odó**: food mortar
ododo ~ adodo: red headtie, red cloth	**òdòdó**: flower, redness
oge: star performer, sweetheart	**oge**: ostentation, a dandy
ogun: war	**ogun**: war
Ogun: "Ogun gave mankind the cutlass, matchet and hoe on which to found civilization"; "there are 4 Ogun: St. Michael, St. George, Uriel, Raphael"; Archangel Gabriel; St. John	**Ògún**: war deity; patron of blacksmiths and users of metal
Ogun *Bwò*: a woodcutter deity	**Ògún Bois** (Fr): Ogun of the forest
ogungu ~ ugungu: ostrich	**ògòǹgò**: ostrich
ohun: voice; pitch, lexical tone	**ohùn**: voice; **ohùn oro**: pitch (of) words/syllables
o jare: good morning (in reply)	**o jàre**: acknowledgement of a casual greeting
o ji ire ~ o jire ~ wo o ji ire o: good morning	**o ~ ìwọ ò jí ire**: you not woke healthy?
ojo: rain	**òjò**: rain
oju: eye	**ojú**: eye
ojuma: daylight	**ojúmọ́**: daybreak
Okiti: a place	**Òkìtì**: hilly district in eastern Yorubaland
oko: farm	**oko**: farm

o ku abọ: welcome	**o kú àbọ̀**: you are greeted (on) approach
o ku alẹ: good evening	**o kú alẹ́**: you are greeted (in) evening
o ku aurọ ~ o ku owurọn: good morning	**o kú àwúrọ̀ ~ òwúrọ̀**: you are greeted (in) morning
o ku jare: good morning	**o kú, jàre**: you are greeted, I heard your greeting
o kuluwu, ọmọ are Afrika: a greeting for Ẹgba people	**o kú Olóòwu, ọmọ àrè Afrika**: you are hailed, King of Owu, child exiled (of) Africa
o kuluwu, ọmọ ọdọ Abẹọkuta: a greeting for Ẹgba people	**o kú Olóòwu, ọmọ ọ̀dọ̀ Abẹ́òkúta**: you are greeted, King of Owu, citizen (of) place Abẹokuta
o ku ọsan ~ o ku asan: good afternoon	**o kú ọ̀sán**: you are greeted (in) afternoon
okun ~ okun o: "keep heart"; good morning	**okun**: strength; greetings (Ek)
okun: rope	**òkun**: rope
okunrin ~ ọkọrẹn ~ okorira: man	**ọkùnrin** (SY) ~ **ọkọ̀rẹn** (Ijb): man ~ **ọkùnrin** *ará*: male person
okunrin didun: black man	**ọkùnrin dídùn**: male black
okunrin fifun: white man	**ọkùnrin fífún**: male white
okurọ: palm nut	**okùrọ́** (Ek): palm nut with pericarp removed
okuta ~ ọkuta: stone, rock	**okúta** (SY) ~ **ọkúta** (Ifẹ, Yagba): rock, stone
ole: lazy person	**ọ̀lẹ**: lazy person
Olodumare: God, Source of Life	**Olódùmarè**: the Supreme Deity
Oluwa: God, Source of Life	**Olúwa**: Lord; euphemism for Shọ̀nkpọ̀nọ́n
Ologbo: a healing deity	**Oloko** (Fon): god of trees
ologun ~ oloro: warrior	**oní ogun > ológun**: carrier (of) war; **oní oro > olóro**; carrier (of) fierceness, terror, provocation
Ologun: mistress of the sea	**Olókun**: male or female deity of the sea
olu: hammer	**oòlù**: mallet
olubọ: cassava flour	**èlùbọ́**: yam, plantain, or cassava flour
(O)luwu: a people	**Olúwu < oní Owu**: chief/lord (of) Owu, a Yoruba town
olori odo: pestle	**ọmọrí odó**: pestle
Olubambi: honorific of Shango	**Olúbámbí**: master who helps me give birth; honorific of Shango
omi: water	**omi**: water

oni: today	**òní**: today
Onire: an honorific for Ogun	**Onírè**: Lord of Ire town in Ekiti
Oranyan: St. Gabriel	**Ọ̀ránỵàn**: Shango's father
ori: head	**orí**: head
orin ~ **ẹrin**: song	**orin** (SY) ~ **erin** (Ek): song
oriṣa ~ **oreṣa** ~ **ọrisa** ~ **oriṣo** ~ **oreṣo**: deity	**òrìṣà**: deity
Oriṣa Oko: mistress of the stars	**Òrìṣà Oko**: patron of the farm and agriculture
oro: bitterness, trouble	**oró**: poison, difficulty, terror
oro: mango	**òro**: wild mango
orofo: kingbird	**orófó**: type of wild pigeon
oru: night	**òru**: night
orukọ ~ **ọrukọ** ~ **oruko** ~ **oluko**: name	**orúkọ**: name
Orumila ~ **Ọrumilẹ** ~ **Erumila**: St. Anthony	**Ọ̀runmila**: deity of divination, also called *Ifa*
orun: cooking fire	**ooru**: heat, cooking fire
Osain ~ **Ọsan**: heavenly doctor; **Osain Dimolẹ, Osain Kiripiti**: various aspects of Osain; **Old Ọsan**: Osain as cripple and hermit	**Ọ̀sányìn**: god of herbal medicine
Oṣala: Holy Ghost	**Òrìṣàalá**: Great Orisha ~ **Ọbàtálá**: Exalted King
Osokbo: Shango	**Sogbo** (Fon): thunder deity
oṣukpa: sun	**òṣùkpá**: moon
otitan: chair	**otita** (Ij, Ọta): bench, chair
otitọ ~ **ọọtọ**: truth	**òtítọ́** ~ **òótọ́** (SY) ~ **ọ̀títọ́** (Ek): truth
oun: and	**òun**: and
ounjẹ ~ **unjẹ**: food	**ounjẹ**: food
owo: money	**owó**: money
owu: lampwick, thread	**òwú**: cotton, thread, lampwick
oyin: honey	**oyin**: honey
oyinbo: European	**òyìnbó**: white person; European
Ọba: St. Elizabeth	**Ọba**: wife of Shango
ọba: king	**ọba**: king
ọbabirin: queen	**ọba obìrin**: ruler female
Ọbatala: Virgin Mary	**Ọbàtálá**: god of purity and patience
ọbẹ: sauce, gravy	**ọbẹ̀**: sauce, gravy
ọbẹ ata: peppery soup or sauce	**ọbẹ̀ ata**: sauce (of) pepper
ọdẹdẹ: drawing room, hall	**ọ̀dẹ̀dẹ̀**: central corridor of house; verandah
ọdun: year	**ọdún**: year, anniversary
ọdun to kọja: last year	**ọdún ti ó kọjá**: year which it passed; last year

ọgba: field	**ọgbà**: yard, cultivated field, enclosure
ọgbọn: wisdom	**ọgbọ́n**: wisdom
ọgẹdẹ ~ **ẹgẹdẹ**: plantain	**ọ̀gẹ̀dẹ̀**: plantain
Ọgẹrẹ ~ **Ogẹrẹ**: St. George	**Ọ̀gẹ́rẹ́**: honorific for earth
ọka ~ **ọkan**: *kuku,* i.e., cornmeal steamed and stirred in water or coconut milk; cassava and plantain pounded together	**ọkà**: cornmeal steamed in water
ọkan: heart	**ọkàn**: heart
ọkẹn: peacock	**ọ̀kẹ́n** (Ijb) ~ **òkín** (SY): peacock
ọkọ: husband, man	**ọkọ**: husband
ọkọn ~ **eni** ~ **ini**: one	**ọkọn** ~ **ení**: one
ọkpọlọkpọ: abundance	**ọ̀kpọ̀lọ́kpọ̀**: abundance
ọkpware: tray	**ọkpọn ọrẹ**: tray with oblation
ọla: tomorrow	**ọ̀la**: tomorrow
ọlọkpa ~ **ọlọpwa** ~ **ọlọbọ**: policeman	**ọlọ́kpa**: policeman < **oní ọkpà**: owner (of) stick; **oní ọgbà**: guardian (of) compound, enclosure
ọlọran: spokesman	< **oní ọ̀ràn**: carrier (of) matters
Ọlọrun: God, Source of Life	**Ọlọ́run**: Supreme Deity
ọlọrun: plant with medicinal properties	**olóòrún**: leaf used as food flavoring
ọmaleko: window	**ọmọ ìlẹ̀kùn**: small door; window
ọmọ ~ **ọma** ~ **ọmọde**: child, descendant	**ọma** (Ọyọ) ~ **ọmọ** (Eg) ~ **ọmọdé**: child, descendant
ọmọbọrẹn: girl	**ọmọ obìnrin**: child female
ọmọdan: lady	**ọmidan**: young woman
ọmọkọrin: boy	**ọmọ okùnrin**: child male
ọna ~ **ọnọ**: road, journey	**ọ̀nà**: road, journey
ọran: matter	**ọ̀rọ̀n**: affair, trouble
ọrẹyẹlẹdẹ: lard	**ọ̀rá ẹ́lẹdẹ̀**: fat (of) pig; lard
ọrọ: word	**ọ̀rọ̀**: word
ọru: heat	**oru**: heat
ọrun ~ **oorun**: sky	**ọ̀run** ~ **ọọ̀run**: sky
ọsan: midday, afternoon	**ọ̀sán**: daylight
ọsẹ ~ **ọṣa**: soap	**ọsẹ**: soap
ọsẹ: week	**ọ̀sẹ̀**: week
Ọṣọsi ~ **Oṣosi**: St. Raphael	**Ọṣọsi**: a hunter deity; as huntress deity, Ogun's wife
ọṣu to kọja: last month	**ọṣù ti ó kọjá**: month which it passed; last month
Ọṣun ~ **Osọn** ~ **Oṣun**: St. Philomen; mermaid goddess	**Ọ̀ṣun**: name of a river; goddess of the waterway named after her
Ọta: a Yoruba town	**Ọ̀tà**: a southern Yoruba town
ọti: alcohol, 'puncheon' (overproof) rum, rum	**ọti**: alcohol; palmwine—the fermented sap of the raffia palm

ọtunla: day after tomorrow	**ọ̀túnla**: day after tomorrow
ọwọ: hand	**ọwọ́**: hand
Ọya: St. Catherine	**Ọya**: the Niger; favorite wife of Shango; goddess of tempestuous winds
Ọyẹ: a Yoruba town	**Ọ̀yẹ**: a town in Ekiti
Ọyọ ~ Ọyọle: a Yoruba town	**Ọ̀yọ́**: capital city of Yoruba Empire and name of its people; **Ọ̀yọ́ Ilé**, Ọyọ homeland
ọyọyọ: shrub, the leaves of which are used as *kalalu*	**ọ̀yọ́yọ́**: *Corchorus olitorius*
pa: wash (of clothes)	**kpa**: rub, bring into contact
pade: meet	**kpàdé**: meet
panṣaga ~ paṣanga: prostitute	**kpańságà**: sexually uninhibited person
Parada: Ọrunmila; St. Joseph	**Parada** (Fon): god of smallpox and disease. Trinidad Catholic counterpart: St. Joseph
paṣan: whip	**kpàṣán**: whip of hippopotamus hide
pẹkpẹyẹ: pigeon	**kpẹ́kpẹ́yẹ**: duck, goose
perogun ~ *pray* ogun ~ orogun: ground altar, also called "stool"	**kpèrègún ~ kpòrògún** (Ek): *orisha* altar formed by mound of earth; a type of plant found in sacred groves and used as an enclosure
pinu: agree	**kpínú**: agree
pokpondo: white beans	**kpòkpòndó**: *Canavalia papilonaccae*
pọrun-kan-de-bọ: news-carrier, gossip	**kpuró**: lie; **ká**: go about; **dé**: reach; **bò**: come
ra: buy	**rà**: buy
ran: send	**rán**: send
ranti: remember	**rántí**: remember
raṣmi: camel	**ràkunmí**: camel
rẹ: be weary	**rẹ̀**: be weary
rere: good, well	**rere**: good
reti: hope, wait for	**retí**: await
ri: see	**rí**: see
rin: walk	**rìn**: walk
rọ: rain	**rọ̀**: rain
rọra: be careful	**rọra**: be careful
sababo: yodel, ululate	**sẹ ababo**: yodel, ululate
Sa Liọnn ~ Sa Lionn: a place, a king	**Sàró**: Sierra Leone
ṣaṣare ~ ṣẹṣẹrẹ ~ ṣẹṣbẹ: broom	**ṣaṣara**: worn-out palm broom, broom; **ṣẹṣẹrẹ**: broom; **ṣaṣa ẹ̀bẹ**: broom for shavings
san: chew	**san**: chew

saraka: religious ceremony to placate ancestors by unsalted food offerings and charitable distribution of food	**sàdákà** ~ **sàráa**: charity, alms; ceremony of annual thanksgiving or special supplication involving the distribution of food to children, friends, and the needy
singbere ~ **singbẹrẹ**: ceremony in which tiny incisions are made on scalp and ritual ointments rubbed in	**sín gbéré**: cut incisions
sare ~ **sure**: run	**sáré** (SY) ~ **súré** (Ek): run
se: cook	**sè**: cook
si: to, into, toward	**sí**: to, into
si: exist—used after negative particle	**sí**: exist, be (location)—used after negative particle
si: preverbal clause conjoiner	**sì**: preverbal clause conjoiner
-si: indicator of spiritual affiliation, e.g., *Ogunsi*: devotee of Ogun	**-si** (Fon): wife of
sibe yi: to this place	**sí ibè yìí** (Ek): to this place
sin: follow, guide	**sìn**: follow, accompany
siọ: exclamation from spectators during stickfights	**síọ̀**: expression of contempt, defiance
so	**so** (E)
sohun: to over there	**sóhùn**: to that place
soke: upward	**sókè**: upward
sun: sleep	**sùn**: sleep
sun daada ~ **sun ire**: sleep well	**sùn dáada**: sleep well; **sun ire**: sleep healthily
ṣagbe: shake calabash rattle	**jí ṣẹ̀kẹ̀rẹ̀**: shake calabash rattle
Ṣakpana: St. Raphael; St. Jerome; deity that brings and removes "copperpox" (*tinea cruris*)	**Ṣọ̀nkpọ̀nọ́n**: smallpox deity
Ṣango ~ **Sango**: St. John of the Cross; god of lightning and the thunderbolt; the system of Yoruba-derived worship	**Ṣàngó**: god of lightning and thunderbolt, once a king of Ọyọ
ṣe: offend, grieve	**ṣè**: offend
ṣe ~ **se**: do, make, be; play an instrument	**ṣé** (SY) ~ **se** (Ọyọ): do, be; play an instrument
ṣẹkẹrẹ: ideophone suggestive of the timbre of the calabash drum	**ṣẹ̀kẹ̀rẹ̀**: calabash drum netted with cowries
ṣẹṣẹrẹ: broom made of cocoyea /kokoye/ (coconut leaf ribs), and used as insignia of certain *orisha*, particularly Shakpana and Ọsain	**ṣẹṣẹrẹ**: broom

ṣi ~ **pa** + NP + **mọ**: shut	**ṣi**: shut; **kpa** + NP + **mọ́**: join + NP + join
ṣibi: spoon	**ṣíbí**: metal spoon
ṣinikafa: rice; *kuku*	**shinkafa** (Hausa): flour
ṣire: play and dance, be merry	**ṣiré**: play, enjoy oneself
ṣiṣẹ ~ **ṣuṣẹ**: work	**ṣiṣẹ́** (SY) ~ **ṣuṣẹ́** (Ek): work
ṣomele: beat the *omele* drum	**lù omele**: beat the *omele* drum
ṣọ: guard, preserve	**ṣọ́**: watch, guard
ṣokoto: trousers	**sòkòtò**: trousers
ṣubu: fall	**ṣubú** (animate): fall
ṣugbọn: but	**ṣùgbọ́n**: but
ṣugudu: image of clay and sticks	**ṣìgìdì**: image used as an avenging agent, but capable of taking revenge on its master if displeased
tẹ: crush, step on	**tẹ̀**: step on, bend, crush, press
ti: of	**ti**: of
tabi: or	**tàbí**: or
tete: soon, just (of time)	**tètè**: soon, just (of time)
ti ~ **ki**: which, who	**tí** (SY) ~ **kí** (Ek, Ij): which, who
ti: not be (of fact)	**tì**: not be (of fact)
titi: a long time, until	**títí**: a long time
tọ: urinate	**tọ̀**: urinate
tun + NP + **ṣe**: renew, help	**tún** + NP + **ṣé**: repair
ule ẹja: fish market	**ulé ẹja**: house (for) fish
ule Ibadan: Ibadan the hometown	**Ilé Ìbàdàn**: home(town) Ibadan
ule ọja: roofed market	**ulé ọja**: house (for) market
ule oriṣa: church	**ulé òrìṣà**: house (for) deities; temple
ule Ufẹ: Ifẹ, the home city	**Ulé Ufẹ̀**: Ile-Ifẹ, Ifẹ, the home
uluṣẹ: place of work	**ile iṣẹ́**: house (for) work
umele ~ **omele**: the medium-sized drum among the three used in *orisha* ceremonies	**umélé** ~ **emélé** ~ **omélé**: type of small drum
Undo: a Yoruba town	**Oǹdó**: an eastern Yoruba town
vudunu: *ẹbọ,* worship ceremony for the *orisha*	**vudunu** (Fon): ceremony in which the *vudũ* ~ *vodũ* are worshipped
vudũsi: person possessed by *vodũ* ~ *orisha*	**vudũsi** (Fon): person possessed by *vodũ* ~ *orisha*
wá: come	**wá**: come
wangu: pounded yam or cassava	**bángún inyọ́n**: pound a boiled tuber together with pounded yam (V)
wara: milk	**wàrà**: milk
warakasi ~ **walakasi**: cheese	**wàràkàsi**: cheese
were ~ **iwere** ~ **rere**: messenger of the *orisha* who behaves in a childish manner; devotee in	**wèrè**: madness, folly; **iwèrè**: mad person

demonic possession; spirits of the air; (adj) disorderly	
wẹ: bathe	**wẹ**: bathe
wẹwẹ: small	**wẹ́wẹ́**: minute
wo: look at	**wò**: look at
wọle: enter	**wọlé**: enter
wu: attract, appeal to liking of	**wù**: catch fancy of, appeal to senses
wura: gold	**wúrà**: gold
wuwo: be heavy	**wúwo**: be heavy
Yasan ~ **Yansa**: Ọya	**Yansan**: mother of nine; honorific of Ọya
Yemanja ~ **Emanja** ~ **Imanja**: St. Ann; St. Mary Magdalene	**Yemọnja**: deity of coastal waters and lagoons
yeye ~ **eye**: mother	**yèyé** (Ọyọ) ~ **èyé** (Ek): mother
Yeye Ilu: Mother of the Earth	**Yèyé Ìlú**: Mother of the town/ community
Yoruba ~ **Yọruba** ~ **Yoroba** ~ **Yooba** ~ **Yuroba** ~ **Yẹraba** ~ **Yaraba**: Ọyọ people; Yoruba speakers	**Yorùbá**: Ọyọ people; Yoruba language speakers
yọ + NP + **lẹnu**: disturb, annoy	yọ + NP + **lẹ́nu**: annoy, disturb

Notes

Introduction

1. Among such recordings are the Caribbean-wide collections by Melville and Frances Herskovits done in the early 1940s and by Alan Lomax in the 1950s. In Curaçao there are extensive collections made by Father Brenneker and Elis Juliana during the 1950s, and more recently by folksong ensembles such as Grupo Rais.

2. See León (1971) for an exposition on the *libreta*.

3. See Baksh-Soodeen (1994).

4. N was not in fact a Yoruba descendant, but had learned Yoruba from her second-generation husband and his first-generation parents.

5. See Warner-Lewis (1994).

6. Mary Morris, née Thomas, of Balthazar Street, Tunapuna. The street itself was named after a freed slave; he had probably bought land in the vicinity.

7. *Obeah*: An omnibus term used in many African-American locales to refer to sympathetic magic, divination, and herbal medicine. All of this is indiscriminately glossed as 'witchcraft', but in Jamaica, for one, there has historically been a differentiation between good and bad *obeah,* the former—*mayal*—being activated for healing purposes, the latter for destructive. For the interconnection between *orisha* ceremonies and *obeah,* see Simpson (1970: 13–16).

8. T, for example, refrained from singing chants to Ogun lest she become possessed. S waited several years before divulging certain prayers and chants, and only consented to their taping when strongly urged. A Congo descendant had a strong objection to Christian hymns in KiKongo being taped because of the sanctity in which she held them, and only did so when, at her request, she was paid.

9. TY tonal configurations are indicated for the TY texts in this chapter.

10. See Bamgboṣe (1969: 163).

1. The Yoruba and Transatlantic Slavery

1. See Greenberg (1963: 8). The Kwa languages include Igbo, Ijo, Edo, Idoma, Igala, Igbira, Gbari, and Nupe—all languages spoken in present-day Nigeria, as well as languages to the west of Nigeria, such as Ewe and Ga of Togo and modern-day Ghana, and Kru (Krao) and Bassa of Liberia.

2. The Portuguese Duarte Pacheco Pereira described the coastal state of Ijẹbu in the sixteenth century. However, accounts of the inland Yoruba-speaking states and even of the coastal kingdom at Lagos date only from the eighteenth century. See Biobaku (1973: 2).

3. Compare the recourse to "primordial ethnicity" as opposed to the "national" self-identification among eastern and southern European peoples during the nineteenth and early twentieth centuries (Fishman 1965: 71).

4. Scholars derive *lucumi* < *oluku mi* (Ijẹsha) 'my friend' and in the same way *aku* ~ *oku* < *ẹ kú* ~ *o kú* 'you are greeted', the two terms hiving off from the familiar greeting *o kú, oluku mi.* A teasing hypothesis I suggest, however, is that *lucumi* may derive from *alkami* ~ *alkumi,* a term for the Ọyọ or the Ọyọ king used at least by the Gun/Popo Ewe-speaking people along the Dahomey coast (cf. Morton-Williams 1982: 169). By analogy with rephonologization such as Arabic *Al-kadi* > Yoruba *Al'ukáádí,* 'the judge', one might hazard an etymology like *lukumi* < *alkami* < *al 'emir* ~ *al kemir* (Arabic) 'the prince'. Classical and Egyptian [?] is replaced by [g] in Gulf and North African Arabic. There were Arabic-speaking officials in the Ọyọ court bureaucracy by the late eighteenth century. Cf. Biobaku (1973: 1).

5. See Peterson (1969: 250–59); Bascom (1972).

6. *Jihad*: A Moslem holy war.

7. See Olmsted (1953: 163) and, following from him, Adetugbọ (1973: 194–99).

8. Cruickshank (1917: 74) lists the Yoruba subgroups in British Guiana as "besides the Yoruba proper—the Ijesa, the Abunu, the Egba, the Yagba, the Ondo (or Doko), the Oyeh and the Effa." The subgroups cited in Cuba are the Ọyọ, Iṣekri, Ijẹbu, Eko (Lagos), Ekiti, Ẹgba-Awọri, and Ijẹsha (Moliner Castañeda 1979).

9. Smith (1965: 33–34) points out that "at the turn of the present century the representative African cult of the Grenadian folk was a type of ancestor ritual known locally as the Big Drum, the Nation Dance, or simply *saraca* (sacrifice). . . . Shango in Grenada was originally the ritual of certain closed communities of Africans and their descendants at Munich, Concorde, and La Mode. Over 1,000 of these Africans came from Ijesha in Yorubaland in 1849 after slavery had been abolished. . . . Within these communities, Yoruba was the spoken language, and numerous elements of Yoruba culture were preserved, including kinship elements, and the basic concepts and rites of Yoruba polytheism." Significantly too, it is an annual

ancestral rite which distinguishes the religious practice of Yoruba in Jamaica—the *ẹtu* 'sacrifice/atonement', while in British Guiana, it was the *s'iku* < *isinku* 'burial'. Cf. Cruickshank (1917: 78).

10. These deities were, however, known to T; see Warner-Lewis (1991a: 125–40). Some Ifẹ deities are retained in Cuba; see Barnet (1961).

11. See Babalọla (1972); Oyelaran (1972).

12. For more on Bishop Crowther, see Ajayi (1967).

13. See Ajayi (1967); Lloyd (1967).

14. See Peterson (1969).

15. Speaking of African descendants in Jamaica, Schuler (1977: 176–77) accurately points out that "even today, although many realize that their ancestors were legally indentured labourers, not slaves, they do not bother to make the legalistic, semantic distinctions of nineteenth-century Jamaica," and therefore "usually describe their grand-parents and great-grandparents, with considerable justification, as slaves."

16. Daaga was a Popo prince, known in the oral tradition as "Langa-langa" because of his height; see Joseph (1838: 259–72).

17. Members of a runaway slave community in Jamaica, defeated in war by the British in 1796, were exiled to Nova Scotia and later transferred to the Sierra Leone Colony; see Hill (1981: 112–13).

18. Schuler (1980: 5) distinguishes between the terms *recaptive* and *liberated Africans. Recaptive* applies to "recent African arrivals in St. Helena or Sierra Leone who still resided in reception depots" at the time of their removal to the West Indies and who were subjected to forced migration. *Liberated Africans* refers to those who actually settled in the villages of Sierra Leone and who migrated voluntarily. In contrast, Fyfe (1961) distinguishes between the Maroon and Nova Scotia *settlers* as against *recaptives*, a general term for slaves freed from impounded slavers.

19. See Kuczynski (1948: 120), quoted in Asiegbu (1969: 31). See also Buckley (1979).

20. For a study of the introduction of African laborers into the French Caribbean, see Schuler (1971).

21. "Two categories of Africans arrived . . . in numbers unanticipated by authorities—children orphaned by the slave trade, and Africans of all ages landed . . . from Cuba-bound slave ships captured by the British navy in the Caribbean" (Schuler 1977: 170).

22. See Asiegbu (1969: 190).

23. See Roberts and Byrne, table entitled "Sources of Indentured and Associated Immigration into Trinidad, 1838–1918," in Harewood (1975: 15).

24. See Cuffie (1963).

25. Certain Africans were delegated to recruit other immigrants. They traveled back and forth between the West Indies and Sierra Leone, bringing supposedly favorable reports of life in the West Indies. They averaged at least two recruiting trips each.

26. See Fyfe (1961: 82).

27. Cf. letter from Adeniyi Williams, to the author, 24 October 1979. The voluntary repatriation to West Africa of self-manumitted Brazilian slaves was fairly substantial and has received documentation; see Verger (1966a), Ralston (1970). An epic fictional recreation is Olinto (1970). For similar repatriation from Cuba to Lagos and Fernando Po from the 1830s to 1897, see Sarracino (1988). Wood (1981: 277–79) refers to the two-way human traffic between the Caribbean and the west coast of Africa.

28. See Schuler (1977: 236–41).

29. See Thomas Peter Norman, Waterloo Estate, Arouca, Trinidad to CMS Committee, and John U. Gammon to same, 4 October 1849. CMS. CA I/020. In Schuler (1980: 92–93).

2. First-Generation Trinidad Yoruba Society

1. Roger Anstey in Higman (1978: 165).

2. *Sobo*: A subgroup of the Urhobo, from west of the Niger Delta.

3. *Moko*: A term for "a diverse range of peoples and cultures shipped from slave ports on the lower Cross River." *Moko* could even carry much the same loose meaning as *Calabari* (Curtin 1969: 188). Spelled *Mocho,* this term is a place-name for sites in Clarendon and Westmoreland parishes in Jamaica.

4. Kanga: Senegambians, but their provenance is obscure. Oldendorp (1987: 162) provides helpful though imprecise information: "Their lands border on those of the Mandinga and the Fula, whose languages, however, they do not understand. On the other hand, they do understand the language of the Mangree, who live deep in the interior of the country. . . . The land of the Kanga is bounded to the west by the sea, though the eastern border is said to be far from it." Perhaps they are Dyula/Diola, famous traders from the city of Kankan in present-day Guinea. See Westermann and Bryan (1952: 40, 56).

5. See Liberated African Register Nos. 75375–84420, vol. 15, 1845–1848; copy of a Report from R. G. Butts, Esq. to the Governor of British Guiana, 23 July to 7 August 1844 entitled "Analysis of new immigrants brought by the *Senator* from Sierra Leone to Trinidad, October 1844," in Report from R. Guppy, Esq. addressed to the Governor of Trinidad, October 18, 1844, Acts and Papers Vol. XLIV. Royal Commonwealth Society Library, London.

6. Copy of a Report from R. Guppy, Esq. to the Governor of Trinidad, October 18, 1844; Copy of a Report from R. G. Butts, Esq. to the Governor of British Guiana, 23 July to 7 August 1844; Copy of Report from R. G. Butts to Governor of British Guiana, 13 March 1845. Accounts and Papers Vol. XLIV. Royal Commonwealth Society Library, London.

7. *Calver* /kalva/ appears to be a syncopated form of *Calabari* /kalabari/, with *v* ~ *b* variation. See also Robertson (1988: 98–99). Calabar comprises Old Town, Creek Town and Duke Town, known collectively as Efik Oboku (*Nigeria Magazine* 52 [1956]: 98). The Efik are one of the Ibibio subgroups. The Kwa and Efut are included among the Efik (Afigbo 1971: 62).

8. Cf. Cruickshank (1917: 74): "The bulk—practically all—of the true Africans in British Guiana are Kongo or Yoruba." Cruickshank thought that there were more Yoruba than Congo alive in British Guiana in 1917.

9. See an 1833 petition for repatriation sent by Jonas Mahomed Bath on behalf of Trinidad Mandingo to the King of England. "The petition is wholly the composition of these people, and was accompanied by a letter in Arabic to the King. . . ." Letter to the Editor, *The Glasgow Courier,* reprinted in the *Port-of-Spain Gazette,* 10 September 1833. C.O. 300/3, P.R.O. Cf. Warner (1967: 48–49); Campbell (1974); cf. also the activities of the Emir Samba Makumba in ransoming Mandingo slave arrivals in Trinidad in Truman, Jackson, and Longstreth (1844: 108–12).

10. Pronounced /ɔlɔ/ in Trinidad.

11. "When Sierra Leone administrators and West Indian emigration officials referred to the Kru in the 1840s and 1850s they meant three main groups on the coast of modern Liberia[:] . . . the Bassa (and kindred De), Grebo, and Krao (Kru)" (Schuler 1980: 126 fn. 13).

12. "For the English on the Gold Coast, Chamba simply meant any slaves brought down from the region north of Ashanti, or anyone speaking one of the Gur languages" (Curtin 1969: 187). The Gurunsi are a people in the north of present-day Ghana and in Upper Volta.

13. *Popo*: A subgroup of the Ewe people resident between Cotonou and Badagry. Also called *Gun, Gunu, Gu,* and *Alada* (Westermann 1930: 197–98).

14. Comparative figures for 1861 are given in the 1891 Census of Trinidad and Tobago.

15. In the nineteenth century the Portuguese were, however, sociologically nonwhite.

16. Under the Crown Colony system, political and economic authority resided in London rather than in a locally elected legislature.

17. Lord Harris to Earl Grey, February 1848, quoted in de Verteuil (1858: 376).

18. See Peterson (1969: 163–64).

19. See also de Verteuil (1858: 322). Wood (1981: 274) estimates that of some 1,000 to 1,200 Kru in British Guiana, Trinidad, and Jamaica during the 1840s and '50s, about 150 settled in Trinidad, but one feels that so small a group could hardly have merited the notice of administrators and commentators and left folk memory of their existence over a hundred years later.

20. P. Keenan, Report on the State of Education in Trinidad, 1869. Sect. 60, pp. 18–19 quoted in Cuffie (1963: 70).

21. Return of Prisoners for 1852. C.O. 295/181. Quoted in Cuffie (1963: 16).

22. Cf. Clarke (1843: 27–28): "The desire to live separately is strongly manifested by the liberated Africans." Towns and hamlets were therefore named after tribal groupings.

23. The term *maroon* implies deliberate escape from socioeconomic domination and was a common response of slaves to their loss of freedom. In the British Caribbean, the best-organized militant maroon colonies were to be found in Jamaica, but there was also a maroon settlement in Grenada; see Carew (1985: 104, 116).

24. Sesame was also called by the Wolof term *bɛnɛ* (though one notes *beni,* perhaps a loan word, in *A Dictionary of the Yoruba Language* [1959: 239]) or the French Creole *žižiwi*. It is still used as an offering to Shakpana and Osain. For its culinary use, see de Verteuil (1858: 273) and Bascom (1951b: 43). For Guinea pepper (*Aframomum melegueta*), see de Verteuil (1858: 274) and Bascom (1951b: 48).

25. See *The Chronicle,* 17 October 1871 and 30 March 1877, as well as Underhill (1862: 25).

26. Collens goes on to identify "these same slaves" with an 1805 insurrection, which is an inconsistency.

27. See Raymond, n.d. She refers to the site as the "Yoruba Cemetery." An informant of Cocorite stated that the land had been jointly purchased by the interrelated Salandy, Marcano, and Vanderpool families.

28. These rituals include anointing of the corpse with oils, depositing items in the coffin representative of the religious status or secular proclivity of the deceased and, to honor a *mọngba,* the rupture of a drum-head and the interment of the drum.

29. See song no. 79, entitled "Caratal," in Warner-Lewis (1994).

30. Yury O. Zhluktenko, *Movni Kontakty,* University of Kiev, 1966: 62. Quoted in Shaffer (1979: 372).

31. Interestingly, T substituted *market* for *San Fernando*—the largest town in south Trinidad—when translating a sentence into Yoruba.

32. Ayò: A game somewhat like dominoes, with the greenish-gray seeds of the *ayò* tree (*Heloptelea grandis*) serving as tabs. The game is commonly known by the Twi name of *warri* throughout the West Indian islands. It is particularly vibrant in Antigua; cf. Zaslavsky (1979: 116–36).

33. As reiterated by several informants, the beaded calabash was the instrument peculiar to the Ẹgbado, and which they used rather than leather-headed drums.

34. In respect of Sierra Leone, Clarke (1843: 37, 40) observed: "The liberated Africans very frequently meet at one another's houses, where groups of merry people spend their time in conversation, carried on amidst heavy peals of laughter, amazing vociferation, volubility, and gaiety. This prattling chit-chat is often prolonged for hours together, and is so seducing that they separate with reluctance. Occasionally they entertain each other

with droll tales, or the wonderful powers of some witch-man. . . . [S]uch liberated Africans as have arrived together . . . as Slaves, contract an eternal friendship, which is beautifully displayed in their coming from great distances to attend one another's funerals."

35. *Headman* is equivalent to S's *ọlọran,* the term she used ascriptively for Dr. Eric Williams, leader of government.

36. *Èsúsú*: a fund to which members contribute and from which each draws the total in rotation; see Bascom 1967: 27. In various parts of the West Indies, this institution is known as *susu* (Trinidad), *pardner* (Jamaica), *box* (Guyana), *sam* (Curaçao), *meeting* (Barbados); see Barrow (1978: 32–40). As regards the operation of the *èsúsú* in relation to trade, Clarke (1843: 40) writes: "The Akoos, who form a great proportion of the liberated Africans, are pre-eminently distinguished for their love of trading, and occasionally amass large sums. . . . From their frugal and industrious habits, the Akoos are called the African Jews. They club together their money to purchase European commodities, which they most perseveringly hawk about the streets of Free Town, and in the villages."

37. See Higman (1978: 171).

38. See Guppy, Royal Franchise Commission 1888.

39. See Carr (1953).

40. Even in differing cultural circumstances, the maternal influence on the language learning process of children has been noted; cf. Haugen (1972: 15).

41. See Beckles (1984).

42. "In 1879 there were . . . as many as 24,000 smallholders of all races with under twenty acres, mostly in cocoa" and about 18,000 peasant proprietors holding between five and twenty acres. West India Royal Commission 1897. Report and Evidence, Cmd. 8565, 8566, 8567. Evidence of C. Leotaud and J. G. de Gannes. In Brereton (1979: 139).

43. Cf. the advice of Ivan Morton, the teacher/politician, to his fellow villagers in Lovelace (1986: 13): "We can't be white, but we can act white."

44. The KiKongo word *malong* 'fellow countryman' was extended to mean 'shipmate'. The word passed into Fr. Cr. See Thomas (1969: 21). A comparable term among the Indians of Trinidad was *jahaji bhai* 'fellow traveler'. See Haraksingh (1985: 160).

45. Brereton's statement is based upon the evidence of Emmanuel Lazare in Royal Franchise Commission 1888.

46. Report of the Inspector of Schools for 1881–1882, *Trinidad Royal Gazette,* 11 October 1882.

47. "The whole machinery of the law and law-enforcement was almost exclusively concerned with lower class persons." "Crimes" included: squatting on Crown lands; defaulting on mortgages; failure to pay hut tax and animal taxes, particularly as they related to donkeys and beasts of

burden essential in a subsistence agricultural economy, and to dogs used for hunting; predial larceny from estates; drum-beating at unauthorized hours; the practice of *obeah* (Brereton 1979: 152–61).

48. From "O Dreams O Destinations" in Brathwaite (1965).

49. Noninteractive language use; see Gorman (1971: 201 fn. 3).

3. Language Attitudes of Second- and Third-Generation Africans

1. The Jamaica-based Africans believed that "Jamaica nigger man da hang them; Jamaica pikni da hang them," i.e., that Jamaican Blacks bring about their hanging; children born in Jamaica bring about their hanging. See also Schuler (1980: 82).

2. Cf. Oyelaran (1978: 22) on the nontransference of Yoruba from parent to child among the Aku (Yoruba) of Freetown, Sierra Leone.

3. See Higman (1978: 170).

4. *Mayo*: A town in the Central Montserrat Range of hills in Trinidad.

5. *The breaking up of the three stones*: A euphemism for marital breakdown.

6. *mani* < *man*; an archaic address of respect. *Willie* refers to Dr. Eric Williams, Prime Minister of Trinidad and Tobago, 1956–80.

7. The translation allows for tonal puns on *rá* 'vanish', *ra* 'perish', *rà* 'rot'. *wa* is interpreted as SY *wọ́* 'be crowded', rather than SY *wá* 'come'.

8. Comparable situations are reported with respect to Jamaica in Carter (1986a) and Adetugbọ (1991) for KiKongo and Yoruba respectively.

9. Despite this reservation, some informants regarded the resurgence of interest in things African as a vindication of their lifelong cultural orientation and involvement. Some, particularly those in the Gasparillo area, had been primary informants for the ethnographic research conducted by Dr. J. D. Elder. Through his connection with governmental cultural agencies at that time, persons such as N and some secondary informants had become involved in government-sponsored folk performance competitions.

10. This remark betrays Z's identification of phonology and orthography with respect to Yoruba, a correspondence that is not absolute.

11. There is a small Chinese population in Trinidad.

12. The only informant who mentioned cannibalism was a Central African descendant. In fact, ritual or nonritual cannibalism was practiced by some of the hinterland peoples in the Congo Basin; see Torday (1925: 80–83) regarding the Bankutu and Kwilu among others; and Lamal (1965: 267) regarding the BaYansi (Babangi). In Trinidad it was also alleged that the Moko were cannibals (see Bridgens [1836, introduction to sketch of Negro Heads]), but this impression had much to do with the filing of teeth

among some northern Bantu peoples, which they considered a mark of beauty.

13. See McKay (1933: 236–39) for an exposition of early twentieth-century African resistance to Indian wage labor in Jamaica.

14. These social changes include the strengthening of oil as the basis of the island's economy at the expense of sugar and cacao, and the presence of American military personnel on bases leased to the United States by the British Government during the Second World War. For fictional recreations of this era, see Selvon (1952) and Naipaul (1961).

15. See Harewood (1975: 172–78).

16. Earlier folk research had been conducted by Olive Walke, leader of La Petite Musicale choral group; Beryl McBurnie, leader of the Little Carib Dance Group; Alan Lomax, American ethnomusicologist; and Andrew Carr and Andrew Pearse, who had both researched the calypso and masquerade traditions. See *Caribbean Quarterly* 4: 3/4 (March/June 1956), reprinted as Besson (1988). Carr (1953) had also documented Rada religious continuities; Mischel (1957), Mischel and Mischel (1958), and Simpson (1970) had investigated *orisha* religion.

17. See Bascom (1969a: 48).

18. See Lucas (1948); Carr (1953); Bascom (1969b).

19. For a discussion of the incorporation of Yoruba rites and deities in Congo-based religion in Cuba, see Lachatañere (1961a, b). Since the 1980s *orisha* religion, called *santería,* has achieved something of national status in Cuba.

20. Popularly known as Papa Neeza, Ebenezer Eliot (1884–1969) was the most reputed *obeah*man in the island during the 1950s and 60s. Eliot would have been a primary informant had it not been that the lengthy tape recording of his chanting is defective, both for technical reasons and because his voice was weakened through illness at the time (1968).

21. *Chapelle*: French and French Creole for 'chapel'. The term pertains to a sacred room in which chromolithographs of Catholic saints, ceremonial drums, and paraphernalia of the *orisha* are locked away.

22. See Fishman (1971: 30–38).

23. Marcus Garvey (1887–1940) was born in Jamaica. In the 1920s his Universal Negro Improvement Association was at its peak. Garveyism called for black economic self-reliance, the liberation of Africa from European partition, and the establishment of a united African state. In Trinidad, colonial authorities took repressive measures against Garveyism, though they eventually allowed him entry to the island in 1937; see Martin (1994).

24. Keenan recommended the methodology proposed by P. W. Joyce in his *School Management,* Dublin (1867: 135ff.; cited by Cuffie [1963: 385–87]).

25. Modeste died in the early 1970s. The author had not sought him out because reports suggested he did not have the makings of a primary informant, and language competence was the major focus of attention in the early stages of the research.

26. Many of the champions of the working class during the 1937 and 1938 labor upheavals throughout the English-speaking Caribbean were Garveyites. See Elkins (1972); Post (1978); Martin (1986).

27. The Shouter Baptists are also called Shouters and Spiritual Baptists and are equivalent to the Nigerian Aládúrà and Jamaican Pukumina, Revival, and Zion.

28. The phrase is grammatically incomplete. There is deletion of V_2 in a necessarily split VP, e.g., *fún NP ní*. See chap. 6, 1.3.21.

4. Residual Language Domains: Names and Ritual

1. Glenn Gilbert, review of Heinz Kloss, *Das Nationalitaten-recht der Vereinigten Staaten von Amerika, Language* 45, 218–24. Quoted in Shaffer (1979: 373).

2. See Laurence (1975) and Baksh-Soodeen (1994) for studies on Trinidad place-names.

3. "The Indians originally spoke several regional dialects of Hindi, but the Braaj dialect, spoken in the North-West Provinces, became the most dominant." Other languages spoken were Tamil and Telugu, belonging to the Dravidian, rather than the Indo-Aryan, language family. . . . [The latter] includes Hindi (Warner 1967: 44, 46). See also Durbin (1973) and Mohan (1978).

4. One of the Nago (Yoruba) sites in Westmoreland parish, Jamaica, was also named Abẹokuta because of the topography.

5. Wilks (1967: 147, fn. 9) indicates that the Niger is "known to the Fulbe as the Mayo."

6. [kunuk ~ konuk]. Cognate with *conuco ~ cunuco ~ cunucu* (Span.) used in Trinidad, the Dominican Republic, Puerto Rico, and Cuba to refer to small cultivated peasant plots. The term was also used by plantation holders in the Spanish Caribbean to designate the '(provision) grounds' allowed for slave cultivation on estate peripheries. The term is also applied to aboriginal cultivated plots. For this reason, some have assumed the word to be of Native American origin, but Pichardo (1976: 180) cites another authority as thinking its origin to be African. Indeed, *kunu* (KiKongo) 'to plant' > *kunuka* 'to become planted'. *-ika, -uka, -uku,* and *-oko* convey a condition attained by an object—here the land—in a passive role in anterior time; cf. Laman (1964: lxxii). *Conuco* is therefore a substantive derived from the verb. Because it describes the cultivated topography of land, Congo *Kunuk* belongs in the (a) category of place-names as well.

Another term from Spanish slave culture with KiKongo etymology is *bozal* 'slave born in Africa' or 'slave undergoing "seasoning" to plantation language, culture, and work regime' < *busalala* 'to be in a condition of subjugation or completely under control of others'.

7. African place-names mentioned in Cruickshank (1917: 74–75) are: Guineve Plantation, "bought by the Kongo, but taken away from them for Polder rates" and therefore known as 'Kongo Heart Burn';" L'Heureuse Aventure, called 'Sabakay' < *asa bá okè,* refuge on a hill; L'Oratoire, called "'Oku tedu' which means 'Oku town' < *Oku (i)tedò,* Oku the townsite.

8. From *The Trinidad Royal Gazette,* 30 September 1870 and 19 April 1871, re land grants.

9. Cf. Koelle (1854: 5–6) in respect of Sierra Leone. There is also evidence from Trinidad that other strategies adopted were (a) phonological modification of names in the direction of accepted European names, for example the modification of Hausa *Goma* to *Gomez* (Spanish) in the case of a third-generation Hausa-Congo descendant; and (b) calquing of African names, for example the adoption of *Boney* as surname of a Congo known as *Dai Bombo.* In KiKongo, *bòmbo* means 'fragility', *dai* may be from *daddy* and be used as a form of address, but also may derive from *dàda* 'tremble'.

10. Yoruba names from British Guiana as mentioned in Cruickshank (1917) are: *Fams'ray* < *Fọmọṣire* 'take child play', *Ajimoko* < *a jí mú oko* 'one who wakes takes hoe'; *Famayadeh* < *Ifámúayọ̀dé* 'Ifa take joy arrive/Ifa brings joy'; *Ol-onuraba* < *oní irungbọn* 'the bearded one'.

11. *Káyìndé*: In SY *Kẹ́hìndé,* that which comes behind.

12. Many Yoruba names are subject to apocope of their initial morphemes. In these cases, the name is likely to have begun with *ọmọ* 'child'.

13. *Egúngún*: The cult honoring family and community ancestors. The cult holds annual public masquerades at different times in different towns.

14. *ẹfun* 'chalk' is one of the symbols of Orishanla or Ọbatala, one of the manifestations of the Supreme God, who is also known as a "white" deity, rather than "red" (tempestuous) deity, since he epitomizes patience and suffering.

15. *Odù*: The palm nuts with which Ifá divination is done.

16. *Akan*: Ethnic name for Twi speakers, and therefore inclusive of the Ashanti and Fanti.

17. Cf. Izutsu (1956: 20): "Nothing is so widespread than [*sic*] the feeling that the word and thing are identical, or that there exists some mysterious natural correspondence between the two. . . . The word is the very 'soul' of the thing." See also Ong (1982: 31–33).

18. See Tanna (1984: 66) where, in the story "John Do Good," Master beats the slave John, but "every stroke dat he gave to John, it registers to his wife h'upstairs. John don't feel any, de wife feel every one."

19. See Schuler (1980: 93–96); Rickford (1987: 245–46); McDaniel (1990); and Warner-Lewis (1991a: 28, 153 fn. 18).

20. *Ze vu sali Mawi pɛn de gas, sɛn tatɛ. Vužɛt bɛni*
I you hail Mary full of grace. . . . You are blessed

antwe tut lɛ fam. Zesi, fu zu antwai, beni.
among all the women. Jesus, fruit your womb, blessed.

Sã	*Mawi,*	*mɛri*	*di*	*Dye,*	*pwie*	*pu*	*le*	*zɔm*	*le*
Holy	Mary,	mother	of	God,	pray	for	the	men	the

pikatwɔ.	*Esi*	*swɔti.*
sinners.	So	be it.

(I. D., Moruga, 1968 interview with Maureen Warner.)

21. See Mischel (1957: 49); Mischel and Mischel (1958: 254).

22. Cf. Parrinder (1969: 67): "Anyone who has listened to African prayers must have been impressed by the sonorous rehearsals of divine qualities."

23. See note 2 to the Introduction.

24. See Schuler (1980: 219), Tanna (1983: 51), and Adetugbọ (1991) for evidence of Christian hymns, in particular "*Ile baba mi,*" "In My Father's House."

25. Cf. a similar claim in Warner-Lewis (1977). This subjective interpretation of the creative verbal act is examined in Finnegan (1977: 236–37).

26. Bromley (1979: 38) found that the interpretation of a glossolalic utterance is "not a translation" but "a random weaving together of fragments of passages of scripture. . . . In many instances, there is no correlation between length of the messages in tongues and length of the interpretation."

27. *Bara* and *Arágbó* are titles of Eshu.

28. For the association of Eshu with fire, see Frobenius (1973: 176–77).

29. While this appears to be the prevailing interpretation of Eshu in Trinidad, see T's depiction of Eshu as amoral in Warner-Lewis (1991a: 125–40).

30. See "Yoruba Religion in Trinidad" in Warner-Lewis (1991a: 125–40).

31. See Abimbọla (1977); Bascom (1969b, 1980).

32. Cuban *babalawo* have been responsible for establishing a network of Ifa priests in Puerto Rico, New York, Miami, and other parts of the United States and Latin America. "Sixteen cowries" divination "is simpler than Ifa divination and is held in less esteem in Nigeria, but in the Americas it is more important than Ifa because it is more widely known and frequently employed. This may be due to its relative simplicity; to the popularity of . . . gods with whom sixteen cowries is associated; and to the fact that it can be practiced by both men and women, who outnumber men in these cults, whereas only men can practice Ifa" (Bascom 1980: 3).

33. Some *orisha* centers, by Act 35 of 1981, have legally registered themselves as the Orisa Movement of Trinidad and Tobago Inc. Its head is Iyalorisa Melvina Rodney of Marabella. Another shrine cluster, headed by Baba Forde, is registered as the Opa Orisha (Shango) of Trinidad and Tobago. These groups have been sponsoring religious classes, and some ceremonies have been telecast.

34. A coalescence of several factors precipitated anti-Establishment protest marches by Trinidad Africans in 1970: an anti-European, anti-discrimination demonstration by West Indian students at the Sir George Williams University in Toronto, Canada; the growing influence of Black Power ideology and rhetoric from the United States; feelings of black economic impotence in the island despite predominantly African political leadership; and increasing unemployment, particularly among the youth.

35. See Simpson (1970: 17).

36. See Henry (1983).

37. See Warner-Lewis (1994).

38. See Ellis (1894: 89).

39. See Odudoye (1971: 5).

40. This etymology is suggested by the honorific in an Osain chant rendered by S: *o-ìmí-ìmí* 'breath of life'.

41. Word-initial *z* is prevalent in French Creole, e.g. *zafe* 'things, complications'; *zorèi* 'ears'; *zami* 'lesbian friends'.

42. Catholic correspondences for Rada/Dahomey deities in this section and the section below on lexical loans are based on Carr (1953).

43. In Trinidad, it is recognized that the same deity may manifest itself with slightly different personalities, though no term is applied to this concept, which is similar to the Hindu concept of the *avatar.* In Yorubaland the term used is *ọnà,* in Cuba *camino,* both words meaning 'road, path'.

44. See *Ọ̀gẹ́rẹ́,* song 11 in Warner-Lewis (1994). *Ọgẹrẹ* is, in fact, a personal name for the earth, and the horse symbolizes the chameleon which, together with a hen, are said to have been the first creatures to descend from heaven to earth.

45. These creatures feature in a fragmentary memory of a creation story recalled by T.

46. A case of the phrase accompanying a ritual action—that of throwing out water in order to eject Eshu from the ritual precincts at the start of the *orisha* devotions—becoming identified with the ritual item so used.

47. See Ojo (1973: 46).

48. See Crowther (1852).

5. Phonology

1. See Hsieh (1974: 253).

2. Forms within parentheses in this chapter are not found within the TY corpus. They signal SY equivalents.

3. See Fresco (1970: 171) re Okìtìkpukpa dialect.

4. See Fresco (1970: 33) re Kétu dialect.

5. See Fresco (1970: 144, 152); Adetugbọ (1977: 386).

6. See Bamgbọṣe (1967: 269).

7. See Ponelis (1974).

8. See Williamson (1973: 73).

9. *ilɛ* < *pẹ̀lẹ́* 'gently'.

10. See Stahlke (1973) and Rowlands (1965: 104–5). The latter points to dialect-based rule generalization in the choice of *n* or *l*, with northeastern dialects opting for *n*.

11. See Rowlands (1965: 105) where he notes that a velar consonant is typical of northeastern dialects where others use the labiovelar semivowel.

12. See Fresco (1970: 128ff); Abimbọla and Oyelaran (1975).

13. In one of a sequence of pronunciations, L's *eyiya* 'comb' comes very close to [eeya].

14. S and to a lesser extent O were more demanding than other informants regarding tonal accuracy in the "learner," since they in part perceived interviews as the researcher's method of learning Yoruba.

15. Syllable-timing results from the mutual reinforcement of French and of West African tone languages.

16. Cf. Warner (1967: 117–18). A study of the speech of a French Creole and English Creole Trinidad bilingual revealed that the two S-final syllables in 57 declarative statements had the following intonation contours: 3, downglides; 12, level pitch; 20, falling pitch; and 22, rising pitch. Of the 54 nondownglides, 26 had a high register, 28 low. With respect to Trinidad Spanish, Laurence (1970: 151) comments on "a marked tendency for the voice to rise on the final syllable in statements as well as . . . questions introduced by interrogatives such as *dónde, cómo.*" In general, the Trinidad Spanish intonation pattern is "characterized by its flexibility; pitch rises and falls with far greater frequency than is the norm in the standard language."

6. Syntax

1. The wide applicability of the singular noun is reflected in TE, which retains the low frequency of formal noun plurality in creoles; cf. TE *it have mango* 'there are mangoes'.

2. See chap. 5, 1.2.152.

3. Fr. Cr. *mwè* 'I'.

4. See chap. 5, 1.1.4.

5. Oyelaran (1971: 145) comments on the frequency of this pronoun form "in the speech of older speakers of the Ọ̀yọ́ (including Ogbomọṣọ) dialects."

6. See Bamgboṣe (1966: 75 fn. 33).

7. E *or.*

8. Either a metathesis of *o yó* 'you FUT', or a case of the future expressed with pro-drop, normative in SY Pr_1 formulations. In the case of the latter, *yóo* would be the FUT marker, with vowel lengthening and an upward tonal

glide on the double mora conveying pronominal assimilation to the FUT particle.

9. In SY, the use of the present continuous marker to imply intention has similarly developed. See Rowlands (1969: 62).

10. See Rowlands (1969: 140–41). Oyelaran (1971: 195–96) further indicates the deletion of *sí* in colloquial Y and in the Ọ̀yọ́/Ogbomọṣọ dialects.

11. The use of *a* rather than SY *ẹ* may reflect a blurring of phonological distinctions between pronouns, observable in some Y dialects. Adetugbọ (1971: 204) instances both *aa* ~ *ɛɛ* as $\text{Pr}_{2\text{ and }3\text{pl}}$ in Ondo. Meaning is no doubt dependent on context.

12. Rowlands (1969: 42) and Oyelaran (1972: 14) note that the relative particle is sometimes omitted in Y.

13. This presently unfamiliar form of query in SY appears to have been normative in TY, given the frequency of its attestation.

14. See chap. 5, 1.2.133.

15. See chap. 5, 1.2.133.

7. Lexicon

1. See the section entitled "Language Competence Testing" in the Introduction.

2. Informants testified to the rarity or even extinction of some of the plant life that had provided food and other materials for the "old Africans."

3. See von Bradshaw (1966), Awobuluyi (1972), and Oyelaran (1978).

4. See *Ó mú mi lọ́wọ́,* song 114 in Warner-Lewis (1994).

5. Rowlands (1965: 106) comments on *t* ~ *d* variation in modern Y.

6. See Afọlayan (1972); Awobuluyi (1972).

7. See Awobuluyi (1971b); Ọkẹ (1974).

8. The informant who cited this entry, O, appears from evidence within her corpus to have had antecedents from northern Yorubaland. One of her grandparents was Moslem; she used northeastern *fa* as a song-line tag; and one of her Shango chants was bilingual with Hausa. *Chambo* itself seems semantically close to Hausa *chambas-chambas* 'in profusion' and *chaba* 'to slash, make notches'.

9. The homophony in TY and TE between this term and *Congo* perhaps suggests a perception that the drum derives from Congo culture.

10. These entries demonstrate the mistaken use of *màrun* 'five (adj.)', for *mẹrin* 'four (adj.)' and vice versa.

11. These examples of fragmentary numeration display defective sequence and correlation with English equivalents, as well as nondifferentiation of numerical forms from adjectival forms. Oyelaran (1978: 26) notes a similar decay in the number system of Krio Yoruba speakers: "Even a good number of those who still speak the language fluently either did not

remember the names of the numbers one to ten, or remembered them imperfectly. Most did not remember beyond twenty."

12. *jù* is usually V_2 in a serial verb construction. However, *jù . . . lọ* expresses superiority in comparative structures.

8. Language Recession within a Creolized Context

1. Thanks are due to Dr. Lise Winer for bringing this collection to my notice and securing me copies of the recorded material.

2. Dorian (1981: 116) comments on the importance of resistant personalities in language survival, but notes that conservative linguistic attitudes do not of themselves retard the rate of language change.

3. For pen portraits and family histories of the primary informants and others, see "Elders and Ancestors: Links to Blood and Culture" in Warner-Lewis (1991a: 61–77).

4. Dorian (1981: 24–25) rightly asserts the nonequation of competency and fluency.

5. Compare this proficiency with that described in Jeffreys (1945: 40).

6. Erroneously used as an indicator of time location whereas a discourse-initial frame was intended.

7. A conflation of *náa* and *la* (Fr. Cr.) 'the' with *yìí* 'this'.

8. Fraser (1971b: 351).

9. Joseph (1970: 264).

10. *nka* can be derived from *kíkà* 'cruel'. A syllabic nasal (here [ŋ̩]) may replace the morpheme which converts V > Adj and which is formed by a high vowel bearing high tone, preceded by the reduplicated consonant-initial of the verb. For the alternation between syllabic nasals and vowels, see chap. 5, 1.2.133.

11. See the section entitled "Dialect Variation" in chap. 7. Note also B's grandmother's disapproval of *agonle* in favor of the unsyncopated *agonile* 'permission to enter, householder'.

12. Writing of British Guiana in 1891, when "the number of Africans in Canal No. 1 is stated to have been ninety-nine," Cruickshank (1917: 74–75) remarks that "the main body were Yoruba. They were 'headman' for the Canal."

13. Ekiti $Pr_{3\ pl\ emph}$. (Armstrong, Ọlayẹmi, and Adu 1969: 91).

14. For more on Trinidad Bhojpuri, see Mohan (1978).

15. See chap. 6, 1.5.2. See also the discussion on equative verb deletion in the section entitled "Interaction of E and TY Syntax" in chap. 9.

16. See chap. 6, 1.2.53.

17. See Dereau (1955: 27):

Mwana *u* *ta* *dila*
Child Pr_3 PROG cry
L'enfant pleure

Ngudi *aku* *mbazi* *ka* *kwiza*
Mother your tomorrow Pr_3 come
Ta mère viendra demain

18. This appears to be a concatenation of *yío,* pre-V FUT particle, and *lọ* 'go'.

19. *ulu ẹja* is apparently a concatenation of *ule ẹja* 'house (of) fish', i.e., 'fish market', and *ulu ọja* 'town (of) market', i.e., 'market town'. For the semantic convergence of 'market' and 'town', see chap. 2, n. 31.

20. Dressler (1972: 454): "Uncertainty in the competence of one language does not necessarily result in the adoption of rules of the victorious language, rather it results in free variation including the introduction of new variants."

21. See Wang (1969), Hsieh (1974). See also Malkiel (1964: 180): "At first contact between . . . two subdialects . . . a certain degree of intermingling of rival forms must have ensued, a process which . . . fell short of disclosing any clear-cut prevalence of one mode over another."

22. See the section entitled "Structural Characteristics of First-Generation English" in chap. 9.

23. See the phonemic descriptions of TE dialects C and D in Warner (1967: 67–69). These are dialects spoken by persons for whom TE is not a first language. While the salience of peripheral vowels in Trinidad Fr. Cr. may be generally valid (although the only description of this language—that by Thomas [1869]—is largely syntactic and lexical), I have noted in the TE of S (a speaker of TY, Fr. Cr., and Eng. Cr.) not only the phonemic indifference of vowel length characteristic of such speakers (see Warner [1967: 135–37]), but also a more frequent use of lax vowels than in the TE of the primary Fr. Cr. speaker analyzed in Warner (1967). Some instances of *boy, meet, stool,* and *talk* in S's idiolect were realized respectively as [bɒɪ], [mɪt], [stʊl], and [tɒk].

24. In a complementary argument, Mufwene (1990: 14) points out that markedness in a system can become relative in contexts of language contact, and is further modified by the frequency factor. Here, salience is shown to be similarly modified by frequency in the language contact situation.

25. It is possible that the term *kashibu* derives from a Carib or Arawak (Taino) language. This suspicion is supported by use of *cachibou* in the late seventeenth-century Caribbean, seeing that Yoruba were negligible in the region at the time. Cf. Labat (1970: 52).

26. See Malkiel (1964: 181). In the context of language decline, Dressler and Wodak-Leodolter (1977: 137) remark that "the polystylism of

a normal language . . . moves to non-stylism." See also Bernstein (1964) and Hill (1973); in both, the correlation between low functional load and loss of elaborate styles is additionally associated, as is appropriate here, with routine, nonintellectual, unofficial registers of living language use.

27. See Dressler (1972: 452).

9. Creolization Processes in Broader Perspective

1. Evidence of African ethnic-based solidarity is plentiful: for the Caribbean, see Schuler (1970); for the Bahamas, see Eneas (1976); for Cuba, see Cabrera (1986a, 1986b), Moliner Castañeda (1986), and Mendoza Lorenzo (1986); for Belize, see Bolland (1987).

2. See Bickerton (1981).

3. See Schumann (1978) with reference to the findings of Michael Clyne in "German and English Working Pidgins," *Linguistic Communications* 13 (1975: 1–20).

4. See Dahlstedt (1972: 346).

5. On the one hand, one needs to remember the dialect and stylistic varieties of European languages that were used in seafaring, military, urban, and plantation contexts in the Caribbean. Furthermore, as Hazaël-Massieux (1993: 111–12) reminds us: "Creole exists when the overgeneralizations tested in the exchange form paradigms accepted by speakers of different origins. They need not have the same forms; it is enough that they have a system of correspondences which ensure mutual intelligibility (more or less approximative) and thus a system which tolerates doublets."

6. See Lynch (1964); Allsopp (1980: 104); and Abrahams (1983: 21–54).

7. Inter- and intrasentential code-switching from KiKongo to English Creole occurs in *kumina* songs in Jamaica; from KiKongo to French Creole and English Creole in *kalinda* and other songs from Trinidad; and from KiKongo to Spanish Creole in *lumbalú* dirges from Colombia. For the latter, see Schwegler (forthcoming).

8. The significance of systemic variation in language convergence and language genesis is the burden of Mufwene (1988).

9. See chap. 6, 1.5.2. See also the discussion entitled "Interaction of E and TY Syntax" in this chapter. Compare the defiant assertion of ethnic affiliation and difference vis-à-vis interlocutors in the pronouncement made in Fr. Cr. by a second generation Yoruba descendant:

mwe *africaine*
I African

10. A Yoruba descendant in Jamaica, during a 1972 interview, used *soup* in the sense of 'gravy'.

11. The first-generation Yoruba who said this sentence may have substituted [b] for [v] since the latter is nonexistent in Y. [aveli] may thus be an imperfect rendition by the granddaughter of the grandmother's articulation.

12. The speakers imitated through these examples were Yoruba and Congo.

13. Could this be linked with glide insertion in respect of Creole rephonologization of West African labiovelars? Cf. chap. 5, 1.2.12.

14. See chap. 5, 1.2.11.

15. See chap. 5, 1.1.11.

16. This exclamation was popular in the 1950s among popular dance band leaders, and I recall hearing it from calypsonians as they were about to begin a stanza.

17. For the variation of *ní* 'at' and *sí* 'to' after *lọ* 'go', and even their optional deletion, see chap. 6, 1.4.0.

18. *How you?*: A calque of *ìwọ ńkọ́?* See chap. 6, 4.0.6.

19. See Awobuluyi (1971a, 1973); Lord (1973); and Ọkẹ (1974).

20. Ricketts (1958).

21. See Boretzky (1993: 86–87).

22. For English, there is not only the adoption by Anglo-Saxon of Norse *she* and *they,* but also the absorption of Latin syntax and lexis, and French lexicon and phonology. Not to speak of more contemporary inputs.

23. See Vega (1969: 29). Among the names for various types of the *bomba* dance in Puerto Rico are *candungo* or *candungué.*

24. See Ryman (1984).

25. See Bilby (1985).

26. See Warner-Lewis (1991b) for the development of this thesis. See also Lalla and D'Costa (1990: 207–15) for further evidence of Ewe influence in *kumina.*

27. The term *lament* is applied to certain types of nineteenth- and turn-of-the-century calypso by Mitto Sampson in Pearse (1956) and by Neville Marcano (The Growling Tiger) in the Trinidad and Tobago Government Broadcasting Unit's 1972 radio series on "The Story of the Calypso."

28. See Goodman (1988: 245–47).

29. See Hazaël-Massieux (1993) for several examples of synchronous variation in Guadeloupe Créole.

30. Among those involved in historical statistics related to the African slave trade are Richard Bean, David Eltis, Robert Fogel, Stanley Engerman, Eugene Genovese, Ralph Austen, Esmond Martin, T. C. Ryan, Paul Lovejoy, and Joseph Inikori.

31. Language contact between Africans and Europeans, between Africans of varying ethnicity, and between various European nationalities took place not only along myriad points of the West and Central African coast, but also at multiple points inland. Klein (1982) indicates that Angola's status as a Portuguese colony from the sixteenth century gave Portuguese traders access to the Angolan interior, in addition to its ports. Thus, aspects

of the slave trade usually handled by African intermediaries in other parts of Africa were, in Angola, undertaken by the Portuguese themselves. On the other hand, Fehdereau (1966: 22–31) sketches the formation of ivory and slave trade routes in the Congo Basin as of 1600 until the nineteenth century. Coastal and hinterland tribes "organized into a long line of intermediaries transferring slaves from the interior to the coast." The routes "reached a thousand miles up the Congo River and more than five hundred miles overland into the interior." And although "by 1870, no European had penetrated very far into the vast interior country . . . the diffusion of European goods carried European influence great distances inland."

R

References

Archival Documents

■ *Annual Report of the Surgeon-General for the Year 1900.* Government of Trinidad and Tobago. Health Department. Council Paper No. 44 of 1901. Parliamentary Library, Red House, Port of Spain.

Annual Reports of the Registrar General of the Vital Statistics for the Years 1901, 1902–3, 1908–9, 1909–10. Government of Trinidad and Tobago. Central Statistical Office, Port of Spain.

Census of Trinidad and Tobago, 1891. Government of Trinidad and Tobago. Registry. Parliamentary Library, Red House, Port of Spain.

Copy of a Report from R. G. Butts, Esq., to the Governor of British Guiana, 23 July to 7 August 1844, re Analysis of New Immigrants Brought by the *Senator* from Sierra Leone to Trinidad, 18 October 1844. Acts and Papers, vol. 46. Library. Royal Commonwealth Society, London.

Copy of a Report from R. Guppy, Esq., to the Governor of Trinidad, 18 October 1844. Acts and Papers, vol. 46. Library. Royal Commonwealth Society, London.

Copy of a Report from R. G. Butts, Esq., to the Governor of British Guiana, 13 March 1845. Acts and Papers, vol. 46. Library. Royal Commonwealth Society, London.

Liberated African Register. Nos. 75375–84420, vol. 15, 1845–1848. Government of Trinidad and Tobago. Registry Library, Red House, Port of Spain.

Libretas de Santería. Government of Cuba. Biblioteca Nacional José Martí, Havana.

The Royal Franchise Commission, To Consider and Report as to the Proposed Franchise and Division of the Colony into Electoral Districts. 1888. Government of Trinidad and Tobago. West Indiana Library. University of the West Indies, St. Augustine, Trinidad.

Newspapers

Port of Spain Gazette, 10 September 1833. C.O. 300/3. Public Record Office, London.

The Chronicle, 17 October 1871, 30 March 1877. C.O. 300/3. Public Record Office, London.

The Trinidad Sentinel, 8 April 1858. C.O. 300/3. Public Record Office, London.

Trinidad Royal Gazette, 30 September 1870, 19 April 1871, 11 October 1882. C.O. 300/3. Public Record Office, London.

Oral Sources (Trinidad)

Alexander, Simon. Caratal, 1972
Alfred, Maureen. Tunapuna, 1993
Anthony, Lucille. Fyzabad, 1991
Antoine, Camilla. Belmont, 1968
Antoine-Modeste, Jane. Valencia, 1968
Atwell, Uwin. Tunapuna, 1968
Babb, James. Marabella, 1968
Bain, Carmen. Belmont, 1971
Baptiste, John. Tunapuna, 1968
Beddoe, Andrew. Laventille, 1968
Bonaparte, Evelyn. Freeport, 1971
Brazle, Benjamin. Moruga, 1968
Cadette, Clarence. Poona Road, 1970
Caesar, Agatha. Port of Spain, 1968
Caesar, Annie. Tunapuna, 1966
Caldera, Mary. Tunapuna, 1968
Charles, Lucy. Fyzabad, 1968, 1971, 1972
Chevalier, Roma. Belmont, 1971
Coker, Philip. St. Anns, 1968
Collins, Edward. Fyzabad, 1991
Cumberbatch, Angelina. Port of Spain, 1971
Daniel, Ishmael. Moruga, 1968
Daniel-Pascal, Vexillia. Manzanilla No. 3, 1971
David, Eldica. Tunapuna, 1980
Dell, Hugh. Princes Town, 1968
Eastman, Rudolph. Laventille, 1989, 1991
Edwards, Victoria. Moruga, 1968
Eliot, Ebenezer. Moruga, 1968

Estwick, Clementina. Sangre Grande, 1979
Euba, Georgiana. Curepe, 1968
Frederick, David. Tortuga, 1971
George, Estalize. Belmont, 1968
Hector, Joseph. Tortuga, 1971
Henry, Octavia. Arouca, 1966, 1968, 1970, 1971, 1972
Howell, Antoinette. Tunapuna, 1968
Jacobs, Macdonald. Princes Town, 1992
James-Cadette, Ruth. Caratal, 1971
Jeremiah, George. Carenage, 1968
John, Cynthia. Cocorite, 1991
Johnson, May. Tunapuna, 1966, 1979
Jones, Gomez. Moruga, 1968
Joseph, Jane-Ann. Bonaventure, 1968
Joseph, Marcius. Caratal, 1968
Julian, Veronica. Tunapuna, 1968
Laurent, Philip. Tunapuna, 1968
LeGendre, Sandrin. Marabella, 1968, 1971, 1972
Lewis, Vera. Tunapuna, 1968
Marcano, Neville (aka The Growling Tiger). Trinidad & Tobago Government Broadcasting Unit. Radio series: "The Story of the Calypso," 1972
Moore, Daniel. Princes Town, 1968
Moses-London, Mina. Moruga, 1968
Mungo, Lawrence. Valencia, 1970
Nelson, Gladys. Gasparillo, 1968
Pablo-Richards, Mary-Ann. Freeport, 1972
Paul-Hunter, Paulina. Barataria, 1971
Philip, Henry. Moruga, 1968
Phill, Mrs. Douglas. Poona Road, 1968
Pierre, Eileen. Moruga, 1968
Roach, Hilda. Princes Town, 1968
Salazar, Andrew. Penal, 1968
Sampson, Arthur. Piparo, 1968, 1971
Sanco, Virginia. Tortuga, 1971
Sherwood, Evans. Princes Town, 1968
Simon, Ann. Mayo, 1970
Swanson, Hugh. Tunapuna, 1968
Thomas, Athanasius. Fyzabad, 1968
Victory, Cecilia. Arouca, 1972
Vidale, Ma. Bonaventure, 1971
Walters, Gladys. St. Anns, 1968
Webb, Edward. Lengua Junction, 1968
Williams, Alphonsine (Nanin). Caratal, 1968, 1971, 1972
Woodley, Roy. Princes Town, 1968
Zampty, Joseph. Diego Martin, 1968, 1971

Articles, Books, Dissertations

Abimbọla, Wande. 1977. *Ifa Divination Poetry.* New York: Nok Publishers.

Abimbọla, Wande, and Ọlasope Oyelaran. 1975. Consonant Elision in Yoruba. *African Language Studies* 16: 37–60.

Abraham, R. C. 1958. *Dictionary of Modern Yoruba.* London: University of London Press.

Abrahams, Roger. 1983. *The Man-of-Words in the West Indies.* Baltimore: Johns Hopkins University Press.

Adetugbọ, Abiọdun. 1971. The Pronoun in Yoruba: Its Function in Three Dialects. *Annales de l'Université d'Abidjan,* série H, vol. 1, 203–19.

———. 1973. The Yoruba Language in Yoruba History. In *Sources of Yoruba History,* ed. Saburi Biobaku, 176–204. Oxford: Oxford University Press.

———. 1977. The Development of Yoruba Vocalic Systems. In *Language and Linguistic Problems in Africa,* ed. Paul Kotey and Haig Der-Houssikian, 374–88. Columbia, S.C.: Hornbeam Press.

———. 1991. African Continuities in the Caribbean: The Yoruba in Jamaica. Preliminary Report to the African-Caribbean Institute of Jamaica.

Afigbo, A. E. 1971. Ibibio Origin and Migrations. *Nigeria Magazine* 107–9: 62–69.

Afọlayan, Adebisi. 1972. The Predicative Adjective as a Grammatical Category in Yoruba. In *The Yoruba Verb Phrase,* ed. Ayọ Bamgboṣe, 73–102. Ibadan: Ibadan University Press.

Ajayi, Ade. 1967. Samuel Ajayi Crowther of Oyo. In *Africa Remembered,* ed. Philip Curtin, 289–316. Madison: University of Wisconsin Press.

Akintoye, S. A. 1971. *Revolution and Power Politics in Yorubaland, 1840–1893: Ibadan Expansion and the Rise of Ekiti-parapo.* London: Longman.

Alleyne, Mervyn. 1971. Acculturation and the Cultural Matrix of Creolization. In *Pidginization and Creolization of Languages,* ed. Dell Hymes, 169–86. Cambridge: Cambridge University Press.

———. 1980. *Comparative Afro-American: An Historical-Comparative Study of English-based Afro-American Dialects of the New World.* Ann Arbor, Mich.: Karoma Press.

———. 1988. *Roots of Jamaican Culture.* London: Pluto Press/Karia Press.

Alleyne, Mervyn, and Beverley Hall-Alleyne. 1982. Language Maintenance and Language Death in the Caribbean. *Caribbean Quarterly* 28(4): 52–59.

Allsopp, Richard. 1977. Africanisms in the Idiom of Caribbean English. In *Language and Linguistic Problems in Africa,* ed. Paul Kotey and Haig Der-Houssikian, 169–86. Columbia, S.C.: Hornbeam Press.

———. 1980. How Creole Lexicons Expand. In *Theoretical Orientations in Creole Studies,* ed. Albert Valdman and Arnold Highfield, 89–108. New York: Academic Press.

Anon. 1956. Calabar. *Nigeria Magazine* 52: 70–98.

Armstrong, R. G., Val Ọlayemi, and Babatunde Adu. 1969. Ekiti Traditional Dirge of Lt. Colonel Adekunle Fajuyi's Funeral. *African Notes* 5(2): 63–94.

Asiegbu, Johnson. 1969. *Slavery and the Politics of Liberation, 1787–1861.* London: Longman.

Awobuluyi, Ọladele. 1971a. "Splitting Verbs" in Yoruba. *Annales de l'Université d'Abidjan,* série H, vol. 1, 151–64.

———. 1971b. On the Status of Prepositions. *Journal of West African Languages* 8: 101–11.

———. 1972. Predicative Adjectives in Yoruba: A Critique. In *The Yoruba Verb Phrase,* ed. Ayọ Bamgboṣe, 103–18. Ibadan: Ibadan University Press.

———. 1973. The Modifying Serial Construction: A Critique. *Studies in African Linguistics* 4(1): 87–111.

———. 1974. Some Traditional Yoruba "Adverbs" in True Perspective. Paper presented at the Linguistics and Nigerian Languages Seminar, University of Ibadan.

———. 1975. On "the Subject Concord Prefix" in Yoruba. *Studies in African Linguistics* 6(3): 215–38.

Babalọla, Adeboye. 1972. The Growth of the Yoruba Language (1770–1970): Problems Encountered and Solutions Essayed. Paper presented to the Tenth West African Languages Congress, University of Ghana.

Baker, Philip. 1993. Assessing the African Contribution to French-based Creoles. In *Africanisms in Afro-American Language Varieties,* ed. Salikoko Mufwene, 123–55. Athens: University of Georgia.

Baksh-Soodeen, Rawwida. 1994. A Historical Perspective on the Lexicon of Trinidadian English. Ph.D. diss., University of the West Indies, Trinidad.

Bamgboṣe, Ayọ. 1966. *A Grammar of Yoruba.* Cambridge: Cambridge University Press.

———. 1967. Vowel Harmony in Yoruba. *Journal of African Languages* 6(3): 268–73.

———. 1969. Yoruba. In *Twelve Nigerian Languages,* ed. Elizabeth Dunstan, 163–71. London: Longman.

Barnet, Miguel. 1961. La religión de los Yoruba y sus dioses. *Actas de Folklore* 1(1): 9–12.

Barrow, Christine. 1978. Meetings: A Group Savings Arrangement in Barbados. *African Studies Association of the West Indies Bulletin* 8: 32–40.

Bascom, William. 1951a. Yoruba Food. *Africa* 21(1): 41–53.

———. 1951b. Yoruba Cooking. *Africa* 21(2): 125–37.

———. 1969a. *The Yoruba of Southwestern Nigeria.* New York: Holt, Rinehart, and Winston.

———. 1969b. *Ifa Divination: Communication between Gods and Men in West Africa.* Bloomington: Indiana University Press.

———. 1972. *Shango in the New World.* Austin: University of Texas Press.

———. 1980. *Sixteen Cowries: Yoruba Divination from Africa to the New World.* Bloomington: Indiana University Press.

Beckles, Hilary. 1984. The Literate Few: An Historical Sketch of the Slavery Origins of Black Elites in the English West Indies. *Caribbean Journal of Education* 11(1): 19–35.

Bennett, Patrick, and Jan Sterk. 1977. South Central Niger-Congo: a Reclassification. *Studies in African Linguistics* 8(3): 241–73.

Bernstein, Basil. 1964. Elaborated and Restricted Codes: Their Social Origins and Some Consequences. *American Anthropologist* 66(6, pt. 2): 55–69.

Besson, Gerard, ed. 1988. *Trinidad Carnival.* Port of Spain: Paria.

Bickerton, Derek. 1981. *Roots of Language.* Ann Arbor, Mich.: Karoma Press.

Bilby, Kenneth. 1983. How the Older Heads Talk: A Jamaican Maroon Spirit Possession Language and Its Relationship to the Creoles of Surinam and Sierra Leone. *Nieuwe West-Indische Gids* 57 (1 and 2): 37–88.

———. 1985. The Holy Herb: Notes on the Background of Cannabis in Jamaica. *Caribbean Quarterly,* monograph, 82–95.

Bilby, Kenneth, and Fi-kiau Kia Bunseki. 1983. *Kumina: A Kongo-based Tradition in the New World.* Brussels: Centre d'Étude et de Documentation Africaines.

Biobaku, Saburi. 1973. Introduction. In *Sources of Yoruba History,* ed. Saburi Biobaku, 1–8. Oxford: Oxford University Press.

Bolland, O. Nigel. 1987. African Continuities and Creole Culture in Belize Town in the Nineteenth Century. *African-Caribbean Institute of Jamaica Research Review* 2, Afro-Caribbean Villages in Historical Perspective, ed. Charles Carnegie, 63–82.

Boretzky, Norbert. 1993. The Concept of Rule, Rule Borrowing, and Substrate Influence in Creole Languages. In *Africanisms in Afro-American Language Varieties,* ed. Salikoko Mufwene, 74–92. Athens: University of Georgia.

Bowen, T. J. 1858. *Grammar and Dictionary of the Yoruba Language.* Washington: Smithsonian Contributions to Knowledge 10:4.

Brathwaite, Edward. 1965. *Rights of Passage.* Oxford: Oxford University Press.

Brenneker, Paul Fr., and Elis Juliana. 1957. *The Zinkinzá Collection.* Institute of Archeology and Anthropology of the Netherlands Antilles, Curaçao.

Brereton, Bridget. 1972. A Social History of Trinidad, 1870–1900. Ph.D. diss., University of the West Indies.

———. 1979. *Race Relations in Colonial Trinidad, 1870–1900.* Cambridge: Cambridge University Press.

Bridgens, Richard. c. 1836. *West India Scenery, with Illustrations of Negro Character, the Process of Making Sugar etc. from Sketches Taken during a Voyage to, and Residence of Seven Years in, the Island of Trinidad.* London: Robert Jennings.

Bromley, Elise. 1979. A Study of the Glossolalia Phenomenon in Jamaica in its Religious Context. Caribbean Studies Project, University of the West Indies, Kingston, Jamaica.

Buckley, Roger Norman. 1979. *Slaves in Red Coats: the British West India Regiments, 1795–1815*. New Haven: Yale University Press.

Cabrera, Lydia. 1970 [1957]. *Anagó: Vocabulario lucumí (el Yoruba que se habla en Cuba)*. Miami: Colección del Chicherekú.

———. 1986a [1979]. *Reglas de Congo, Mayombe, Palo Monte*. Miami: Ediciones Universal.

———. 1986b [1954]. *El Monte: Igbo-finda, Ewe Orisha, Vititi Nfinda*. Miami: Colección de Chicherekú.

Campbell, Carl. 1976. Immigration into Trinidad in the Middle of the Nineteenth Century: A Note on Race Relations in a West Indian Colony. *Journal of Indian History* 54(2): 407–39.

———. 1974. Mohammedu Sisei of Gambia and Trinidad, c. 1788–1838. *African Studies Association of the West Indies Bulletin* 7: 29–38.

Campbell, Lyle, and Martha Muntzel. 1989. The Structural Consequences of Language Death. In *Investigating Obsolescence: Studies in Language Contraction and Death*, ed. Nancy Dorian, 181–96. Cambridge: Cambridge University Press.

Carew, Jan. 1985. *Grenada: The Hour Will Strike Again*. Prague: International Organization of Journalists.

Carr, Andrew. 1953. A Rada Community in Trinidad. *Caribbean Quarterly* 3(1): 36–54. Reprint. Port of Spain: Paria Publishing, 1989.

Carter, Hazel. 1979. Some Considerations of Tone in Jamaican Creole. Paper presented to the Conference on Caribbean Linguistics, University of the West Indies, Kingston, Jamaica.

———. 1986a. The Language and Music of Kumina: Report of Research Visit to Jamaica, January–April 1985. *The African-Caribbean Institute of Jamaica Newsletter* 12: 3–12.

———. 1986b. Annotated Kumina Lexicon. Typescript. Kingston: African-Caribbean Institute of Jamaica.

———. 1987. Suprasegmentals in Guyanese: Some African Comparisons. In *Pidgin and Creole Languages: Essays in Memory of John Reinecke*, ed. Glenn Gilbert, 213–63. Honolulu: University of Hawaii Press.

———. 1993. Vowel Length in Afro-American: Development or Retention? In *Africanisms in Afro-American Language Varieties*, ed. Salikoko Mufwene, 328–45. Athens: University of Georgia.

Cassidy, Frederic. 1971. Jamaican Creole and Twi: Some Comparisons. Paper presented to the Conference on Caribbean Linguistics, University of the West Indies, Jamaica.

Cassidy, Frederic, and Robert LePage. 1967. *Dictionary of Jamaican English*. Cambridge: Cambridge University Press.

Chapman, J. K. 1964. *The Career of Arthur Hamilton Gordon, First Lord Stanmore, 1829–1912*. Toronto: University of Toronto Press.

Clarke, Robert. 1843. *Sierra Leone: A Description of the Manners and Customs of the Liberated Africans*. London: James Ridgway.

Collens, J. H. 1888. *A Guide to Trinidad: A Handbook for the Use of Tourists and Visitors*. London: Elliot Stock.

Comhaire-Sylvain, Suzanne, and Jean Comhaire-Sylvain. 1955. Survivances africaines dans le vocabulaire religieux d'Haiti. *Études Dahoméennes* 14: 3–20.

Courtenay, Karen. 1969. A Generative Phonology of Yoruba. Ph.D. diss., University of California, Los Angeles.

Crowther, Samuel. [1843] 1852. *A Grammar of the Yoruba Language*. London: Seeleys.

Cruickshank, J. Graham. 1916. How the Later Negro Learned His English. In Cruickshank, *Black Talk, Being Notes on Negro Dialect in British Guiana, with (Inevitably) a Chapter on Barbados,* 13–16. Demerara: Argosy Co. Reprinted in *Festival of Guyanese Words,* ed. John Rickford, 222–26. Georgetown: University of Guyana, 1978 [1976].

———. 1917. Among the "Aku" (Yoruba) in Canal No. 1, West Bank, Demerara River. *Timehri* 3d series, 4(21): 70–82.

Cuffie, Daphne. 1963. Problems in the Teaching of English in the Island of Trinidad from 1797 to the Present Day. M.A. diss., University of London, Institute of Education.

Curtin, Philip. 1969. *The Atlantic Slave Trade: a Census*. Madison: University of Wisconsin Press.

D'Costa, Jean, and Jack Berry. 1971. Some Considerations of Tone in Jamaican Creole. Paper Presented to the Conference on Caribbean Linguistics, University of the West Indies, Jamaica.

Daeleman, Jan. 1972. Kongo Elements in Saramacca Tongo. *Journal of African Languages* 11(1): 1–44.

Dahlstedt, Karl-Hampus. 1972. Mother Tongue and the Second Language: A Swedish Viewpoint. *International Review of Applied Linguistics in Language Learning* 10(4): 333–50.

Dalby, David. 1971. Ashanti Survivals in the Language and Traditions of the Windward Maroons of Jamaica. *African Language Studies* 12: 31–51.

Dalphinis, Morgan. 1985. *Caribbean and African Languages: Social History, Language, Literature and Education*. London: Karia Press.

Dalziel, J. M. 1937. *The Useful Plants of West Tropical Africa*. London: The Crown Agents for the Colonies.

de Verteuil, Louis A. 1858. *Trinidad: Its Geography, Natural Resources, Administration, Present Condition, and Prospects*. London: Ward and Lock.

Dereau, Léon. 1955. *Cours de Kikongo*. Namur: Maison d'Éditions Ad. Wesmael-Charlier.

Deschamps Chappeaux, Pedro. 1967. El lenguaje abakuá. *Etnología y Folklore* 4: 39–47.

Devonish, Hubert. 1989. *Talking in Tones: A Study of Tone in Afro-European Creole Languages*. London: Karia Press/Caribbean Academic Publications.

Diaz Fabelo, T. 1956. *Lengua de Santeros (Guiné Gongorí)*. Havana.

———. 1958. *Yoruba Ikaye: la Numeración Yoruba*. Havana.

A Dictionary of the Yoruba Language. 1937. 6th printing. London: Oxford University Press.

Dorian, Nancy. 1981. *Language Death: The Life Cycle of a Scottish Gaelic Dialect*. Philadelphia: University of Pennsylvania Press.

Dressler, Wolfgang. 1972. On the Phonology of Language Death. In *Papers from the Eighth Regional Meeting of the Chicago Linguistic Society*, ed. Paul Peranteau, Judith Levi, and Gloria Phares, 448–57.

Dressler, Wolfgang, and Ruth Wodak-Leodolter, eds. 1977. *Language Death*. The Hague: Mouton.

Durbin, Mridula Adenwala. 1973. Formal Changes in Trinidad Hindi as a Result of Language Adaptation. *American Anthropologist* 75(5): 1290–1304.

Edwards, Walter F. 1978. Tantalisin' and Busin' in Guyana. *Anthropological Linguistics* 20(5): 194–213.

Elder, Jacob D. 1988. *African Survivals in Trinidad and Tobago*. London: Karia Press.

Elkins, W. F. 1972. *Black Power in the Caribbean: The Beginnings of the Modern Nationalist Movement*. New York: Revisionist Press.

Ellis, A. B. 1894. *The Yoruba-Speaking Peoples of the Slave Coast of West Africa*. London: Chapman and Hall.

Eneas, Cleveland. 1976. *Bain Town*. Nassau: Cleveland and Muriel Eneas.

Fehderau, H. W. 1966. The Origin and Development of Kituba. Ph.D. diss., Cornell University.

Finnegan, Ruth. 1977. *Oral Poetry: Its Nature, Significance and Social Context*. Cambridge: Cambridge University Press.

Fishman, Joshua A. 1965. Varieties of Ethnicity and Varieties of Language Consciousness. *Language and Linguistics* 18: 69–79.

———. 1971. National Languages and Languages of Wider Communication in the Developing Nations. In *Language Use and Social Change: Problems of Multilingualism with Special Reference to Eastern Africa*, ed. W. H. Whiteley, 27–56. Oxford: Oxford University Press.

Franklin, C. B. 1910. *After Many Years: A Memoir, Being a Sketch of the Life and Labours of Rev. Alexander Kennedy, First Presbyterian Missionary to Trinidad, Founder of Greyfriars Church, and Its Pastor for Fourteen Years—January 1836–December 1849*. Port of Spain: Franklin's Electric Printery.

Fraser, Lionel M. 1971 [1891]. *History of Trinidad, 1781–1813*. Vol I. London: Frank Cass.

———. 1971 [1896]. *History of Trinidad, 1814 to 1839*. Vol II. London: Frank Cass.

Fresco, Edward Max. 1970. *Topics in Yoruba Dialect Phonology. Studies in African Linguistics*, Suppl. 1. Los Angeles: University of California.

Frobenius, Leo. 1973. *Leo Frobenius: an Anthology*, ed. Eike Haberland. Wiesbaden: Franz Steiner Verlag.

Fyfe, Christopher. 1961. Four Sierra Leone Recaptives. *Journal of African History* 11(1): 77–85.

Gamble, W. H. 1866. *Trinidad: Historical and Descriptive, Being a Narrative of Nine Years' Residence in the Island with Special Reference to Christian Missions*. London: Yates and Alexander.

García Gonzalez, José. 1973. Remanentes linguisticos munsundis: Un estudio descriptivo. *Islas* (Revista de la Universidad de las Villas, Cuba) 44, 193–246.

García, José, and Gema Valdés. 1978. Restos de lenguas bantúes en la región central de Cuba. *Islas* 59: 4–50.

Gilbert, Glenn. 1986. Oldendorp's *History* . . . and Other Early Creole Materials in the Moravian Archives in Herrnhut, East Germany. *The Carrier Pidgin* 14(1): 5–7.

González Huguet, Lydia, and Jean René Baudry. 1967. Voces "Bantú" en el vocabulario "palero." *Etnología y Folklore* 3: 31–64.

Goodman, Morris. 1993. African Substratum: Some Cautionary Words. In *Africanisms in Afro-American Language Varieties,* ed. Salikoko Mufwene, 64–73. Athens: University of Georgia.

Gorman, T. P. 1971. Sociolinguistic Implications of a Choice of Media of Instruction. In *Language Use and Social Change: Problems of Multilingualism with Special Reference to Eastern Africa,* ed. H. Whiteley, 198–220. Oxford: Oxford University Press.

Greenberg, Joseph. 1963. *The Languages of Africa. International Journal of American Linguistics* 29(1).

Grupo Rais. 1988. *Yabi Yaotina: un antalogia di musika di seu di Korsou.* Raimy Sound and Recording Studio, Curaçao.

Hall, Beverley. 1976. Introduction to a Jamaican Ethno-botany. Typescript.

Hall-Alleyne, Beverley. 1984. The Evolution of African Languages in Jamaica. *The African-Caribbean Institute of Jamaica Research Review* 1: 21–46.

———. 1990. The Social Context of African Language Continuities in Jamaica. *Caribbean Languages: Lesser-known Varieties,* ed. Velma Pollard. *International Journal of the Sociology of Language* 85: 31–40.

Hancock, Ian. 1971. A Study of the Sources and Development of the Lexicon of Sierra Leone Krio. Ph. D. diss., School of Oriental and African Studies, University of London.

———. 1978. Yoruba Lexical Behaviour in Sierra Leone Krio. Paper Presented at the Eleventh Annual Conference on African Linguistics, East Lansing, Michigan.

———. 1987. A Preliminary Classification of the Anglophone Atlantic Creoles with Syntactic Data from Thirty-three Representative Dialects. In *Pidgin and Creole Languages: Essays in Memory of John E. Reinecke,* ed. Glenn Gilbert, 264–333. Honolulu: University of Hawaii Press.

Haraksingh, Kusha. 1985. Aspects of the Indian Experience in the Caribbean. In *Calcutta to Caroni: The East Indians of Trinidad,* ed. John La Guerre, 155–69. St. Augustine: University of the West Indies Extra Mural Studies Unit, Trinidad and Tobago.

Harewood, Jack. 1975. *The Population of Trinidad and Tobago.* Port of Spain: Giuseppi's Printery.

Haugen, Einar. 1972. *The Ecology of Language: Essays by Einar Haugen.* Stanford: Stanford University Press.

Hazaël-Massieux, Guy. 1993. The African Filter in the Genesis of Guadeloupean Creole: At the Confluence of Genetics and Typology. In *Africanisms in Afro-American Language Varieties,* ed. Salikoko Mufwene, 109–22. Athens: University of Georgia.

Henry, Frances. 1983. Religion and Ideology in Trinidad: The Resurgence of the Shango Religion. *Caribbean Quarterly* 29(3 and 4): 63–69.

Herskovits, Melville, and Frances Herskovits. 1939. Trinidad and Tobago. Folk Archive Collection, Library of Congress, Washington, D.C.

Higman, Barry. 1978. African and Creole Slave Family Patterns in Trinidad. *Journal of Family History* 3(2): 163–80. Also in *Africa and the Caribbean: Legacies of a Link,* ed. Margaret Crahan and Franklin Knight, 41–64. Baltimore: Johns Hopkins University Press, 1979.

———. 1984. *Slave Populations of the British Caribbean, 1807–1834.* Baltimore: Johns Hopkins University Press.

Hill, Daniel. 1981. *The Freedom-Seekers: Blacks in Early Canada.* Agincourt: Book Society of Canada.

Hill, Donald. 1977. *The Impact of Migration on the Metropolitan and Folk Society of Carriacou, Grenada.* New York: American Museum of Natural History, vol. 54, pt. 2.

Hill, Jane. 1973. Subordinate Clause Density and Language Function. In *You'll Take the High Node and I'll Take the Low Node,* ed. Claudia Corum, T. Cedric Smith-Starke, and Ann Weiser, 33–52. Chicago: Chicago Linguistic Society.

Holm, John. 1993. Phonological Features Common to Some West African and Atlantic Creole Languages. In *Africanisms in Afro-American Language Varieties,* ed. Salikoko Mufwene, 317–27. Athens: University of Georgia.

Hombert, Jean-Marie. 1974. Universals of Downdrift: Their Phonetic Basis and Significance for a Theory of Tone. *Studies in African Linguistics,* suppl. 55: 169–83.

Hsieh, Hsin-I. 1974. Time as a Cause of Phonological Irregularities. *Lingua* 33: 253–63.

Huttar, George. 1971. Some Kwa-like Features of Djuka Syntax. Paper presented to Conference of Caribbean Linguistics, University of West Indies, Jamaica.

———. 1985. Sources of Ndjuka African Vocabulary. *Nieuwe West-Indische Gids (New West Indies Guide)* 59: 1 & 2, 45–71.

Hyman, Larry, and Russell Schuh. 1974. Universals of Tone Rules: Evidence from West Africa. *Linguistic Inquiry* 5(1): 81–115.

Igue, John, and Olabiyi Yai. 1973. The Yoruba-Speaking People of Dahomey and Togo. *Yoruba* 1(1): 1–29.

Iwu, Uzoamaka. 1978. Similarities in Language and Culture between Nigeria and Guyana. In *Festival of Guyanese Words,* ed. John Rickford, 163–69. Georgetown: University of Guyana.

Izutsu, Toshihiko. 1956. *Language and Magic: Studies in the Magical Function of Speech.* Japan: Keio Institute of Philological Studies.

Jeffreys, M. D. W. 1945. The Death of a Dialect. *African Studies* 4: 37–40.

Joseph, E. L. 1838. *A History of Trinidad.* Reprint. London: Frank Cass, 1970.

Klein, Herbert. 1982. The Portuguese Slave Trade from Angola in the Eighteenth Century. In *Forced Migration: The Impact of the Export Slave Trade on African Societies,* ed. John Inikori, 221–41. New York: Africana Publishing.

Koelle, Sigismund Wilhelm. 1854. *Polyglotta Africana.* London: Church Missionary Society.

Kuczynski, R. R. 1948. *Demographic Survey of the British Colonial Empire.* Oxford: Oxford University Press.

Labat, Jean Baptiste. 1970. *The Memoirs of Père Labat, 1693–1705.* Trans. and ed. John Eaden. London: Frank Cass.

Lachatañere, Rómulo. 1961a. La influencia bantú-Yoruba en los cultos afro-cubanos, *Actas del Folklore* 1(6): 3–8.

———. 1961b. El sistema religioso de los Lucumís en Cuba, *Actas del Folklore* 1(7): 9–20.

Lalla, Barbara, and Jean D'Costa. 1990. *Language in Exile: Three Hundred Years of Jamaican Creole.* Tuscaloosa: University of Alabama Press.

Lamal, F. 1965. *Basuku et Bayaka des districts Kwango et Kwilu au Congo.* Tervuren: Musée Royal de l'Afrique Centrale.

Laman, Karl Edward. 1964 [1936]. *Dictionnaire Kikongo-Français.* Ridgewood, N.J.: The Gregg Press.

Laurence, Keith. 1958. Immigration into Trinidad and British Guiana, 1834–1871. Ph.D. diss., University of Cambridge.

Laurence, Kemlin. 1970. Spanish in Trinidad: The Survival of a Minority Language in a Multilingual Society. Ph.D. diss., University of London.

———. 1975. Continuity and Change in Trinidadian Toponyms. *New West Indies Guide* 50 (2 and 3): 123–42.

La Velle, Carl. 1974. An Experimental Study of Yoruba Tone. *Studies in African Linguistics,* Suppl. 5: 185–93.

Law, R. C. C. 1973. Traditional History. In *Sources of Yoruba History,* ed. S. O. Biobaku, 25–40. London: Oxford University Press.

Lawton, David. 1963. Suprasegmental Phenomena in Jamaican Creole. Ph.D. diss., Michigan State University.

León, Argeliers. 1971. Un caso de tradición oral escrita. *Islas* 39–40: 139–51.

Lewis, Antony. 1978. Possible Bantu Linguistic Survivals in the Palenquero Creole Dialect. Paper presented to the Conference of the Society for Caribbean Linguistics, University of the West Indies, Barbados.

Lloyd, Peter C. 1967. Osifekunde of Ijebu. In *Africa Remembered,* ed. Philip Curtin, 217–88. Wisconsin: University of Wisconsin Press.

Lomax, Alan. 1959. The Lomax Collection of Caribbean Music. Radio Education Unit, School of Continuing Studies, University of the West Indies, Jamaica.

Lord, Carol. 1973. Serial Verbs in Transition. *Studies in African Linguistics* 4(3): 269–88.

Lovelace, Earl. 1986 [1982]. *The Wine of Astonishment.* London: Longman.

Lucas, Olumide. 1948. *The Religion of the Yorubas.* Lagos: Church Missionary Society Bookshop.

Lynch, Louis. 1964. *The Barbados Book.* London: André Deutsch.

Mabogunje, Akin, and J. Omer-Cooper. 1971. *Owu in Yoruba History.* Ibadan: Ibadan University Press.

Mahabir, Kumar. 1991. *Medicinal and Edible Plants Used by East Indians of Trinidad and Tobago.* El Dorado: Chakra Publishing House.

Malkiel, Yakov. 1964. Some Diachronic Implications of Fluid Speech Communities. *American Anthropologist* 66(6, pt. 2): 177–86.

Martin, Tony. 1994 [1986]. Marcus Garvey and Trinidad, 1912–1947. In *Garvey, Africa, Europe, the Americas,* ed. Rupert Lewis and Maureen Warner-Lewis, 47–77. Trenton, N.J.: Africa World Press.

Martínez Furé, Rogelio. 1986. Patakin: Sacred Literature of Cuba. In *African Cultures,* 41–83. Paris: UNESCO.

McAndrew, Wordsworth. 1978. Some Possible Africanisms in Guyanese Speech. In *Festival of Guyanese Words,* ed. John Rickford, 153–62. Georgetown: University of Guyana.

McDaniel, Lorna. 1990. The Flying Africans: Extent and Strength of the Myth in the Americas. *New West Indies Guide* 64(1 and 2): 28–40.

McKay, Claude. 1961 [1933]. *Banana Bottom.* New York: Harcourt, Brace, Jovanovich.

Mendoza Lorenzo, Leidy. 1986. Estudio sobre el cabildo de Congos reales "San Antonio" de Trinidad. *Islas* 85: 49–73.

Mercier, Paul. 1950. Notice sur le peuplement Yoruba au Dahomey-Togo. *Études Dahoméenes* 4: 29–40.

Mischel, Frances. 1957. African "Powers" in Trinidad: The Shango Cult. *Anthropological Quarterly* 30: 45–60.

Mischel, Walter, and Frances Mischel. Psychological Aspects of Spirit Possession. *American Anthropologist* 60(2): 249–60.

Mohan, Peggy Ramesar. 1978. Trinidad Bhojpuri: A Morphological Study. Ph.D. diss., University of Michigan.

Moliner Castañeda, Israel. 1979. Los Iyessa. *Semanario Yumurí* 4:35, 2 September.

———. 1986. Las sublevaciones de esclavos en Matanzas. *Islas* 85: 24–48.

Morton-Williams, Peter. 1982. The Oyo Yoruba and the Atlantic Trade, 1670 to 1830. In *Forced Migration: the Impact of the Export Slave Trade on African Societies,* ed. John Inikori, 167–86. New York: Africana Publishing.

Mufwene, Salikoko. 1988. Why Study Pidgins and Creoles? *Journal of Pidgin and Creole Languages* 3: 265–76.

———. 1990. Transfer and the Transfer Hypothesis in Creolistics. *Studies in Second Language Acquisition* 12: 1–23.

Naipaul, Vidia. 1961. *A House for Mr. Biswas.* London: Deutsch.

Oduyoye, Modupẹ. 1971. *The Vocabulary of Yoruba Religious Discourse.* Ibadan: Daystar Press.

Ojo, Afọlabi. 1968. *Yoruba Culture.* University of Ifẹ/University of London Press.

Ojo, J. R. O. 1973. Orìṣà Oko, the Deity of the "Farm and Agriculture" among the Ekiti. *African Notes* 7(2): 25–61.

Ọkẹ, Ọla. 1974. Syntactic Correlates of Notionally Defined Adverbial Types in Yoruba. *Studies in African Linguistics,* suppl. 5: 232–52.

Oldendorp, Christian Georg Andreas. 1987 [1777]. *History of the Mission of the Evangelical Brethren on the Caribbean Islands of St. Thomas, St. Croix and St. John.* Ed. Joh'ann Jakob Bossard; trans. Arnold R. Highfield and Vladimir Barac. Ann Arbor: Karoma Press.

Olinto, Antonio. 1970. *The Water House.* Trans. Dorothy Heapy. London: Rex Collings.

Olmsted, David. 1953. Comparative Notes on Yoruba and Lucumí. *Language* 29(9): 157–64.

Ong, Walter. 1982. *Orality and Literacy: the Technologizing of the Word.* London: Methuen.

Oroge, E. A. 1975. Iwofa: An Historical Survey of the Yoruba Institution of Indenture. Paper presented to Seminar on Sociology and History: Their Inter-relationship in the Nigerian Context, University of Ifẹ.

Ortiz, Fernando. 1921. Un catauro de cubanismos. *Revista Bimestre Cubana* 16: 1–6, 17: 1–5.

———. 1922. Los afronegrismos de nuestro lenguaje. *Revista Bimestre Cubana* 30(117): 5–35; 30(118): 126–64.

Oyelaran, Ọlasope. 1971. Yoruba Phonology. Ph.D. diss., Stanford University.

———. 1972. The Characterization of a Standard: Yoruba. Typescript.

———. 1978. Notes on Yoruba Culture in Krio Setting. Seminar Paper, Department of African Languages and Literatures, University of Ifẹ.

Parrinder, Geoffrey. 1969. *Religion in Africa.* Harmondsworth: Penguin.

Pearse, Andrew, ed. 1956. Mitto Sampson on Calypso Legends of the Nineteenth Century. *Caribbean Quarterly* 4(3 and 4): 250–62.

Peterson, John. 1969. *Province of Freedom: a History of Sierra Leone, 1787–1870.* London: Faber and Faber.

Pichardo, Estebán. 1976 [1875]. *Diccionario provincial casi razonado de vozes y frases cubanas.* Havana: Editorial de Ciencias Sociales.

Ponelis, Fritz. 1974. On the Dynamics of Velarization and Labialization: Some Bantu Evidence. *Studies in African Linguistics* 5(1): 27–57.

Post, Ken. 1969. Tribalism in West Africa. *Jamaica Journal* 3(1): 2–6.

———. 1978. *Arise Ye Starvelings: the Jamaican Labour Rebellion of 1939 and Its Aftermath.* The Hague: Nijhoff.

Price, Richard. 1975. Kikoongo and Saramaccan: A Reappraisal. *Bÿdragen tot de Taal-Land-en Volkenkunde van Neerlandsch Indië* 131: 461–78.

Quesada, Cándida Judith. 1973. Remanentes de una lengua africana utilizada por la sociedad secreta de los Abakuá en Cuba. *Islas* 45: 143–66.

Ralston, Richard. 1970. The Return of Brazilian Freedmen to West Africa in the Eighteenth and Nineteenth Centuries. *Canadian Journal of African Studies* 3(3): 577–92.

Raymond, Ursula. N.d. The Yorubas of Diego Martin. Typescript. University of the West Indies Library, St. Augustine, Trinidad.

Reddock, Rhoda. 1984. Women, Labour and Struggle in Twentieth-Century Trinidad and Tobago, 1898–1960. Ph.D. diss., Institute of Social Studies, University of Amsterdam.

Relouzat, Raymond. 1971. Structure comparée de la phrase ewe et de la phrase créole. Paper presented to the Conference on Caribbean Linguistics, University of the West Indies, Kingston, Jamaica.

Ricketts, Sam. 1858. Foo Massa Headhitter Sentiwel. Letters to the Editor, *Trinidad Sentinel,* Thursday, 8 April.

Rickford, John, and Angela Rickford. 1976. Cut-eye and Suck-teeth: African Words and Gestures in New World Guise. *Journal of American Folklore* 89: 294–309.

Rickford, John. 1987. *Dimensions of a Creole Continuum: History, Texts and Linguistic Analysis of Guyanese Creole.* Stanford: Stanford University Press.

Roberts, George, and Joycelyn Byrne. 1967. Summary Statistics on Indenture and Associated Migration Affecting the West Indies, 1834–1918. In *Trinidad and Tobago Central Statistical Office Research Papers* 4: 59–68. Port of Spain: Government Printing Office.

Robertson, Ian. 1993. The Ijo Element in Berbice Dutch and the Pidginization/Creolization Process. In *Africanisms in Afro-American Language Varieties,* ed. Salikoko Mufwene, 296–316. Athens: University of Georgia.

Rowlands, E. C. 1955. The Mid Tone in Yoruba. In *Afrikanistische Studien,* ed. Johannes Lukas, 333–36. Berlin: Akademie Verlag.

———. 1965. Studies Devoted to S. W. Koelle's *Polyglotta Africana*: Yoruba Dialects in the *Polyglotta Africana. Sierra Leone Language Review* 4: 103–7.

———. 1969. *Yoruba.* London: English Universities Press.

Ryman, Cheryl. 1984. Kumina: Stability and Change. In *African-Caribbean Institute of Jamaica Research Review* 1: 81–128.

Sarracino, Rodolfo. 1988. *Los que volvieron a África.* Havana: Editorial de Ciencias Sociales.

Schuler, Monica. 1970. Akan Slave Rebellions in the British Caribbean. *Savacou* 1(1): 8–31.

———. 1971. African Immigration to French Guiana: The *Cinq Frères* Group, 1854–1860. *African Studies Association of the West Indies Bulletin* 4: 62–78.

———. 1972. The Experience of African Immigrants in Nineteenth Century Jamaica. Paper presented to the Fourth Conference of Caribbean Historians, University of the West Indies, Kingston, Jamaica.

———. 1977. "Yerri, Yerri, Koongo": A Social History of Liberated African Immigration into Jamaica, 1841–1867. Ph.D. diss., University of Wisconsin.

———. 1980. *"Alas, Alas, Kongo": A Social History of Indentured African Immigration into Jamaica, 1841–1865.* Baltimore: Johns Hopkins University Press.

———. 1991. Liberated Africans in Nineteenth-Century Guyana. Elsa Goveia Memorial Lecture, University of the West Indies, Kingston, Jamaica, May.

Schumann, John. 1978. *The Pidginization Process: A Model for Second Language Acquisition.* Rowley, Mass.: Newbury House Publishers.

Schwegler, Armin. Forthcoming. La descodificación de las canciones fúnebres afrohispanas "lumbalú" del palenque de San Basilio (Colombia). *Thesaurus* (Bogotá).

Seaforth, C. E., C. D. Adams, and Y. Sylvester. 1985 [1983]. *A Guide to the Medicinal Plants of Trinidad and Tobago.* London: Commonwealth Secretariat & and Caribbean Industrial Research Institute (CARIRI).

Selvon, Samuel. 1952. *A Brighter Sun.* London: Alan Wingate.

Shaffer, Douglas. 1979. The Spread of English over Immigrant Languages in the United States. In *Linguistic and Literary Studies in Honor of Archibald Hill,* ed. Mohammed Jazayery, Edgar Polomé, and Werner Winter, 371–77. The Hague: Mouton.

Simpson, George. 1970 [1965]. *The Shango Cult in Trinidad.* In George Simpson, *Religious Cults of the Caribbean: Trinidad, Jamaica, and Haiti.* San Juan: Institute of Caribbean Studies, University of Puerto Rico.

Smith, M. G. 1965. *The Plural Society in the British West Indies.* Berkeley: University of California Press.

Smith, Norval, Ian Robertson, and Kay Williamson. 1987. The Ijo Element in Berbice Dutch. *Language in Society* 16(1): 49–90.

Stahlke, Herbert. 1970. Serial Verbs. *Studies in African Linguistics* 1(1): 60–99.

———. 1973. The *n/l* Alternation: A Minor Rule in Yoruba Phonology. In *Issues in Linguistics: Papers in Honor of Henry & Renée Kahane,* ed. Braj Kachru et al., 854–62. Urbana/Chicago: University of Illinois Press.

Stark, James. 1897. *Stark's Guide Book and History of Trinidad.* Boston: James H. Stark.

Stevick, Earl, and Ọlaleye Aremu. 1963. *Yoruba Basic Course.* Washington: Foreign Service Institute, Department of State.

Swadesh, Morris. 1955. Towards Greater Accuracy in Lexicostatistic Dating. *International Journal of American Linguistics* 21: 121–37.

Tanna, Laura. 1983. African Retentions: Yoruba and Kikongo Songs in Jamaica. *Jamaica Journal* 16(3): 47–52.

———. 1984. *Jamaican Folk Tales and Oral Histories.* Kingston: Institute of Jamaica Publications.

Thomas, John Jacob. 1969 [1869]. *The Theory and Practice of Creole Grammar.* London: New Beacon Books.

Tinelli, Henri. 1973. Generative and Creolization Processes: Nasality in Haitian Creole. *Lingua* 33: 343–66.

Torday, E. 1925. *Causeries congolaises.* Brussels: Librairie Albert Dewit.

Truman, George, John Jackson, and Thomas B. Longstreth. 1844. *Narrative of a Visit to the West Indies in 1840 and 1841.* Philadelphia: Merrihew and Thompson.

Underhill, E. B. 1862. *The West Indies: Their Social and Religious Condition.* London: Jackson, Walford and Hodder.

Valdés Acosta, Gema. 1974. Descripción de remanentes de lenguas bantúes en Santa Isabel de las Lajas. *Islas* 48: 69–85.

———. 1986. Algunos fenómenos semánticos en los remanentes africanos del centro de Cuba. *Islas* 85: 104–13.

Vega, Hector. 1969. Some Musical Forms of African Descendants in Puerto Rico: *Bomba, Plena,* and *Rosario Francés.* M.A. diss., Hunter College, City University of New York.

Verger, Pierre. 1966. Retour des "Brésiliens" au Golfe du Bénin au XIXe siècle. *Études Dahoméennes* 8: 5–28.

von Bradshaw, A. T. 1966. A List of Yoruba Words in Krio. *African Language Review* 5: 61–71.

Wang, William. 1969. Competing Changes as a Cause of Residue. *Language* 45(1): 9–25.

Warner, Maureen. 1967. Language in Trinidad with Special Reference to English, M.Phil. diss., University of York, England.

———. 1970. Some Yoruba Descendants in Trinidad. *African Studies Association of the West Indies Bulletin* 3 (December): 40–49.

———. 1971a. Trinidad Yoruba: Notes on Survivals. *Caribbean Quarterly* 17(2): 40–49.

———. 1971b. A Preliminary Analysis of Syntax in Two Idiolects of Trinidad Yoruba. Paper presented to Caribbean Conference on Linguistics, Jamaica.

Warner-Lewis, Maureen. 1977. *The Nkuyu: Spirit Messengers of the Kumina.* Mona: Savacou Publications. Also in *Savacou* 13: 57–78.

———. 1979. The African Impact on Language and Literature in the English-Speaking Caribbean. In *Africa and the Caribbean: Legacies of a Link,* ed. Margaret Crahan and Franklin Knight, 101–23. Baltimore: Johns Hopkins University Press.

———. 1982. The Yoruba Language in Trinidad. Ph.D. diss., University of the West Indies, Kingston, Jamaica.

———. 1991a. *Guinea's Other Suns: the African Dynamic in Trinidad Culture.* Dover, Mass.: The Majority Press.

———. 1991b. The Ancestral Factor in Jamaica's African Religions. In *African Creative Expressions of the Divine,* ed. Kortright Davis and Elias Farajaje-Jones, 63–80. Washington: Howard University School of Divinity.

———, comp. 1994. *Yoruba Songs of Trinidad.* London: Karnak House.

Westermann, Dietrich. 1930. *A Study of the Ewe Language.* Oxford: Oxford University Press.

Westermann, Dietrich, and M. A. Bryan. 1952. *The Languages of West Africa.* London: Oxford University Press.

Wilks, Ivor. 1967. Salih Bilali of Massina. In *Africa Remembered,* ed. Philip Curtin, 145–69. Madison: University of Wisconsin Press.

Willett, Frank. 1973. Archeology. In *Sources of Yoruba History,* ed. S. O. Biobaku, 111–39. London: Oxford University Press.

Williamson, Kay. 1973. More on Nasals and Nasalization in Kwa. *Studies in African Linguistics* 4(2): 115–38.

Wood, Donald. 1968. *Trinidad in Transition: The Years after Slavery.* Oxford: Oxford University Press.

———. 1981. Kru Migration to the West Indies. *Journal of Caribbean Studies* 2(2 and 3): 266–82.

Zaslavsky, Claudia. 1979 [1973]. *Africa Counts: Number and Pattern in African Culture.* Westport: Lawrence Hill.

Index